CHOOSING *Joy*

Our Walk through Tragedy

CHRIS AND NATALIE SWANSON

WESTBOW
P R E S S®
A DIVISION OF THOMAS NELSON
& ZONDERVAN

THE HOLY BIBLE, NEW INTERNATIONAL VERSION, NIV Copyright 1973, 1978, 1984, 2011 by Biblica, Inc. Used by permission. All rights reserved worldwide.

WestBow Press books may be ordered through booksellers or by contacting:

WestBow Press
A Division of Thomas Nelson & Zondervan
1663 Liberty Drive
Bloomington, IN 47403
www.westbowpress.com
1 (866) 928-1240

ISBN: 978-1-5127-0904-9 (sc)
ISBN: 978-1-5127-0905-6 (hc)
ISBN: 978-1-5127-0903-2 (e)

Library of Congress Control Number: 2015913275

Print information available on the last page.

WestBow Press rev. date: 9/4/2015

For Caleb, Emma, Grace, and Gavin.

We love you with all our hearts and pray you
choose joy when the going gets tough.

CONTENTS

Part Three

INTRODUCTION

I can do all this through him who gives me strength.
Philippians 4:13

*May the God of hope fill you with all joy and peace
as you trust in him, so that you may overflow
with hope by the power of the Holy Spirit.*
Romans 15:13

In 2005, an amazing woman, Barbara Robinson, had been invited to minister at our church's yearly women's retreat, and we were excited to hear her message. Her husband, Mickey Robinson, shared his amazing story on television prior to this retreat and I knew she also had led an incredible life. She set her hand on my shoulder, prayed for me and then said she saw me as a strong pillar, gathering and linking arms with other women, full of joy, rejoicing and with laughter. She told me that Jesus had given me a mantle (cloak or blanket) of strength. I was comforted and intrigued.

What was especially amazing was that Barbara and I had never met and she had no idea what the last year had been like for my husband and me. She didn't know our oldest boy had been killed in an accident at our home, and that I had felt fragile and lost. It encouraged and strengthened me at a time when I really needed it. From that moment on, I felt like we were supposed to share our story. I dreamed of being able to spread hope to others. I wanted them to know that if they were broken and alone, too, that there was a God that could put them back together again and they could have real joy again.

That summer, Chris and I spoke at a multi-church gathering in Duluth, sharing about what had happened and how we could see God working this awful situation for good in our lives and in others. The message was well received.

Over the next few years I shared our story with local women's groups. Amazingly, when I was finished speaking, ladies would come to me and tell how they were inspired after hearing this story, that they had needed to hear it. One girl I met with was in awe that I had survived such a loss and said she could never imagine something so horrible. God had divinely connected us; only 16 months later, her own little girl died. It was a hard phone call to make, but I shared my condolences and had a connection, she knew I validated her pain. Sadly, she's not the only weary-soul we've crossed paths with over the years.

Chris has talked with many of his students over the years about things that go on in their lives and that there's hope even in the midst of pain. Countless students and parents have expressed their appreciation for his care and concern over the years. It's the kids who have lost a sibling or who are trying to make it on their own that really touch his heart. He's doing a different form of ministry work; there are so many kids with so many needs.

During a two-year leave from teaching to work as a railroad conductor, our story touched even more lives. It was no surprise that people on the railroad need encouragement from time to time, as well. Once, he came home feeling exhausted after an overnight job on the railroad, but was happy to tell me that he'd struck up a conversation with a grieving mother who was driving crews to and from their home terminals. She seemed touched that he had empathized with her and left the terminal cheerier than when she had arrived.

Now, back in the classroom, Chris is proud to continue teaching his students about social studies and life. We couldn't imagine it any other way.

As the years have gone by, it has become easier to help others by talking about the loss of our own child. Nobody should have to go through an experience like this alone. We, who have made it, need to lift up and support them; this journey is long and exhausting. When parents lose a child no matter what the age, they don't want the memory to be stolen away, too. They don't want to weird people out by always talking about their missing loved one. It's tough getting through this stuff. We can walk lighter, worry less, and love more when we know this life is temporary and that eternity awaits. That's what this book is about.

Part One, chapters one through seven are about us and our life with Cameron. Part Two, chapters eight through 18, walk through the story of the accident and the days following. This was the toughest part to dredge up, we choked up as we wrote and talked about that sad, sad stretch of days. Part Three, chapters 19 through 24 are about working through the insecurity and the struggle to choose joy daily.

Part One

Chapter 1

TRAGEDY

I t was a sunny day in May and the countryside was coming alive. I (Natalie) remember the wide open sky, crisp clean air, and the sound of birds. Frogs and crickets were now going to put us to sleep at night instead of the cars and dogs we often heard at bedtime. It was refreshing to think we had a new beginning and all sorts of family adventures ahead of us. With three little kids, we looked forward to experiencing the life of country dwellers. On this particular day, May 19, 2004, we had planned for cleaning up the old farmhouse and property we now called home. My family was visiting and available to help on a Wednesday, but Chris still needed to go to work. My uncles, grandparents, parents, brother, and sister were all there working to get us set up and clean all the dangers of an unoperated old farm. We had an old pond that needed to be drained, chicken wire rolls in random places, holes that needed to be filled, dog kennels that needed dismantling and sharp, rusty pieces of equipment we needed to get rid of. It seemed that it was going to be a glorious day full of productivity.

The boys, Cameron, Caleb, and my nephew Alex, were also outside gathering bugs. Worms, ants, ladybugs and slugs were available by the dozens now, and being squashed in their little hands. They ran around our property with squeals of delight and were determined to catch all they could. We had a bug catcher that was going to house their new friends and the boys wanted to find as many as they could. I remember telling them, "If you squeeze them too hard they will die." Instantly, they slowed down their run to a fast walk and focused on softening their squeeze. Once they finished looking around the edge of the pole barn, which sat on the lower southeast corner of our property, they headed toward the pond. I immediately was uncomfortable with that idea, so I hopped on the three-wheeler that was close by in effort to get there quicker, as the distance from where I was seemed too far away to stop them from getting too close to the edge if I were to run. When I scooped the boys up, they were thrilled to have a ride in the attached trailer, so I did a few circles around our property.

I can remember the giggles and excitement in their little voices as we went through puddles and sped over little hills. I was peaceful and looking forward to more times of having fun together. When we finished our ride, I strategically placed them in a spot I thought would be safe. It was close to the house and away from everything I thought was dangerous, on a cement slab at the end of a long line of dog kennels that were eventually going to be removed. They quickly started to spread out all of their bugs and compare their new treasures. I told them to stay there so they wouldn't get hurt. I hopped back on the three-wheeler and headed toward the pole barn to park it. There was more work to do.

My sister was mowing the lawn, and one of my uncles was preparing to tear down all of the dog kennels that ran along the side of the addition. He had already taken the fencing off the top. The only part left was the seven walls made from cinder blocks that stood about four feet high, each four feet from the next. He tested the sturdiness of the first wall about 30 feet away from the kids, and to his surprise, it moved a lot easier than he thought it would. It fell out of his grasp, into the next wall. The cinder block walls crashed down on each other in a domino effect, and in seconds, the place I put the boys to keep them safe became the most dangerous place on the property. The cinder blocks fell closer and closer to where they were playing until there was nothing left to stop them from toppling onto the boys. Our nephew, Alex, was on his knees with his back to the walls, so when the walls fell on him, his body braced the weight. He was injured. Our son Caleb was out far enough that the walls missed him completely. Over the noise of the lawnmower, I heard my dad scream, "Call 911!" as he pulled Cameron out from the under cinder blocks. Cameron was wearing an Incredible Hulk costume backwards and pink mud boots, easy to spot. He was limp like a sleeping child would be. All the noise around was silenced and time stood still as I heard Cameron's sweet voice in my head say, "I am alright, Mommy."

Chapter 2

LOVE

Every girl dreams of being whisked away by their knight in shining armor. I know I did, and I was one of the few lucky ones who-stumbled upon him during my 10th grade year in high school. Chris was unusually peaceful, genuinely sincere, and seemed to have a truly joyful spirit. He lived for something more than just the next football game or the next party. I remember a fight breaking out in the classroom next door to my homeroom. Everyone started to gather around watching and cheering for one of the kids, while the other boy seemed to have no one for support. Conflict of any kind makes me uneasy, so I didn't want to stick around and engage in the wildness or cheering. However, there was something else happening. There seemed to be someone stepping in that was trying to stop the fight. Chris was standing in between an angry junior and a raging sophomore who was holding a chair above his head. I don't know what he said to them, all I know was that my heart skipped a beat, and I was intrigued. Looking back now, he was like Jesus in that story when he silenced the storm out on the raging sea with his disciples, and I could not stop thinking about him. Ladies, if you ever see someone step in and break up a fight, marry him. This was one of many unique things he did that was different from others and showed me that he was a real gentleman.

With him on my mind a lot, I asked him to the Sno Ball, our winter dance, and he accepted. We had a really great time together, and from that moment on we became inseparable. As our friendship grew, he led me to the Lord and showed me what it was to have a relationship with the real God. I grew up knowing about the church and attended a Methodist and Lutheran church periodically, but was not aware of a personal relationship with Jesus. Chris's first assignment for me was to write the Lord's Prayer in my own words and memorize it. I found the challenge kind of fun and was excited to show him I could do it, I think I got a sticker for my achievements, but who needs rewards when you get the butterflies every time you see someone? For my 16th birthday, he and some friends bought me my first Bible. I was thankful for the gift and determined to impress them all by reading the whole thing, but by the time I had reached the story of Cain and Abel, I found myself uninterested. For your information, Cain and Abel join the Bible in chapter four of the book of Genesis. Genesis is the first book of over 60, so you can see I didn't get very far. To this day, I still have not read the whole thing.

After four years of growing our friendship, Chris and I were married in August of 1997. The thrill and excitement of moving in together was so huge, I still get butterflies thinking about it. I remember being swept off my feet, and I truly believed we could live on our love alone. Very quickly, reality seemed to settle in, and I realized that while love was amazing, it did not pay for our rent, groceries or the gas for our little red Chevy. Chris worked part-time as a janitor at the Cloquet Middle School and was going to school full-time to become a social studies teacher, while I was working other jobs. We had planned on having a family, but we didn't want to start until Chris was done with college.

In October, shortly after Chris resumed his busy school schedule, I found myself severely fatigued. After lying in bed for days and not being able to do anything, I went to the doctor sure I had Mono. I had never slept so much in my life, and I still never felt rested. I actually was surprised when the doctor asked if I could be pregnant. The thought hadn't crossed my mind. Pregnancy was supposed to be fun and dreamy and I did not feel that way. A quick test confirmed I was and the due date was June 25. My lips quivered as I held back tears. I was not crying because I was disappointed, but because I was shocked, nervous, excited, and hormonal. I left the clinic with all sorts of pamphlets and the book, *What to Expect When You're Expecting*. Still crying, I drove straight to Chris's work, and I spilled the news. Being the gentleman he was and still is, he was excited and assured everything was going to be alright. I was thinking it would be fun to keep it a secret for a bit, but there was nothing graceful about my early pregnancy and everyone would know something was up. The same time I told my sister Sarah, she was planning on telling me that she was pregnant too. She, on the other hand, kept her beauty and glow in the early months of pregnancy.

The next few months I spent rushing to nearby bathrooms everywhere. The suggestion or thought of food created an instant reaction and I would need to vomit. When I couldn't make it to a bathroom, I used the little blue bags on airplanes, grocery aisle floors, flower buckets at the flower shop I worked at (sorry George and Shelly) and curbs on the side of the road. Yes, it was apparent I had morning sickness. I remember thinking I would never do this again. My mom and dear friend recently reminded me that I said that all five times I was pregnant.

After 16 or 17 weeks, the sickness finally left and my belly grew. The rest of my pregnancy I enjoyed kicks, hiccups and the glorious stretching of my whole body. My body was no longer my own and every decision I made from then on was not about me, but about another human being living inside of me. I love how God prepares us to be ready to love and provide for another human's life. We learned all we could from friends and family that had little ones already. We studied up on nutrition, safety precautions, breastfeeding, toys, car seats, discipline techniques and delivery room preferences. We talked about baby names over and over again, and we finally settled on Hannah Lynn for a girl or Cameron Michael for a boy. My thoughts were consumed with what our life was going to be like once the baby arrived.

Chapter 3

ABUNDANT LIFE

As a boy, the interesting collection of information and Hallmark "welcome to earth" cards collected in my baby book gave me a wonderful sense of the love and pride my mom must have had for me in the two years we were together. She died before I am able remember, but my dad and aunts and uncles have shared pictures and stories of her. Knowing that she spent time making note of the first time I rolled from my back to the front and then back again helped me when I was young to know I had been loved by her. I wondered what it might have looked like, her at the table with the book, me in the high chair with a toy, my older brother and sister doing their own thing... My dad remarried years later and I grew to love her as any boy would love a mom, but life was complicated sometimes as I tried to figure things out and that baby book was a source of comfort when times were tough. I wanted the same for our child.

We set out early, keeping track of details of the pregnancy and all the gifts and cards received at baby showers, but I thought we could do something more. Cameron's babybook is more of a collection of anecdotes and silliness than a more traditional "book."

I had come across a pair of 3 inch locking rings that could hold together a stack of unprinted cereal box cardboard. (I had all sorts of interesting things squirreled away for projects not yet dreamed of.) This "book" would be the sort of curious ramblings I imagined a kid would enjoy reading or laughing about later on. I wanted it thick with craziness.

The entry in black pen from January 17, 1999: "Possibly felt the baby move. Felt like a tap or a flutter - like the brush of a butterfly wing... This is also the day of Bob & Lynn Hunt's 25th wedding anniversary. This [is] also the day that the Minnesota Vikings football team lost the NFC championship game to go to Superbowl XXXIII to the Atlanta Falcons. The score was 27 to 30. (Gary Anderson's kicking streak broke, effectively losing the game.) Also, Natalie lost a game of Scrabble to me. The score was 234 to 153." On the facing page the running scrabble scorecard is taped. I really slaughtered her.

Two weeks later, the entry reads: "Clumsiness was the order of the day. A couple broken glasses over the last few weeks, and two falls. Neither severe, but potentially deadly. The first was from the car into the garden next to the parking space. A three foot drop. Natalie said that she was surprised to be looking at the bottom of the car and standing up to her waist in the snow. The second was on our way out the door for a walk to Pinehurst Park and back. I was in the lead, opening the door to walk out, and I heard a scream. Natalie had taken a three-step step. If I hadn't been there, she would have put her head through the window of the door, and I would have found her looking like this:" (I drew a cavewoman hanging through a door at the bottom of the stairs. "Inside," "outside," and "a pool of blood" were all appropriately labeled.) Sometimes morbid humor is funny.

The months went by in that tiny little apartment, with me going to school, cleaning the middle school at night, and Natalie working at Skutevik's floral.

Even though I didn't know it at the time, the preciousness of young life was fully imprinted in a small hospital in the hill country of Northern Haiti in February, only months from Cameron's birth.

Through a long series of events, some wrangling with my college professors over deadlines and due dates and with a backpack full of school supplies from the basement storeroom at the middle school, I was fortunate enough to find myself in Pignon, Haiti, a geographically tiny mountain town that had become a base of operations for a humanitarian mission organization, Haiti Outreach. There were several folks from the Twin Cities and a bunch of us from Cloquet. We all had been connected through the churches we were attending at the time and it was good to be someplace warm, doing good work for good people in a place far from the blizzards of home.

Natalie was pregnant with Cameron for five months at this time. We had planned to both go on this trip together, and it had been a tough decision to go to Haiti without her, but the plane travel and pickup ride through the pitted roads, swollen rivers and sweltering heat made a pregnant young American woman's trip through Haiti's third-world infrastructure a tough sell. The fact that we had to buzz the runway to clear it of a small herd of goats before setting down in Cap Haitien was enough to make even the hardiest of our travelers a little nervous.

There was so much to learn, see, and do in Haiti. I loved the adventure of it all. One morning, I got up early to climb the side of one the high hills that contains Pignon so I could get a better perspective of how big the place was. Nobody came with, but many of the ladies I saw that morning beginning their preparations for the day probably wondered what the pasty white kid was doing marching up into the scraggly brush of the hillside. Little did they know that I was armed with a disposable camera to get a panoramic view of their city. They didn't stop me, nor did the bleating of goats and smells of the breakfast beans and rice being cooked over charcoal fires. I wondered just how devastated this place had been over the years, the rocks and crags I was climbing upward through were clearly not the soil that had once held down a jungle paradise. A few hundred feet above the city I snapped a few shots and wondered aloud how such a beautiful people could go through so much. The tin roofs seemed to stack up on each other, tiny paths winding their ways through a sea of rust and the way to the marketplace and city center.

We had come to help build a house for a family on the outskirts of town and to be "ambassadors of goodwill" to this tiny place. The construction was primitive, and the walls held a tin roof. The roughly 400 square foot structure was several times larger than the hut this family of eight had been living in. Their banana-leaf roof would no longer need constant repair. Daniel, one of the boys in the family, and I enjoyed being around each other. He showed me what a pineapple plant was and how to roast cashews plucked from the tree that shaded us from the sun. I had to learn where it was okay to use the bathroom, the proper ways to speak Creole words, and especially how to make the children wonder and laugh. He and his friends tried to show me how to open a Coke bottle with their teeth, warned against petting the little distended-bellied dogs that roamed around the town looking for a scrap or handout and to stay away from the witch doctor and his followers when they came through the public square.

This was a place like no other, exotic and strangely familiar at the same time. People laughed and talked over cold drinks in the late afternoon. Mothers worried about their little ones and old men told stories, lots of stories. We haggled for trinkets in the market, ate our beans and rice and enjoyed the cool night breezes when they came. The most fun I had, though, was to laugh and play with the kids. They seemed so free. A rolled-up ball of socks and a couple stones in the middle of the street would be enough for the most exciting time. Some rolled and raced "hoops" of blown out bicycle tires with their sticks. Some whipped rocks out into the sugarcane and many just waited around for something, anything, to happen.

The beauty of the jungle exposed the ruggedness of the land, long stripped of its soil by erosion after being clear-cut by farmers needing the charcoal that heated their food. The wild music and dancing of the molasses-covered, rum-guzzling stilt-walkers and carnival parade made the eerie, above-ground tombs on the edge of town seem all the more imposing and fearsome. The liveliness of the children during our impromptu street soccer games was tempered by how carefully they would attack the bananas and mangoes delivered by an older brother or sister. This was a people and place without the luxury of being able to miss a calorie or two. The reality of the poverty and emptiness of the homes was overshadowed by the generosity of their spirits and the fullness of the lives they did have. I'm not sure I'd really taken my life for granted back home, but it was clear to me from then on that I didn't want it wasted.

One afternoon, after the work had been completed, one of our leaders arranged a visit to a hospital run by an American-trained Haitian doctor. Desperation marked the faces of the patients and their families packed into a one-room triage and recovery ward. Our leader had told us a little about what to expect and warned that most people in this town didn't go the hospital to be healed; they often never made it out alive. It was a strange thing for us from Northern Minnesota, the land of the Mayo Clinic and decent health coverage to realize so many that we would see that day wouldn't see daylight from the comfort of their own homes again.

Everything changed for me that afternoon. After handing out the mints and other candies I had been assigned, I peeked behind the curtain where soft whimpers and the whines of hungry babies indicated young life. The nurse's eyes caught mine and she motioned for me to step in. She was holding the tiniest baby I had ever seen. With the help of some simple interpretation, we talked about how this child had been born prematurely and needed medicine. As I felt the feather weight of the baby's little body I imagined a future with my own child, still months away. All the hopes and dreams of a young family and the exciting times to come flashed before me. Another nurse prepared the IV as we chatted and I was dumbfounded as these young ladies pierced the child's tiny arm with an adult-sized needle. Blood and tiny screams went out as they nervously tried again and again. It was too much for me, I got choked up and excused myself. Without any medical training myself, I knew this wasn't going to work, and that this one would give up its last breath before we left that forsaken place. We came to that hospital bearing pieces of candy and I left with a heavy heart. I carried on with the work we had set out to do, but I was downcast the rest of the trip. I was tired and saddened. It just wasn't fair.

When I came through the door of our apartment back in Cloquet, all the frustration with American complacency, the shock of experiencing so much destitution and the very real grief I was experiencing as a result of the death of this child converged as I saw my beautiful wife. Through tears and photos I explained to Natalie what I'd seen and experienced and how it had affected my sense of self, our family and what our lives were really about. I committed in my mind and heart that the time we had as a family would not be wasted. Life is short, sometimes too short, and there was no guarantee that our baby would have it any better than one born thousands of miles away to a woman I did not know.

Getting back to the rhythm of life after traveling took a while. I had been affected by what I had seen and experienced. As time went on, though, so did my schooling and the work at the school. I kept up on the journaling for the baby book. Natalie's belly got bigger and bigger. I was anxious for the baby. I think she was, too.

On June 14, 1999, I recorded the story of Cameron's birth for posterity. I wrote to him: "After Martha Krhin and Mike Laulunen's wedding on Saturday, June 12, 1999, we decided to go out for the day. We bought bread at the Positively 3rd Street Bakery. Two loaves and some bagels to be exact. From there we went to Park Point and a two mile walk... One woman was so concerned about us walking in the heat of the day she went into her house, filled a glass with water and ice and gave it to us for your mother to drink. What a blessing. After that jaunt, we spent a couple hours looking at books (baby books) and magazines (Country Living, Home, and other assorted house and home decorating magazines) at Barnes and Noble... Since this was getting toward the end of Natalie's pregnancy, she would get hungry frequently, so we ate BLT Bread-Bowl salads at Perkin's. When we got home that night the contractions she had been feeling started to seem to hurt. (She'd been having them for a couple weeks infrequently, so it didn't seem like a big deal.) We played a game of cribbage and lay down. At around 10:00, I started timing the contractions to see if they were regular and they were. So we called the hospital (St. Mary's) in Duluth and they told us to come down; Natalie was dilated to two centimeters before, so we thought it might just be a practice run.

This is a list of stuff we needed to put in the bag before we left. (It had been packed for two weeks before.) [Taped to the page is a 1.5 X 2 inch vanilla colored piece of cardstock that lists in pencil: "Going-home clothes, toothbrush, brush, pony-tail holders, tape recorder, tape, camera and film, food for me, popsicles"] We never did put that stuff in before we left.

When we got to the hospital, they attached the fetal heart monitor and checked the dilation and decided to keep us overnight. (We thought we'd be going home in the morning.)

When we woke up they reattached the monitors and found that she had dilated another centimeter, and that this could be very early labor. To make the process go a bit quicker, they encouraged us to go for a walk. We kept passing another couple in the hall that was doing the same thing... (It turned out to be Nathan and Jean McParlan, future friends of ours. Their oldest boy, Michael, and ours shared a birthday.)

At around noon, the doctor broke her bag of waters. This is supposed to help labor along faster. It didn't. At 3-3:30 they decided to give her Pitocin, 'The Pit,' a drug that makes contractions closer and stronger. They hurt intensely. (Genesis 3:16) I had to press her back to counter the pressure of the contraction. This is called back labor. We wanted to be completely natural with the birth, but she couldn't bear the pain. Around 5:00 the guy with the epidural block came. He was a loud Italian man. The needle was about six inches long.

Labor progressed from that point on, nearly painless. A little before 9:00 p.m. the nurse felt to see how much longer the head would be in there and she was surprised to realize that the baby was already coming down the birth canal. She could start pushing anytime! So from then until 9:24 she pushed. Nicole and Sarah (our sisters) were in the room during this time and the rest of our crowd was behind the curtain by the door, sneaking peeks the whole time. It took a little work to get the baby out. "It's a boy!" Cameron Michael Swanson. 9:24. 6-13-99. 7lbs. 12 oz.

What a day and night. We were worn out after all the people and pictures. Someone brought Kentucky Fried Chicken, so we ate a bunch around 11:30 before heading for bed. You were purple-headed, a little slimy, and screaming upon arrival... The most beautiful child I've ever seen. We cried together, you, your mom and me, that day, our family."

Chapter 4

CAMERON

He was perfect! God created a perfect little baby just for us. He had all his toes, fingers, tear ducts, fuzzy hair, a loud cry and beautiful eyes. Every yawn, coo and Cheerio mouth brought us pure joy. We could stare at him for endless hours and for the next few weeks we adored all his little movements and noises.

When Cameron was about 2 weeks old I was rocking him and adoring his little face. During this sweet moment, I imagined God handing over His one and only Son to die for me. I couldn't even handle the thought of giving up my precious baby like God had done. I started sobbing and was overwhelmed with love. I was affected by two thoughts in these moments of God showing me this deeper love. First, I could not imagine ever giving Cameron up for anything. I loved Cameron more than I thought was even possible. Second, God loved me so much, that he gave His Son to die for me. Just imagine how much God must love each one of us. He loves us more than we can even comprehend. *For God so loved the world that he gave his one and only Son, that whoever believes in him shall not perish but have eternal life.* John 3:16 This is a scripture I had read multiple times before this moment, but in this little revelation, I grasped it more than I had before. Looking back, I believe God was using this moment to prepare me for bigger plans.

Chris and I got to enjoy all the firsts with Cameron. His first belly laugh was from something as simple Chris swinging a pillow case above his head. We only replayed the same action 200 times so we could hear it over and over. Cameron's first time rolling over, crawling, sitting up on his own, cutting his first tooth and his first steps were all our most exciting moments at the time. He taught us how to slow down and enjoy small moments like any first-born would. Every time we danced to the silly songs from The Wiggles or sang along with the cartoon, "Caillou," he would light up as if it was the first time all over again. I think we rediscover that childlike love and joy when we have children. I am thankful for those days and the time we had to spend with just Cameron. I am also so grateful we took hundreds of pictures of him so we can still enjoy seeing his beautiful face.

Since we were having so much fun with one child, we thought, "Why not two?" Cameron graduated to big brother and our family grew on August 13, 2001. Caleb Robert, weighing exactly 7 lbs, was beautiful in all the same ways as Cameron. Before Caleb was born, I was worried that I would not have enough love for more than one child. How can you possibly love that much again? What I learned instantly when he was born, is that our hearts are more than capable of loving more than one. It was explained to me that parents' love for their kids is like a flame of a candle. It can spread to other wicks endlessly and keep its flame. There was enough flame for all of our candles to glow brightly.

Caleb and Cameron became quick friends and it was great to have two sons. I often found myself saying, "Those boys!" Caleb was quick to walk so he could keep up with his big brother. Needless to say, our hands were very busy. One summer day, the boys were playing outside while my husband was cleaning the garage. We had a second floor in our garage, and apparently a bird had flown up there. The boys decided to chase it around and around. I remember thinking that this game of tag was just the start of all the crazy moments we would have. One of my favorite memories of Cameron and Caleb together happened one night at bedtime. Cameron (4) was telling Caleb (2) the story of David and Goliath. I found myself standing at the bottom of the steps listening and swelling with pride. Cameron did such a good job telling the story just like his Daddy had told it to him. When I thought it was an appropriate time for the story to end I was surprised to hear it continue. My little 4-year-old had finished telling the story by saying, "And they cut his head off!" I gasped and my husband calmly said, "It's true." I didn't think that my little boys should know things like that. Their pure little minds now had a vision of yuck in them. However, Goliath was a bad guy and David was victorious because of God's' strength, so this time I let it slide. That is what I hoped they would remember, "And they cut his head off," is probably what stuck.

Our family grew quickly and we welcomed Emma Lynn a short 18 months after Caleb on March 21, 2003. We had three kids in diapers. As you can see, our plan for waiting until school was finished didn't really pan out. Sleep was definitely a thing of the past for me, and so was a clean house. Somehow, God made it so moms can get by on little sleep for a long time. I remember getting up nightly for at least one of our three kids. Cameron had a not-so-welcomed habit of waking in the middle of the night and putting a movie on for himself. People often say, "Enjoy these years when they are little, because they will go by fast." When you are in the years of endless diapers, lack of sleep and baskets of laundry, those years seem to drag by. Now that our kids are older, I wish I could make time pass more slowly.

Cameron was often described as more serious than other children. It would take more work to make him smile than others. He was very inquisitive and I liked to think he was a deep thinker. People would also comment to us that he seemed mature for his age. Chris had found some really unique wood, and built a coffee table Cameron could pound nails into, and use a cordless drill on. This independence made him feel like he was a big boy. He spoke well and could carry a conversation with adults. In addition to that, he seemed to be quite focused when he worked on projects. He would sit for long periods of time drawing pictures or playing with playdough. He created one of my most cherished little pieces of art, a picture that says "I Love You Mom." I was thoroughly impressed and pretty sure he was the smartest 4-year-old there ever was.

Cameron was definitely a morning person. I remember sounding like a broken record, asking him daily to be quiet because Caleb and Emma were still asleep. He wanted to start the day playing with toys that made noise or sneaking some sort of sugar from on top of the fridge. Sneaking Tootsie rolls or fruit snacks upon waking is another trait one of his little brothers would inherit. One morning, I came out of our bedroom and Cameron had pulled a kitchen chair to the fridge, stacked a smaller chair on top of it and piled a foot stool on top of that so he could get on the refrigerator where the Tootsie rolls were. He was always on the ball with how to solve a problem; when you couldn't reach a Tootsie roll, you needed to create a ladder.

Cameron had four male cousins around the same age that he enjoyed spending time with. Alex, who lived nearby, was one month younger and a ball of fun. He was always the more charismatic one and smiled a lot. He would sing and dance on command, and Cameron would just stare at you with a blank look. Those two boys came up with some interesting activities to keep them busy. They would dress up as superheroes, use their imagination, laugh a lot and compete for the same toys. Cousins were such a big part of my upbringing and I was glad that my kids would get to grow up with theirs as well.

In addition to relatives, we belonged to an active church family. They taught us a lot about parenting and how to show our kids how to live a faith-filled life. At a young age, Cameron had good friends who already shared a common faith and love for things like worship music. Our church family provided a lot of support when we had little ones. Without them, surviving Cameron's accident would have played out much differently.

Another of my favorite memories of Cameron is when he would see someone being mad or yelling about something he would get concerned. Cameron would whisper in my ear, "They have fire in their heart, and they need Jesus in the heart." He knew that Jesus could bring joy. Looking back, I see he was wise beyond his years. I loved how he thought the local paper mill was a cloud-making factory.

I could go on and on about all the things I remember about our firstborn child. Talking about and remembering him is so healing for me and helps me to not forget him. Even though it has been almost 11 years I want to remember everything about him. I can even recall smells and giggles. It is almost like they are etched so deep in my mind that they are truly a part of me. When my kids do something that Cameron did, or say something he said, I instantly make the connection.

Cameron was a very strong-willed boy, and if he did not want to do something he would put up a fight. I asked him to pick up the backpack he dropped in front of the bottom step once. I wanted it on the bottom step and out of the way. Since I had just recently talked to one of the mothers I often went to for parenting advice and she told me to be strong and finish the battles, I knew I needed to follow through with the request to move his bag. It took him 45 minutes to move it for me. He was really good at getting me exhausted purely with stubbornness. He didn't want to try the food, take the Tylenol, put his shoes on or pick up the toy unless it was his idea and timing.

With busy days and sleepless nights most of the time, it was hard to always remember to teach the kids to pray. One thing we would try to do with our kids is pray for people before bed. At one point, Cameron and I prayed for the same person night after night. We had a friend named Alicia that nannied a precious little boy named Jonathan who was the same age as Cameron. Jonathan had been adopted from Russia and had been fighting Leukemia. I remember praying so earnestly for this little boy to be healed and crying just at the thought of what the parents must have been going through. I still remember where I was sitting and the heaviness that was on my heart when we were asking God to be with his parents. I sat with Cameron, rubbing his head and just weeping while praying for them. In January 2004, we heard from Alicia that Jonathan had taken a turn for the worse and was only given weeks to live. We would always check in with Alicia on the latest information for Jonathan and pray for him and his parents.

As a family, we participated in Early Childhood Family Education and school readiness programs and Cameron attended from birth through preschool. Cameron loved school! He was always ready to learn new things and enjoyed being involved in activities. According to one of his teachers, Patrice, she could count on him to always follow directions. Patrice first met Cameron when he was only a few months old. She volunteered through a program called "Books For Babies." When she recalled that first visit, she said, "As I left that day, I remember thinking what a blessing that sweet, fair haired angel was, and how blessed he was to have been born into such a loving and dedicated family." She continued to work with him every year through preschool. Patrice wrote us a letter sharing her memories about the time she spent with him in her class. She said Cameron would regularly inquire about what they would be making in art class and he could most likely be found at the art table or play dough station. She noticed his effort and persistence in learning how to write every letter of his name and he did not give up until he accomplished it. He always had something to contribute during circle time and it would get everyone's attention because it was pertinent to the subject. Shy and gentle is what he came across as, but once you got to know him you would see that he was determined and persistent, knowing exactly what he wanted.

Cameron, like any other 4- year old, liked to help and get his hands into everything. I still love to share one of my favorite memories of him helping out at a kitchen show. At the time, I was a consultant and would go into other homes preparing food while demonstrating their products. Sometimes Cameron would come with me and be my little helper. While I was demonstrating, he asked if he could peel an onion for me. Since I was distracted, I nodded yes. I'm guessing five minutes passed before I looked over, and to my surprise the onion was peeled. He had many tears running down his face and the onion was about the size of a bouncy ball. Not once did he stop to ask why his eyes burned or why there were tears running all over. We all had a great laugh and he never asked to peel another onion for me again.

Chapter 5

BWCA, SUMMER 2004

W eekends when I (Chris) was quite young were spent
tagging along fishing and hunting with my dad. I
cherish the gift he gave me of memories of frying
rainbow trout at the campsite or the smell of a 16-gauge shotgun
shell after it takes down a grouse or clay pigeon. It's because of my
dad that I like the feel of a Duluth Pack on my back and the sound
and resistance of a canoe paddle slicing through the water on a
misty morning. He showed me where to find the wild strawberries
for breakfast and the agates that emerged from the gravel after a
rain. I still admire how my dad has always been a hard worker on
the job, honest in his assessment and a straight talker. I've learned
all sorts of other valuable stuff from my dad, too, but as a father
now, myself, I am grateful for all those times when I was able to

see a bit of the wild world around us and have always hoped to pass that same joy of the outdoors along to my own kids.

The trip to the Boundary Waters in the summer of 2003 with Cameron and my dear friend Doug Olsen was one of those legacy-building times. Truth be told, Cameron had no idea what he was in for, but he thought that whatever it was going to be, it was going to be fun. We spent a restless night at Doug's parent's place south of Ely and then headed out early the next morning. I packed our gear in ZipLoc Bags in one of the large green packs so familiar in our neck of the woods. His was filled with the stuff a kid thinks to take: a rubber ball, a plastic sword, a matchbox car, some fruit snacks and a swimsuit. We had brought along a small fishing pole and some tackle on the off-chance that we might have the chance to catch something. He had never canoed before, but looked forward to swimming in a lake with his new life jacket. The possibility of catching fish nagged at him as we paddled along, a challenge any canoeing family can attest to. It was wonderful to be in this part of the country with my son and a friend. We were making memories.

One of my favorite pictures of Cameron is from that trip when we took a break to let the water rush over us in the rapids on the west end of Knife Lake. It's border country and fairly rugged, but we had a great time lying in the cold clear water, splashing around in the early afternoon sun. His delight and the squeals of laughter have stuck with me over the years, and I smile when I hear those same sounds from other kids playing with their dads.

I tried to explain the story of the "Root Beer" lady, Dorothy Molter, a local legend among canoeing-types in the Ely area. We anticipated camping at a favorite site near where the remnants of her former home site now remain. Our entire family enjoys the taste of cold root beer and the froth when you pour it over ice cream, and so it was no surprise that he was intensely curious about Dorothy. What he really wanted was the root beer, but every twenty minutes or so, he'd ask if we were close to where she lived.

I imagine him thinking he'd pull up to her spot and down a bottle or two. Sadly, the homestead has been disassembled and is now in Ely and Dorothy and her drinks are long gone. Cameron didn't get it. Even after we walked the grounds and seen the overgrown roses and lilacs, he couldn't understand how the "Root Beer" lady wasn't able to quench his thirst.

His frustration and the feeling of being ripped off came out the next afternoon as we headed through the jack pines and thistleberry south of Knife. He'd had enough. The walk was too long. His pack was too heavy. The sun was too hot. The root beer wasn't flowing. He was finished. He hadn't slept well the night before and I think he was missing the comforts of home and his mom. As I looked out toward the lake and the path down the hill toward it, I imagined what Doug might have heard. He was ahead of us carrying the canoe, so I doubt he did, but it was the argument of a young father and son about when and how he was going to get down the hill one way or another and that he couldn't possibly stay put forever. It'd get cold at night and Doug and I were moving on. We had to keep going, we'd run out of food, and the fish don't live on land.... It went on and on until he stopped and threw down his pack. He demanded that I carry him. I tried to rationalize with him, but he was spent. I'd packed this trail multiple times as a canoeing guide years before, so I knew that we only had a couple hundred yards to go, but it didn't matter. I told him to stay where he was if he wanted to and I walked off. He was shocked and a little angry. His wailing was almost unbearable, but I knew he was going to be okay; there was nobody else nearby and I'd be back in a few minutes. He'd have to deal with it. Doug laughed when I reached the water and told him about the tantrum and then I headed back. Cameron was relieved and grateful that the ordeal was over, but it had scared him and I was glad to have "saved" him. He was strong-willed, but a quick learner; that was the last time he got left behind.

Chapter 6

THE MOVE

When February 2004 rolled around, my parents found themselves needing to downsize immediately because my dad was forced to retire early. He had been working for the local "cloud making factory," or paper mill. We have a good relationship and wanted to help, so we decided to have them move in with us. On their new income, we knew it would take a couple years until they would be set to buy again so we would figure out a way to make it work. With our three small kids and four adults in the house, we quickly realized we needed a bigger place. My husband worked tirelessly to finish up any house projects so we could sell and start our search for the perfect place. In Moose Lake, Minnesota, a small town about thirty minutes south of where we lived, we found an old dairy farm that had a huge barn, pole barn and milk house. It was a two-story three-bedroom farmhouse with a large heated slab addition that had been used as a kennel. We would call it home for the next five years, and it was perfect for all of us to fit and live in comfortably. We moved in on May 4, 2004. We planned on making the addition an apartment for my parents and fixing the existing farmhouse to meet our needs. This was going to be a slow project that we would work on over the next year. We were excited about our new adventure and the possibilities of what country life could be for us.

Cameron was quick to scout the place out and enjoyed the freedom of running without caution. We were surrounded by rolling hills that would be hayed twice each summer. It was easy to picture the fields full of roaming cattle. This was quite different from all the cars and busy streets we were accustomed to. We were looking forward to agate hunting on our own road, the enjoyment of watching the cows and horses across the road from us, listening to crickets and coyotes at night and stargazing without any light interfering. The boys had so much exploring to do and they didn't waste any time. There was an old silo behind the barn that Cameron discovered and decided to make into a fort. He planned to call the silo "The Echo" because it echoed when you talked in it.

Another great perk of our new place was that we had room for animals and lots of them. We had planned to get egg-laying chickens so the kids could gather eggs, ducks just for fun, guinea hens to eat the wood ticks, a dog and whatever else we could talk Chris into. We just had to clean up the place first and get our feet on the ground. However, I let the thrill of starting a mini hobby farm get the best of me, and on May 18, my sister, my mom and I set out to experience our first chicken swap. At first I thought there would only be chickens there, but farmers brought their young livestock of all kinds. I was so ecstatic! I saw goats, lambs, rabbits, kittens, puppies and even miniature donkeys. I contained myself and only left with a dozen baby chicks, two ducks and a pair of goslings. Who knew there were multiple types of chickens and ducks to choose from? You had choices of what color eggs you wanted your chickens to lay and what hairstyle your chicken would have. I preferred the ones that had a perfect Mohawk down the middle; they were hilarious. That was the first of many swaps we attended. Later, I swapped a bunny for a goat! It was so much fun. We had an exciting time getting them all settled at our new home and the boys fell in love with the little birds instantly.

Chapter 7

NIGHT CRAWLER PICKING

As for God, his way is perfect: The Lord's word is flawless;
he shields all who take refuge in him.
Psalms 18:30

I love how God has a way of prompting our spirit. I did
something way out of the ordinary the night before the
accident, one of the most cherished nights of my life.
I decided to let Cameron stay up late, even after his dad had
gone to bed. We were going to have a special night and I was
going to give him much needed attention after the big move. We
made ourselves ice cream sundaes, and I gave him permission
to create his own ice cream masterpiece. We had chocolate,
sprinkles, butterscotch, whipping cream from a can, bananas and
marshmallows. Cameron's sundae was not complete however until

he added some maple syrup! I cringed at the amount of sugar he was about to put down, but shook it off as "our special night." In addition to the sundaes, we watched the movie *Cheaper by the Dozen* together. I remember staring at his little face and just swelling with love at who he was becoming. He sat on my lap for most of the movie, and at one point he told me how bad he felt for the little boy who had to sleep way up in the attic. He felt bad that the boy did not get much attention and seemed to get in trouble when it was not his fault. He told me that he wanted to have a lot of brothers and sisters, but did not want to sleep in the attic. I thought it was sweet that he noticed the little boy was sad and was feeling left out. I reassured him that I would never make him sleep in an attic, and he was content with knowing that.

Our biggest adventure that last night was hunting for night crawlers, though. I am not sure where this idea arose from - maybe it was something they did in the movie. This is not something I typically would think of as a fun thing to do, but I am grateful the idea was there that night. It was raining out, so we put on our mud boots and rain coats. Now, we were in the country, so it was a lot darker than what I was used too. We hunted down a few flashlights and a bucket, and as we were walking in our front yard, you could see the ground squirming with night crawlers. Cameron was so excited that he darted towards one close to us, and if you have ever tried grabbing for a night crawler, you know how fast they move. He missed it, and another, and another. The challenge was on; I needed to show Cameron how to catch one without it getting away. I didn't even care that they were disgusting and slimy; I just went for it. I loved how he was proud of me for being good at catching them. He didn't give up and finally started to catch them as well. We had lots of laughs and caught many gross night crawlers. We talked about fishing with them and even selling them. When it was time to go in, I told Cameron that we needed to keep the worms in the bucket outside, so we left it on the porch steps and went in to dry off. After getting Cameron tucked in and giving him lots of kisses, I slept satisfied with the extra time I spent with him that night.

Because Cameron required little sleep to function, he rose earlier than everyone else the next morning. He came running into the house and was upset about something. He said, "Mom, all the night crawlers are dead!" He then accused me of drowning them because I was the one who told him to keep them in the bucket outside. The rainwater filled the bucket and all of our chubby night crawlers had drowned. I felt awful, but he seemed to have gotten over it quickly, and was already planning his next night crawler adventure. I recently brought our youngest boy, Gavin, out to find night crawlers, and I was giddy with joy because I knew we were making memories. I also used it as an opportunity to talk with Gavin about the older brother he never met. I think moments like these help to connect the dots a little better.

Part Two

Chapter 8

OUR DARKEST DAY

God is our refuge and strength, an ever-present help in trouble.
Therefore we will not fear, though the earth give way and the
mountains fall into the heart of the sea, though its waters roar
and foam and the mountains quake with their surging.
Psalm 46:1-3

I t was a sunny day in May and the countryside was coming
alive. I (Natalie) remember the wide open sky, crisp clean air
and the sound of birds. Frogs and crickets were now going to
put us to sleep at night instead of the cars and dogs we often heard
at bedtime. It was refreshing to think we had a new beginning and
all sorts of family adventures ahead of us. With three little kids,
we looked forward to experiencing the life of country dwellers. On
this particular day, May 19, 2004, we had planned for cleaning up

the old farmhouse and property we now called home. My family was visiting and available to help on a Wednesday, but Chris still needed to go to work. My uncles, grandparents, parents, brother and sister were all there working to get us set up and clean all the dangers of an old farm. We had an old pond that needed to be drained, chicken wire rolls in random places, holes that needed to be filled, dog kennels that needed dismantling and sharp, rusty pieces of equipment we needed to get rid of. It seemed that it was going to be a glorious day full of productivity.

The boys, Cameron, Caleb and my nephew, Alex, were also outside gathering bugs. Worms, ants, ladybugs and slugs were available by the dozens now, and being squashed in their little hands. They ran around our property with squeals of delight and were determined to catch all they could. We had a bug catcher that was going to house their new friends and the boys wanted to find as many as they could. I remember telling them, "If you squeeze them too hard they will die." Instantly, they slowed down their run to a fast walk and focused on softening their squeeze. Once they finished looking around the edge of the pole barn, which sat on the lower southeast corner of our property, they headed toward the pond. I immediately was uncomfortable with that idea, so I hopped on the three-wheeler that was close by in effort to get there quicker, as the distance from where I was seemed too far away to stop them from getting too close to the edge if I were to run. When I scooped the boys up, they were thrilled to have a ride in the attached trailer, so I did a few circles around our property.

I can remember the giggles and excitement in their little voices as we went through puddles and sped over little hills. I was peaceful and looking forward to more times of having fun together. When we finished our ride, I strategically placed them in a spot I thought would be safe. It was close to the house and away from everything I thought was dangerous, on a cement slab at the end of a long line of dog kennels that were eventually going to be removed. They quickly started to spread out all of their bugs and compare their new treasures. I told them to stay there so they wouldn't get hurt. I hopped back on the three-wheeler and headed toward the pole barn to park it. I set off to get more work done. My sister was mowing the lawn, and one of my uncles was preparing to tear down all of the dog kennels that ran along the side of the addition. He had already taken the fencing off the top. The only part left was the seven walls made from cinder blocks that stood about four feet high, each four feet from the next. My uncle was testing the sturdiness of the first wall about 30 feet away from the kids, and to his surprise, it moved a lot easier than he thought it would. It fell out of his grasp, into the next wall. The cinder block walls crashed down on each other, and in seconds, the place I put the boys to keep them safe became the most dangerous place on the property. It was a domino effect. There was nothing to stop the wall from toppling onto the boys. My nephew, Alex, was on his knees with his back to the walls, so when the walls fell on him, his body braced the weight. He was injured. Our son Caleb was far enough out that the walls missed him completely. Over the noise of the lawnmower, I heard my dad scream, "Call 911!" I immediately looked up from a distance and saw him pull Cameron out from the under the brick walls. Cameron was wearing an Incredible Hulk costume backwards and pink mud boots. He was easy to spot. When my dad lifted Cameron, he was limp like a sleeping child would be. All the noise around was silenced and time stood still as I heard Cameron's sweet voice in my head say, "I am alright, Mommy."

I was way over by the pole barn, which was probably two hundred feet away from them. I ran as fast as I could to call 911. My hands were shaking so badly I could barely hold the phone. I was sure he would be alright because his voice was audible. I *heard* him, but he looked lifeless. When the dispatcher answered, I tried to explain that we needed help fast, but I started to fall apart. I hung up, thinking Chris needs to get here; I need my husband!

Since we had only lived in this house for a few days, we did not have long distance service yet. I looked at the clock and it was 3:00. Chris would not be leaving work for 45 more minutes. I tried dialing the long calling card number, and I kept on messing up. My hands were shaking too much and my heart was racing; adrenaline was being released into my body. My body still shakes when I go through this story, even though I have told it a thousand times. After many tries, I got through to the school and the secretary, Pam Schimenek, bless her heart, answered the phone. I screamed a blood-curdling scream, "Our boy is hurt!" For years after this incident, Pam was nervous when she saw my name on the caller I.D. She went to get Chris.

While I was making the phone calls, there was chaos all around me. My mom was in the front yard on the ground screaming, crying and praying. My grandma was pacing and praying, and my sister kept telling me I needed to get out there to be with Cameron. There was something in me that prevented me from going outside to see him. I did not want to see our son fighting for his life, or see his little broken body. At that point, I was scared that this is how I would remember him. My brother, Justin, my dad, my grandpa, and my uncles were all out there with him. I picked up the phone again thinking I have to get the prayer chain going. Panicking, I struggled to get the calling card numbers dialed, and fell apart again. I kept asking my grandma, "Is he going to be okay?" She kept repeating, "All you can do is pray, dear."

I fell against the wall by the phone and sat on the floor. The numbers kept getting dialed wrong for my friend Katie. I would go back and forth between crying and fighting to dial correctly. When she answered, all I could do was scream again, but this time it was more murderous and uncontrolled. I hung up, leaving her uneasy and confused about who had called. Because of the calling card, she did not recognize the number. Thank God she was smart and called the phone company to figure it out. She was

YOU MAY ALSO LIKE...

Song of Hartgrove Hall
    by Solomons, Natasha

Flying Circus
    by Crandall, Susan

Inheritance: How Our Genes Change Our ...
    by Moalem MD, PhD, Sharon

Essentials of Evidence-Based Academic ...
    by Mather, Nancy; Wendling, Barbar...

be exchanged at the store in accordance with the applicable warranty.

Returns or exchanges will not be permitted (i) after 14 days or without receipt or (ii) for product not carried by Barnes & Noble or Barnes & Noble.com.

Policy on receipt may appear in two sections.

Return Policy

With a sales receipt or Barnes & Noble.com packing slip, a full refund in the original form of payment will be issued from any Barnes & Noble Booksellers store for returns of undamaged NOOKs, new and unread books, and unopened and undamaged music CDs, DVDs, vinyl records, toys/games and audio books made within 14 days of purchase from a Barnes & Noble Booksellers store or Barnes & Noble.com with the below exceptions:

A store credit for the purchase price will be issued (i) for purchases made by check less than 7 days prior to the date of return, (ii) when a gift receipt is presented within 60 days of purchase, (iii) for textbooks, (iv) when the original tender is PayPal, or (v) for products purchased

Barnes & Noble Booksellers #2098
1600 Miller Trunk Highway
Duluth, MN 55811
218-786-0710

STR:2098 REG:005 TRN:2270 CSHR:David T

Choosing Joy: Our Walk through Tragedy
   9781512709049   T1
   (1 @ 11.95)   11.95

Subtotal   11.95
Sales Tax T1 (8.375%)   1.00
TOTAL   12.95
CASH   20.00
CASH CHANGE   7.05-

A MEMBER WOULD HAVE SAVED   1.20

Thanks for shopping at
Barnes & Noble

101.37A   01/26/2016 11:30AM

CUSTOMER COPY

purchased from other retailers or sellers are returnable only to the retailer or seller from which they are purchased, pursuant to such retailer's or seller's return policy. Magazines, newspapers, eBooks, digital downloads, and used books are not returnable or exchangeable. Defective NOOKs may be exchanged at the store in accordance with the applicable warranty.

Returns or exchanges will not be permitted (i) after 14 days or without receipt or (ii) for product not carried by Barnes & Noble or Barnes & Noble.com.

Policy on receipt may appear in two sections.

Return Policy

With a sales receipt or Barnes & Noble.com packing slip, a full refund in the original form of payment will be issued from any Barnes & Noble Booksellers store for returns of undamaged NOOKs, new and unread books, and unopened and undamaged music CDs, DVDs, vinyl records, toys/games and audio books made within 14 days of purchase from a Barnes & Noble Booksellers store or Barnes & Noble.com with the below exceptions:

A store credit for the purchase price will be issued (i) for purchases made by check less than 7 days prior to the date of return, (ii) when a gift receipt is presented within 60 days of purchase, (iii) for textbooks, (iv) when the original tender is PayPal, or (v) for products purchased at Barnes & Noble College bookstores that are listed for sale in the Barnes & Noble Booksellers inventory management system.

Opened music CDs, DVDs, vinyl records, audio books may not be returned, and can be exchanged only for the same title and only if defective. NOOKs purchased from other retailers or sellers are returnable only to the retailer or seller from which they are purchased, pursuant to such retailer's or seller's return policy. Magazines, newspapers, eBooks, digital downloads, and used books are not returnable or exchangeable. Defective NOOKs may not sure what was going on, but she knew it was bad and started spreading the word to our church's prayer chain and praying herself.

Lifting my hands, I prayed to God. My grandma told me to just sit and pray and don't stop. My mind seemed to be in a state of peace as my heart was being torn into a million pieces. During this time, a lady I had never seen before came running in my house that I had never seen. She asked me what my son's name was and ran back outside. I remember thinking she must be an angel. Her name was Corrine and she was our neighbor we had not met yet. She had heard the screaming and was a first responder. Apparently, no one outside could tell her his name because everyone was such a mess.

My dad and brother had been doing CPR on Cameron and doing everything they could think of for him. My heart still breaks into a million pieces when I think about what they were all going through. My grandpa had not been a stranger to tragedy. My grandparents had lost three of their own kids tragically. The uncle that knocked the wall over had previously lost two of his own kids in a tragic car accident. It must have been awful.

Justin, my brother, came in the house with my son's blood on him after working on him and holding him. He looked defeated, confused and helpless. I was told Cameron had blood coming from his ears, nose and mouth. I knew that is never a good sign, but at the moment I dismissed all doubt and just hoped for the best because I heard his little voice tell me he was okay. However, I was feeling nervous because I had not heard much from anyone. No one had come out and said that Cameron was not breathing or any specifics. I felt like my sister, Sarah, knew something because she kept urging me to go be with him.

After what seemed hours, but was really only minutes, a lady from the ambulance came in and said, "We have Life Flight in route and if your son gets a pulse, they will land and transport him." "What?" I thought, "**If** he gets a pulse?" Still unable to get myself to go out to him, I just cried. I think what kept me from going out was that I knew deep down he was gone and I was not ready to accept that reality.

Hope felt more comfortable and I needed to deal with it this way. During these moments, I thought about everything I had learned about God. God is always with us. He has a plan for everything and everyone. God has our days numbered. God will never abandon us. God will turn all things for those who love Him into good. All these things I grasped at and continued to pray. At the same time, I fought back the lies that I didn't love God hard enough or this was happening because I didn't pray well enough. I struggled to understand how this could be happening to me; after all, I loved God with all my heart and so did Chris. Cameron loved God; we dedicated him, we were faithful churchgoers and we prayed daily. For some reason, I thought I should be exempt from this kind of pain and tragedy. As you know, none of us is given a free pass for a painless life. One thing we can count on though is that God is with us even in our darkest moments and He has our future in his hands.

My brother came back in and said "Come on, the ambulance is taking him. Let's follow them." I knew this was bad because the helicopter hovered, but never landed. All the way to the hospital I kept asking my brother if there was still hope. He wanted to believe as much as I did, so he would try to encourage me. He would say that Cameron was a fighter and if anyone could pull through this, he could. He told me to keep thinking positive and that they were going to help him.

Back at home, our other children were being watched over by whomever could function. Our daughter, Emma, had been napping, which is a blessing because she was safe and missed all the loudness and chaos. Caleb, our 2- year- old, was spotted by a deputy sheriff, who was a friend of ours. He received a call that a young child had been under a falling dog house and it did not look good. Cale had been the deputy sheriff on duty and came out to our farm to write up a report and see what had happened. When he arrived, he saw little Caleb in a diaper by himself crying on the front steps and found someone to take care of him. Caleb was so little and had seen all the first scenes of the accident. Who knows what his little brain stored away or thought when it all happened. Cale found my father and could clearly see that he had been holding Cameron's body closely because of the condition of his clothing. He asked my dad to explain what happened. It was obvious my dad was in shock; he had a hard time replaying the accident. He had a glazed over look that would stick around for a few days to follow. My poor family had been through it.

Chapter 9

THE CALL

*Do be anxious about anything, but in every situation, by prayer
and petition, with thanksgiving, present our requests to God.
And the peace of God, which transcends all understanding,
will guard your hearts and your minds in Christ Jesus.*
Philippians 4:6-7

I (Chris) had been teaching a government class to seniors
during the last period of the school day. Pam, our school's
secretary, flung my classroom door open in a panic, eyes
wide, to tell that Natalie had called and that I needed to leave
right away because there had been an accident where one of my
boys had been hurt. She didn't have any more information at that
point. I said goodbye to my students as I grabbed my bag and
headed for the door. I remember running down the long sidewalk

to my car as panic engulfed me. I wasn't sure if it was Cameron or Caleb, and I didn't have any way to know. At that point I didn't have a cell phone and the half-hour drive was going to be long. I drove as quickly as I safely could west on Doddridge Avenue and south onto Highway 33. The most efficient way home was south on I-35 to the Moose Lake exit and then east to County Road 13. At somewhere between 70 and 90 miles per hour on the straight, clear stretches, I was pushing it to get home as quickly as possible.

It was hot and I was stressed. The car was rattling as I went faster and faster. Tears came to my eyes as I choked out a prayer that everything would be okay, that Natalie would be able to get our wounded boy to the doctor and that nobody else had been hurt. The others cars seemed to stand still as I raced homeward. It was somewhere between the Black Bear Casino and Mahtowa exit when I felt what can only be described as the "peace that passes understanding" I had sung about in Sunday School so many years before. I've heard about this before with people in stressful situations, but I also believe that God, through his Holy Spirit, granted me a window of complete peace to concentrate on speeding to my destination and to calm my nerves for the onslaught of emotion I would soon encounter. It was like a wave of calmness rushed over me. I was in the zone.

As I slowed to exit the highway toward Moose Lake, I saw an ambulance and fire trucks heading under the overpass toward town. We lived in the opposite direction, so when I saw a familiar vehicle following along, I knew which direction to turn. Other vehicles with lights and horns blaring followed and I chased toward the hospital. I was frustrated that they had to slow down and stop at the lights in town and how it seemed like they couldn't have driven slower. I was honking and shouting out my window as we got closer to the hospital. I actually had no idea where it was. We'd only recently moved to the area, and I needed to find out as soon as possible. I wasn't sure we were headed in the right direction, but the volunteer fire fighters led me straight to the emergency room doors. I must have seemed like a crazy person, frantic and panicked, yelling, "That is my son." (I learned later it was the ambulance carrying my nephew, Alex, I didn't know that he'd been injured as well.)

By this time, Natalie and the other members of her family were already inside and Cameron was being cared for by the good people at Mercy Hospital. I had no idea what to expect. My wife and her family were in a room next to the entry. Everyone looked dazed and scared. There were lots of tears, hand-wringing and concern as I tried to piece together what happened. Natalie was inconsolable. Her dad and brother told me through tears how they had done everything they could to save him. Emotions were high and everything said seemed to be louder than normal and hit harder than it otherwise would have. I borrowed a cell phone and called my family to tell them what I knew and that we were at the hospital and to come if they could. I made a call to our pastor, Dave Ballard, and to one of the people on the prayer chain. The message was pretty short, we were at the hospital, there had been a terrible accident with Cameron and we weren't sure if he was going to make it.

When a doctor emerged, I suspected that it wasn't going to be good. Sunken shoulders and a furrowed brow betrayed the message that he was "still being worked on."

We were invited in. His blood-stained Hulk costume had been cut off and was lying in a heap on the floor. The boots he had worn were there, too, but he had been stripped to his underwear. There were tubes and wires attached to his motionless little body. At a glance, he looked like he was just sleeping, but his head was propped up by gauze and cloth. They had prepped him for this moment. I knew he was broken. So were our hearts.

The hospital staff had backed off when we entered, but I thought that they might still have more they could do or try. After a small time with him, we were escorted to an adjoining room and we sobbed and hurt together. We were joined by other family members as they began arriving, and the hugs and tears began again.

Chapter 10

MERCY

But he said to me, "My grace is sufficient for you, for my power is made perfect in weakness." Therefore I will boast all the more gladly about my weaknesses, so the Christ's power may rest on me.
2 Corinthians 12:9

My brother pulled up to the doors of the Mercy Hospital in Moose Lake, and I couldn't get inside quick enough. Shear panic and despair took over as I ran through the doorway of the hospital. There were a bunch of people working at the nurse's station. I screamed that they needed to help my little boy and they needed to start praying right away. I fell to my knees in the hallway, feeling helpless. Everything was getting drawn out and the suspense and trauma was wearing me out. I felt a sense of relief being at the hospital and I just let go of every emotion I was trying to keep in check. Someone quickly pulled me up off the ground and walked me to a waiting room that had doors. Clearly, I was being a little loud. In this room, my family started to quickly gather, and my husband finally was able to get there. Cameron's grandparents, aunts, uncles, and whoever could get there came. We all just sobbed and waited.

At one time a nurse came in and said they were trying to do everything they could and walked back out. She returned minutes later to say that the doctors were still trying to pump water through his little aorta to see if there would be a connection made to make his heart pump, but they thought it was a long shot. At that point, my entire body was numb and I felt like I could just lie down and die. She asked Chris and me if we wanted to see him. I am not sure why, but this was the scariest part for me. I was faced with seeing my injured, lifeless son, and I was going to have to control myself. I couldn't take him from the table. As we slowly walked behind the curtain, the first thing I noticed was a pink mud boot sitting on the table. Doctors and nurses were very quiet and working around us. I am sure they were past the fact that he was not going to pull through, so I didn't notice any urgency. He was so still, perfect and peaceful. I didn't see a single bruise on his body. They had cleaned off any blood that may have been on his face and he just looked like he was sleeping. I remember putting my mouth to his and trying to breath for him.

His skin was so soft and he still had his little blue Spiderman underwear on. I touched him and caressed his hair. I did not want to forget the sweetness of his smell, the feel of his hair in my fingers, and the size of his little hands. When I pressed my face to his, I closed my eyes and said "I know you are okay." I didn't want to leave the room and move on from this moment. Walking out meant never seeing him in our house again. It meant I couldn't tuck him in at bedtime, or force him to brush his teeth. We didn't get to hear his voice, feel his hugs, hold his hand or cuddle with him anymore. This moment was so heartbreaking that I actually thought I was having a heart attack. I kept saying, "I think I am having a heart attack, my heart hurts so badly."

I didn't want the time to keep going on. I didn't want to leave the hospital and get further away from our baby boy being alive. I didn't want to accept our new reality, a reality that meant our little boy died.

The only thing that could have carried me through those moments was God's grace. People say God doesn't give you more than you can handle. Actually, he does. He gave me way more than I could handle. The shear heartache and sorrow that took over my body could have killed me that day, but He sustained me. God helped me to continue breathing. My grandpa actually had a heart attack two weeks later, and my dad had triple heart bypass two months later. I am sure if you opened me up and looked at my heart there would be an actual physical scar from that day.

There are parts of the day I don't remember, and I believe it is for my protection, so I don't have to live those exact moments over and over again. *But he said to me, "My grace is sufficient for you, for my power is made perfect in weakness." Therefore I will boast all the more gladly about my weaknesses, so that Christ's power may rest on me.* 2 Corinthians 12:9. I love this promise and we went on to name our next child Grace because of it.

My last memory of the hospital is from when we had all gathered back in the waiting room. A lot more family had shown up. Lots of sobbing was going on as Chris told them he was gone. I noticed my sister-in-law was curled up on one of the beds. Everyone was trying to figure out how to process this news. I was hugging my brother when over his shoulder I saw the hearse pull up. I was angry. We weren't even gone yet and a hearse had come to take our boy away? I couldn't believe how fast things were happening and how I was being forced to move on. I had just left his side! I have learned since then that it was obvious to the officials and medical staff that Cameron had died instantly and the ball had been rolling already. I think, in hindsight, that they were prolonging the process along for our sake, because it had been a long time from the bricks falling, my family working on him, the first responders working on him, the helicopter coming and leaving, the ambulance ride and the time at the hospital. If they would have revived him it would have been close to an hour after the accident. Either way, I did not want the hearse to take Cameron's body away. I wanted to be the one to bring him home in our car. It twisted the knife for me and I had to be consoled again.

Chapter 11

EMPTY-HANDED

Just four years and three hundred and forty days earlier, we were bringing Cameron home from the hospital. Now, on what was supposed to be a beautiful spring day, we were leaving our child behind. How do you even go on and take the next steps when your heart has been ripped out of you? Chris and I rode home together in the same car and neither of us can recall that drive. When we pulled up to the country house we were excited to call home yesterday, we were empty, confused and not sure we would ever enjoy it again. Our large driveway was filled with cars and people filled our home. They were family and friends coming to do all they could, and getting everything cleaned up so there were no dangers left. People were coming constantly to hug us and let us know they were there for us. Friends were bringing meals for us and all the company they knew we would be having. We were exhausted and lost.

I can't recall seeing our other children that day, I think grandparents were hugging them and watching them close. My sister, Sarah, and her son, Alex, were still at the hospital getting checked out. The ambulance had taken him after Cameron and he was getting tests done to see what damage had been done. When Alex was in the ambulance still, he said, "Mom, why did Cameron's angel look different than mine?" Alex saw something, and when I heard this I knew Cameron was taken care of and that he was okay. Alex suffered a great blow to his lower back and could not walk for a few days.

I sat down in our living room, and remember my aunt Leslie sitting by me on the couch. She hugged me and reassured me that Cameron was in Heaven, and that Chris and I raised him well. She told me that time was the only thing that would probably make the hole in my heart smaller. That must be true, because shortly after she talked to me, my grandma sat with me and told me the same thing. I asked her how she survived losing her nine-year-old to a drunk driver. She said, "There is no easy way, you just need to continue living and let time heal you." After grandma, it was my mother-in-law, then my cousins and then my friends. They were all worried about us and none of them knew how we would handle this. My friend, Katie, thought we would need a miracle to survive that day. We all sat in the living room and talked about Cameron, about the fact that he was wearing a hulk costume and pink rubber boots. We even laughed. We talked about how sad I was and we cried together. Our pastor was there taking care of anything he could for us. He had received a call from another pastor who had heard the news and wanted to share that he believed that God had big plans for our family. I clung on to that promise and thought, "He better have big plans for us because we just lost our child." I still wonder sometimes what God's plan for our family is. I can't help but to think that this book is part of it.

I had no idea where Chris was during all this time I was with the ladies in the living room. I was coping with the moment by talking about Cameron, how the day unfolded and being with friends and family. I needed to talk through the facts and be reassured over and over that Cameron was in a better place. I needed to cry and be encouraged that we were going to make it.

Chapter 12

PICKING UP PIECES

I (Chris) spent the evening wandering in and out of the house. I was in shock. The place was full of family and friends, all trying to figure out what to do and how to deal with such a devastating loss. And so was I! Our children were cared for, but not by Natalie and me. The bloody mess had been hosed down and much of the outside brick removed to a corner of the property, as far away from where kids were going to be as possible. We'd later have to remove them to another spot, but for the meantime, it was fine. There was so much to do and now I wasn't sure if I had the will to do it. I looked at all the people and their faces and thought about how my dad and my wider family must have felt when my mom died. I knew just a little more about his pain in that moment. I probably seemed a little detached. I prayed for peace in my house and for all those affected; they'd done what they could, and now they'd still be left with a nagging feeling and questions about the wisdom of moving to this place or the project we faced. I knew that some felt a responsibility for what had happened, and that they'd need mercy and grace, not condemnation or judgement.

As a husband and father, I knew it was my responsibility to protect Natalie and the kids from any other dangers I could. So I cleaned up Cameron's bedroom since the immediate physical threats would have to wait for the morning. It took about ten minutes to box up the toys, his drawings and all the clothes. There were Legos all over, some rubber bouncy balls and Matchbox cars. A stray snorkel and goggles and a container of Tic-Tacs were under a pile of blankets. Random pieces of paper with stick people and animals were gathered up. Maybe he could have been a great artist or builder or teacher someday... Clothes went into a blue plastic bin. Dirty or clean, didn't matter, I didn't want to sort it out until later; they'd inevitably be washed again before Caleb would wear them anyway. The boxes went into the closet. Vacuuming the floor and the bits of fishy crackers would have to wait. I was tired. I knew there would be a time and place to go through all of this stuff, but it would be less overwhelming in the months and years to follow than it would have been in the morning.

I imagined Natalie trying to clean up the mess of stuff in his room as ripping off a bandage over and over again, regenerating the pain of loss, and I was already numb. I didn't want to find her there crying over every object, struggling with whether to save it or not, or deciding where it should go until we might be able to use it again. I didn't want Caleb and Emma to wander in and inadvertently get hurt with a toy not intended for them, or think that because all his stuff was still there that Cameron was coming back. It was going to be confusing enough already, no use delaying the inevitable. One less thing to think about. There were going to be lots of questions and I wanted to close the door on the remnants of his short time in this house. So, I did.

Chapter 13

SAMANTHA'S DREAM

This night seemed to go on forever. However, more and more bits of hope were given to us. We had Alex, who had seen an angel. We had the reminder that I (Natalie) spent a special night with him just the night before, and we had the pastor's phone call saying God had big plans for our family. Another life changing moment happened to us that same night that I believe God orchestrated just so we could glorify Him and continue to believe that He truly has the whole world in His hands. Remember Alicia, the nanny? She had a sister, Samantha, who just happened to be turning 16 on this night. Samantha had recently been feeling depressed and struggling with her faith. She was seeing a lot of her friends doing big things, like joining the worship team at church, being called in to missions work or leading bible studies. Samantha just wanted to be used by God and she was not sure what she could do.

On her sweet 16th birthday, which was the day Cameron died, she drove with her parents to our house to share with us a dream she had a few weeks prior. She dreamt that two little blonde boys ran toward each other at the bottom of a hill. When they came together, they joined hands and ran up to Jesus at the top. Jesus took them up on his lap and there was a lot of joy. We found out that same night that Jonathan, the little boy that Cameron and I prayed for many times, died the same day. Cameron and Jonathan joined hands and went to Jesus together. We believe God needed Cameron so Jonathan would not have to go alone. This dream gave us a great sense of peace and we were thankful she was willing to share it with us; it was pivotal in our healing. It somehow made things a little easier to manage. Cameron was clearly okay. They could be friends forever.

God heard our cries as we prayed for that boy. He knew that Chris had not been taking our time as a family for granted. He knew that I imagined giving our son to die when Cameron was two weeks old, and I felt a deeper connection and love then I had ever felt that day. He also knew that Cameron believed in heaven. Cameron talked about how when he went to heaven, he would have a chocolate skateboard and a chocolate house. He would never be told to stop eating sugar and he would never get a stomachache. Cameron was excited about heaven and knew that Jonathan would like it especially since he would be whole and healthy when he was done suffering on earth.

Chapter 14

THE CHOICE

"Rejoice always, pray continually, give thanks in all
circumstances; for this is God's will for you in Christ Jesus."
1 Thessalonians 5: 16-18

After taking care of Cameron's stuff, I (Chris) went back downstairs and talked with the others for a bit. That said, weariness had set in. Thankfully, the young ones had been put to bed. I said, for Natalie and the others to hear, "Everyone else can fend for themselves, we need to go upstairs." Some stayed for a little longer, putting food away and cleaning up dishes. Most drove away shortly after we left the room.

As we sat in the darkness at the edge of our bed, the house quickly quieted. The yard light filled the room with a soft glow. We were exhausted. Clothes were strewn about. The tops of the dressers were filled with things that hadn't found their place yet, and everything seemed to be in disarray. It felt like life had been blown apart. This room would have to wait.

God had answered our prayers before, but this time we needed something more. We asked for strength and wisdom for parenting Caleb and Emma, assurance of His love for us, peace in our home as people from all over would come in the morning, answers to "Why us, why now?" and imagination for what would have to become the new normal. There were plans to be made, an obituary to write, people to call, a deconstruction mess to clean up and an apartment to build. It was hard to breathe.

In that moment of desperation, having known the brokenness of losing loved ones prior and having seen the devastation of tragic death on other families, I was prompted to set us on a path to healing. Our boy was gone and there was nothing we could do about it, but we could decide how to respond and recover. We talked about if we were going to be angry at Natalie's uncle for being the one that pushed that first domino, at ourselves for being at this house at this time in the first place or for unwittingly putting the boys in harm's way that afternoon. Should I have taken time off of school to work on the project, or demanded that the deconstruction phase wait for my arrival an hour later? Why didn't the doctors keep working on him? Were we going to blame God for this loss? There were unanswered questions swirling around in both of us.

The pain of seeing the afternoon play out the way it did shook everyone, and I knew how bearing that burden was going to weigh heavy for a long time. We talked about how the people invovled needed grace and we needed to give it. Maybe even more than that, we needed to consciously commit to overcoming the darkness. We needed each other and to have the space to grieve in our own ways as long as we needed to. In short, as we sat there, numbness setting in and salty tears streaming down, we decided to choose joy.

Chapter 15

DECISIONS

Within days of the loss of a loved one, regardless of the violence or peacefulness of a death, there are innumerable and sometimes weighty decisions to make. For us, there were decisions over whether to have a burial or to have the body cremated, to have a memorial service or a funeral, to speak or not to speak at the service and to find a place that would accommodate the crowd we anticipated. Where would we be and what would we do immediately prior to the actual service? What would we say when the tears started to flow? How would we carry ourselves through the day and who would hold our squirmy son and daughter? Somehow, we had to determine how much space was going to be reserved for family at the front of the sanctuary, and which of Cameron's items to display in the foyer as people entered the sanctuary. We had to decide which pictures to show, which clothes to wear and what songs to sing. We had to decide how to respond to the flood of well-wishers and their cards. Our kids needed help understanding what was going to happen. People were dropping off meals and asking what they could do to help with the house project. The stream of humanity in and out would eventually stop, and we wondered how quiet it would be after everyone left or began to forget. We thought about the farm animals it would be interesting to have, whether to buy a long-discussed puppy and the problem of not having a table in the dining room large enough for our family and guests.

At one point in the days prior to the memorial service, I got to spend a few quiet moments with our pastor, Dave, walking the property. It was one of those clear, late spring days when everything is starting to come alive. The mosquitoes hadn't come out yet, and it was comfortable in a long-sleeved t-shirt. I showed off the gigantic pole barn and outbuildings, already scattered with stuff that didn't fit in the house and Natalie's parent's furniture and belongings that would soon be inside. He got to see the shed we expected to use as a chicken coop, the old manure pit that would need to be emptied and filled in, the place where the trees would be close enough to have a rope bridge or treehouse for the kids and the spot I imagined getting set up for deer season. I thought there was a lot of potential for the barn, garage and milk house to be used in other ways, and I shared those thoughts as we walked. The hayloft of the barn was quite a sight, like a cathedral in our own backyard. I liked the way the dust of old hay had settled over the wooden floor and how the pigeons scattered every time we peeked into the loft. The sun glinted in through cracks and knotholes in the walls and windows. It was a rugged space, perfect for the kids to mess around in. After scaring off the resident pigeons, Dave and I looked out onto the field beyond as the sounds of saws and drills hummed a hundred yards away. I was reminded of our boys scaring the bird out of the garage at our old place in town and what a thrill it must have been. They would have really liked making racket in this old barn.

It was decision time. Natalie and I had discussed using MercyMe's ballad, "I Can Only Imagine," at the memorial service. Dave thought it was a good choice. We talked about gathering up all the photos we had of Cameron to scan and put in a slide show. Our friends would tackle that project for us. Dave would speak and so would I. Luke Krhin, our church's young worship leader, would be asked to sing. The songs, "Jesus Loves the Little Children," and "We Will Dance," both upbeat and hope-filled songs, were planned for. After some time had passed, I stared off, looking at nothing in particular in the distance and said, "I'm going to miss that boy." It was a bittersweet realization. We anticipate a time when we'll get to see him again, not in this life, but beyond. I wonder what it'll be like.

We talked about channeling the goodwill and outpouring of support from so many people by requesting that in lieu of gifts of flowers we'd like maple, birch, or spruce saplings to plant on our land. We liked the idea of the relative permanence of planting trees over flowers that would eventually die and be tossed aside. It seemed a more fitting tribute considering our circumstances and probably was one of the better decisions we made. We wanted people to come out to the place, to walk with them on the property, to dirty a shovel together and then see their gift grow over time. Our hope was that the property would eventually be blanketed with trees planted as a living memorial to our boy and we thought about how wonderful it would be to look back years down the road at the oasis that had grown up since that time. There was a row of old cottonwoods, some elm, box elder and a maple or two, but short of the few spruce and an old crabapple tree close to the house, the place could have been pictured in any other windswept field. The property was mostly bare, treeless pasture land, eaten down by the deer and cows that used to roam on it and the surrounding fields.

Chapter 16

SAYING GOODBYE

For I know the plans I have for you," declares the Lord, "plans to prosper you and not to harm you, plans to give you hope and a future.
Jeremiah 29:11

The days after Cameron died, I (Natalie) struggled to find the strength to keep moving. Looking at our other kids, I would try to imagine what their lives would now look like. Caleb would no longer be Cameron's sidekick. Cameron would no longer tell Caleb bedtime stories, and he was now forced into being an oldest child. Who was going to teach him how to do all the things little boys do? Caleb and Emma would no longer look to Cameron to be the ring leader of their little posse. We worried that Caleb would be lost and bored without having Cameron to follow around all day. Who would he play with? After all, Emma was our little girly princess and Caleb was all boy. How could he sword fight her, and who would wrestle with him? Looking back I now know that kids are the most resilient little beings on earth and they figure out a new way quickly.

There was a lot of talk going on around about how everyone could help us and keep us moving forward. We had many visitors and friends stop in to share their condolences and bring food. Some people were so taken back by what happened we found ourselves comforting them and telling them that we would be OK. It didn't take long at all before we found ourselves making the decision that Cameron's body would be cremated. These decisions needed to be made quickly and I wasn't ready for it. Chris is definitely the more level-headed of the two of us in emotional situations, so he was able to make a lot of these decisions. He was tender with me knowing I needed his strength and wisdom to make this whole process smooth and meaningful.

When Chris and I arrived at the Cremation Society in Duluth, we had no idea what to expect. I remember sitting down in a small room with an associate to discuss all the details. I imagine we had less to go through since we did not need a coffin or cemetery plot. I have been asked over the years why we decided to cremate Cameron. It was a simple decision for us, if there is such a thing, when making final arrangements for a lost loved one. For us, Cameron's body was dead and he would receive a new one in Heaven. To put his remains in a coffin in a cemetery plot that we may someday move far away from did not sit well with us. Having his ashes with us to do what we felt led to later made more sense. Now we have heard of places that make ashes into diamonds. Someday, we may look into that option, but for now we are sitting tight.

After that, the same associate led us through the process of writing the obituary. It was another daunting task no parent should have to do. How could we summarize Cameron's life so quickly and with so few words? We wanted to share our boy's very essence and have everyone understand who he really was in a few short paragraphs. After much difficulty finishing that process, the associate offered for us to see Cameron one last time. I remember freezing with fear and did not know if my heart could handle it. The biggest wound of my heart would be touched again.

It would be the last time we would get to look at him and this time I wanted to etch every detail about him in my brain. We walked into what I remember as a large empty room with just our boy up on a table. He was so still and peaceful, and he looked perfect to me. I remember having the thought that maybe he would awaken, and rise from the dead, so we would have a miracle to share with the world. After I left the room Chris and a friend prayed for it to happen, but it didn't. (At least they tried.) During the last visit with Cameron, I touched his sweet soft skin that once had a nice olive tone to it, but was now pale and colorless. I looked over his "special marks" our name for moles, and touched all of his fingers for the last time. His teeth were adorable and little; he had not lost any. He had beautiful light blonde hair that was thick and about an inch and a half long. I remember feeling it and smelling it. It had a damp scent like he had just had a bath, and to this day when I smell my other kids' hair when it's wet, this picture runs through my mind. I survived the last visit, but it did not go without a lot more tears and agony. It never feels good walking away from someone you love so incredibly much, knowing it will be the last time for a long while. The comfort comes when we can realize it was only the last time on earth, and when we join up again in Heaven it will be forever. Cameron was set to be cremated on May 22, 2004, Chris's 27th birthday.

After we left, we still had other decisions to make; even trivial decisions were tough. Like what to wear to the memorial service. What do you wear to celebrate the life of your son? I didn't have the energy to look through stores at all of the options. My mom and sisters took me shopping and I found a simple black and white dress that was springy, yet formal. I still have that dress and it is one of the dresses I wear most often.

We wanted this whole nightmare to be over with, and to go back to how things were. There were too many reminders forcing us to relive the moment. I was emotionally and mentally exhausted and had anxiety about making it through the memorial service. When we arrived at the church early, we were directed to the family room to wait for everyone to arrive. I could hear the sound of people gathering and once in a while, I would catch a glimpse of people coming in. Just seeing people that we knew cared about Cameron would put me into tears. They seemed to always tilt their head to the side and make a face that showed they could never imagine going through this and they were so sorry. In the entrance of the church were many pictures and trinkets of Cameron's that I don't really remember gathering. My husband was really good about taking care of things he knew would be hard for me to deal with.

Our Savior's Lutheran Church in Cloquet was the best available option for the memorial service. We had been part of a church in Duluth, living in Moose Lake and working in Cloquet, so our hometown was going to be the best place for everyone to converge. We knew that a lot of people were intending to attend, and we knew that the church I had grown up attending, the Presbyterian Church, wasn't going to be big enough. Pastor Morreim and his staff and the volunteer ladies were especially kind to allow us the use of their space.

When it was time to get the service started I was really nervous about keeping it together. There was no way to escape my own son's memorial service. I tend to want to flee when I am having feelings I can't control. Our family walked with the pastor to the front of the sanctuary and we took our seats. There were over 600 people in attendance watching us come in, and we were overwhelmed with love and support from all of the people who had been part of our lives. This service was going to make an impact on the lives of everyone that showed up and we hoped it would stick. While we were writing this book, I learned that Chris somehow managed to get up in front of everyone and share his heart with the congregation. For some reason, my mind draws a complete blank when I try to remember this detail. I am certain Chris's words were amazing and he captured many hearts that day. Pastor Dave led the whole service and shared an excellent message about getting to Heaven and seeing our dear boy again. It was important to us that people knew life was short, but there was an eternity promised to us and we wanted to see everyone there. I am sure it was difficult for Dave to memorialize our little boy who he had seen often and was the same age as one of his own children. Bless his heart for walking with us through that whole process and doing a wonderful job.

Many people have asked if we allowed our younger children to attend the memorial service. We did for the entirety and they ended up sitting on their grandparent's laps. I remember wondering what was going on in Caleb's mind at the time. Did he know we were saying our final goodbye and celebrating the life of his brother? I wondered if he knew why everyone was crying. He tells me now he doesn't recall any of it, so it did not have a lasting effect on him.

While we watched a slideshow of Cameron's life, I could hear sobs and sniffles all around the room as everyone looked at our spunky, sweet and handsome little boy. This is a cherished collection of photos put to a great song and we have watched it many times since then. At first, Chris would watch it with the kids when I couldn't yet. It took a couple years for me to get the courage to allow the heartache. Now I love watching it and sharing it when I speak to groups. I still cry, but I find myself loving the memories and seeing my other kids in him.

When the memorial service was over, we shared food, fellowship, and more tears together. I remember seeing a bunch of ladies taking care of the food in the kitchen and cleaning up, one more task we couldn't have orchestrated, and didn't even think of. We were well taken care of and felt loved. Chris and I stood in the fellowship hall and an endless line of people came to give us hugs and words of encouragement. We hugged so many people I think both of us had numb arms in the end. We were blessed with the freedom to be a mess and receive love abundantly.

Chapter 17

REMEMBERING

I (Chris) wanted to honor the memory of our son by sharing a few words with those attending the memorial service. I wanted them to hear something more intimate than they might have otherwise. The text was typed, double-spaced, and printed in 16 point font so that I could see it through teary eyes. Here's what was said:

"I've described on the phone and in conversations with folks that have come to visit how it seems like we have been in the middle of a big storm that just seems to be swirling around us. There has been a tremendous amount of activity, preparation of meals, lessons planned and executed and work that has been done to make life for my family and me much more bearable. We have heard from several circles that there are people praying for our family from all across the United States and other parts. My brother and sister-in-law have flown in from their posts in Iraq and the UK to be here today. And others have come from parts near and far. You honor us by coming to be here today, and for that, I thank all of you.

My wife and I have been thinking over the course of the past six days about what a blessing it is to have people love us so completely. Since Cameron's death there has been a crew of family and other people working at our house almost nonstop to make the place more safe and livable. What a blessing that has been. To go through all of that without so many others is unimaginable. And we appreciate all the food and encouraging cards and letters that have been sent to us, thank you.

There have been, and I expect that there still will be, many times of intense feeling in the days ahead. My heart aches and leaps within me when I think about all of the little things that I remember and little ways that Cameron has had an effect on our family and those around us. Every time I pick up something in our house that reminds me of him, or see a special place or trinket that is significant, the memories come flooding back, and I am wracked with a mix of emotion. Through the tears and laughter, a real peace has set in, and it's the peace that God has given in order for us to bear this burden.

I think that the most difficult part for us is simply missing him. It's those little things that have endeared him to so many that we hang on to as precious. I remember the day that Natalie told me she was pregnant. It was on a lunch break when I was working at the Middle School as a cleaner. He was our first child. We were so excited and scared about the whole thing, and I remember how proud we were to strap this tiny little baby in our car and drive him home. It all seems like yesterday to me. He grew up very quickly as our family also grew and of course was very special to us.

He and I were the early risers in our house, and now everything is really quiet in the house for quite a lot longer in the morning.

This is compounded by the fact that we now live on a quiet country road. We're gonna miss that energy in the morning.

Cameron got a kick out of wrestling whenever the opportunity presented itself. It didn't matter if I was on my way out the door to school or long after he should have been in bed. He loved to do art; he would make precious little drawings for us and for the refrigerator. There were always piles of pictures for the refrigerator. He liked rub-on tattoos, and he would put them all over his arms and belly. It didn't really matter what kind they were, the whole package of them was on his body somewhere within the day. Caleb, our other son, has sort of picked up that mantle; he has a half a dozen on his belly right now.

Every time we had a new food, he thought we were having a "tasting party." That's what we called it a long time ago to make him eat new foods. He tried lettuce for the first time a few weeks ago, and actually liked it. He loved maple syrup on ice cream and popcorn on Sunday nights.

Cameron was surrounded by people that loved him and that he loved back. In fact, when driving past Pinehurst Park, here in Cloquet, Cameron would see Dean Levinski working on the field and say, "Hey, there's Uncle Dean!" He loved the Levinskis and being with them and their family. He wanted Barb Cook, his teacher at ECFE, to be his teacher forever. She really had a profound impact on his appreciation for school. He wanted to name some of the chickens we just got after our old neighbors Don and Rose, and Barney and Edna. He enjoyed them and going to get the egg that mom needed for something they were cooking together. He couldn't wait to see or hear from Mike "Test" (Tess), a good friend from high school who is here today with his wife Kirsten, on a short leave from Fort Campbell, Kentucky.

One of the things that I am especially touched by is that Cameron understood "need" when he saw it. Once, not too long ago, he saw one of those world hunger information programs on television and determined to send lots of money so the little girl on the TV could have food. He had Natalie write a letter to his cousin, Alex, encouraging him to do the same. This was a serious deal for him and he genuinely wanted to help.

He was very protective of his brother and sister, always making sure that risk was measured carefully.

He, I suppose, like most kids, was filled with wonderment and awe. As a two-year-old he asked, "Mom, why did God only make part of a moon." (I guess it wouldn't be so significant unless you realize that it was a half-moon that he had seen.) He was fascinated by bugs and things he could dig out of the ground. We had a critter cage for him to carry around, which he did, very proudly. It was always Cameron that would find the agates on the road at the cabin or at our new home. He thought they were so cool. Along with other rocks that weren't agates, but he thought they were neat anyway, and so we would hang on to them.

He would remind us to sing the Johnny Appleseed prayer song at meals if we hadn't already. Sometimes he thought it was funny to sing the first few words and then stop, leaving the rest of us to finish; he got a kick out of that.

He loved helping out with projects around the house, whether it be planting tulips on the side of the house, or moving garbage from a construction project. He was quite a helper.

It makes me smile when I think about how he would run in to the school that I work at during my lunch break if I had forgotten something or needed something from home. I could see him get out of the van and run all the way in because the windows to my classroom face the parking lot. Little legs running, and arms pumping, racing his brother. It was so precious. He was really a lot of fun to have around. Always curious and so full of energy.

We loved him with all our might. God has blessed us in so many ways in the almost five years he was with us. He was a very nice, well-mannered, adventurous, fun-loving boy, and we are very proud to remember him here today. Thank you for coming."

Initially, we had discussed and planned for the tree-planting to occur the day of the service. I had bought some shovels and staked out an area for trees to go. As it turned out, the weather did not cooperate and we thought the better of it until another day. There was a bunch of trees to plant, some from friends, some from family, some from colleagues. One was mailed to us, a beautiful little spruce. Others were transplanted from friends' properties to ours. It was a beautiful thing. Sadly, the winters and deer have taken their toll on the lovely hardwoods, but the willows brought in by some of my students and most of the spruce we set in have continued to thrive and now provide cover for young and old alike.

Once we returned home that day we had family and friends come over to continue visiting. I needed some down time to try and unwind and my friends wanted to help. The fellas and I left to talk and have pie. We are thankful for this group of God fearing, selfless and humble friends whom I have had for much of my life. Natalie was surrounded by her own great friends, wonderful cousins and amazing family and it was good. The next day would be harder.

Chris and baby Cameron at our first apartment, college
textbooks and story-time reading material piled high.

Nothing beats chomping ice cream on any day ending in "Y."

Grinning Cameron, Sam, Belle, Ted, Ethan and Nick, all cousins.

The dudes visit Mom and brand new sister, Emma,
at the hospital, fruit snacks in hand.

Goofing around with cousin Alex. The horned hat
and rub on tattoo were family favorites.

On a well-traveled Boundary Waters portage
trail the day before melting down.

Natalie and Cameron snuggled in a tender moment
on the couch while visiting family in North
Carolina a few weeks prior to the accident.

Cameron, Bella, Alex and the critter cage riding
in the back of the trailer at the new place hours
before the accident that would claim his life.

Natalie and Cameron, heading out for a walk in early fall.

Chapter 18

THE NEW NORMAL

*Your word is a lamp for my feet, a light on my path. I have taken
an oath and confirmed it, that I will follow your righteous laws.
I have suffered much; preserve my life, Lord, the willing praise
of my mouth, and teach me your laws. Though I constantly take
my life in my hands, I will not forget your law. The wicked have
set a snare for me, but I have not strayed from your precepts.
Your statutes are my heritage forever; they are the joy of my
heart. My heart is set on keeping your decrees to the very end.*
Psalm 119:105-112

T he hustle and bustle of everything revolving around
Cameron was over and our family needed to start being
four rather than five. This day was the start of me getting
lonely for Cameron's voice and longing for his hugs. I panicked

as the days started to get further away from him being alive, and I didn't want to forget the sound of his laugh or what he looked like. These moments took extra effort to push through and I had to consciously choose to not let anger start to take over. I didn't like how life kept going on around us and I was forced to move on. I have heard from other people over the years that they also wished time would have stood still for a while so they could have processed slower. I had to constantly fight feelings of doubt that things would be okay. I was afraid of everything now. If Cameron could be gone that fast, so could our other kids. Fear was something I faced every day all day for a long time. The only way I could fight it was talking it through with friends and actually confronting it. I had to refuse the fear a thousand times a day and choose to put one foot in front of the other. I had been taught a few years earlier to rise above what is not true and keep believing what you know is the truth. During this deep struggle, I had to sort out what was fear and what was truth, and it was exhausting. Believing God had a plan for me and trusting that He would pull me through had to be written on my heart every day. I had to do things like listen to uplifting worship music, call encouraging friends, meditate on God's promises, tape scripture up around the house and be around people who were positive. Even with all of these venues of encouragement, some days were too much for me to handle. I remember collapsing in the shower just days after the funeral, wondering how I was going to go on. We had two other children who needed me to be their mom, but how was I going to be happy again? I had too many questions and I was weak. I wanted to know if Cameron would recognize me in Heaven as his mom. I wanted to know if Cameron would run to me calling me "Mommy" or would I just be his friend. I was losing ground and I was starting to feel cheated.

In these moments, and I had a lot of them, I needed to remember that I didn't need all the answers. I needed to trust just like I had before that God had these details worked out and that his strength could get me through this. I tend to want control and answers, and when I live life in my understanding and abilities, I struggle. The devil wanted me feeling anxious, inadequate, crippled and full of guilt. He was very strategic about placing bad thoughts in my mind at the right moments. I needed God's Spirit to be my guide daily, to keep me moving forward, to help me to walk in victory and claim joy. My community of friends and family held me accountable by checking in on me. They would encourage me, assure me that we were loved and they were there for us. They would also give me scriptures to meditate on and memorize. Even though most of our questions will remain unanswered, when you need something positive to get stuck in your head, the promises of God are uplifting. It is hard when our heart is feeling one thing and our mind another, but practice will help the two line up. Our other children needed a mom and dad, and we needed them.

Each moment with Caleb and Emma was different now. Their hugs were embraced longer, their smiles meant more and our patience with them had grown. We wanted to slow everything down and live each moment fully. Soon, we bought a little floppy-eared goat with blonde hair and blue eyes we named Sampson for Caleb to run around with. He pranced around the yard and Caleb practiced butting his head with the goat a few times. Our animal count was on the rise and we added a bunny, two turkeys and a puppy. My dad had also purchased a new parakeet. The goat was Sampson, parakeet Sammy and the bunny Samantha. Our little nephew, Sam, had impressed Caleb during his last visit by showing us his muscles. He had quite a six-pack for a 5-year-old, and he had become Caleb's new super hero. His name came first in Caleb's mind when it was time to name the animals.

We had a quiet and peaceful month at home with just our family. We found that every time we went out, people would tilt their heads to the side with sympathy and let us know they were sorry. This was only natural, but each time we would be reminded that we should be sad and had a hard time trying to be happy. We didn't go out in public often because we knew, coming from a small town, we would see people we knew. We were trying to figure out our new life and we needed to keep to ourselves for a while. One time, I went to Walmart with the kids, and I found myself looking around at all the moms with children. I felt bits of anger creep in every time I found someone with three kids. We worked hard to raise Cameron and we had many, many sleepless nights parenting him. I felt cheated and thought I deserved to have as many as them. I constantly felt like someone was missing and realized I was not ready to be around a lot of people yet.

About four weeks after Cameron died, we received a Death Certificate in the mail. We hadn't expected it, so it was a little bit of a surprise and interfered with our attempt to have only positive thoughts. It had said that the cause of death was a brain injury. The nurse at the hospital had mentioned that his aorta was ripped from his heart just like it can be when a kid is in a car accident and their chest hits the seat belt too hard. My husband knew Cameron was broken in other ways, but I didn't like to admit that. It made sense because of the blood my brother and dad had on their clothes, but that is a place my mind didn't like visiting. We did learn that he never had a pulse from the moment my dad pulled him out, so he died instantly. This letter had brought back an icky feeling for me, but my husband reminded me that it didn't matter and we couldn't bring Cameron back regardless of the cause. He was right, and I needed his bits of wisdom to refocus.

Meanwhile, my parents' apartment had been getting finished up way quicker than planned because of all the help from everyone. Family thought we would need our privacy, so they wanted to get it finished as soon as possible. My father-in-law, Ken, headed up the project with the help of my father, brother, brother-in-law and our good friend Doug. They worked hard to finish it quickly.

Things were cleaned up around the farm and Chris was home for the summer. We decided that is was a good time to go on a lengthy family vacation. My sister, Sarah, her husband, Chad, and their children, Alex and Bella, had moved to North Carolina and we thought we could make it a fun road trip on the way to visit them. We packed up Caleb and Emma and headed out. Our friends like to remind us of how radical we are by sharing a memory from this trip. On the second day of our three week trip we stopped in Jacksonville, Ohio at a Pottery Barn outlet store, and we found a super great deal on a tan velvet sofa and a black coffee table. So we decided to buy them and strap them to the top of our van. These great pieces of furniture traveled with us through Pennsylvania, Virginia, North Carolina, Tennessee, Kentucky, Illinois, Wisconsin and back to Minnesota. Chris had to tighten the straps often and at one point in Tennessee we had to stop at Lowe's to get a tarp because it was raining. Now, thinking back, I imagine that we spent way more on gas lugging these things around for three weeks than we might have otherwise. We had a great time together going to the Hershey factory in Pennsylvania, seeing the Liberty Bell in Philadelphia, touring Thomas Jefferson's estate, Monticello, in Virginia and spending time with my sister's family. It was and is always special to visit with our nephew, Alex, because he was the same age as Cameron, and was also involved in the accident. I imagine they would have similar interests, so it is really fun watching Alex grow up. I couldn't help but think about how much Cameron would have loved all the things we had seen. Caleb and Emma were amazing travelers making our time very delightful. Caleb decided on this trip it was time to grow up and he potty-trained himself.

Months passed and I went through a lot of different emotions. Some days were great while others I still struggled to get out of bed. I remember one day I decided to look at the lock of hair the man at the Cremation Society had cut for us. I touched it, and smelled it, and all I could do was lie on my bed and sob. I called Katie and cried, telling her how I was struggling with missing him so much. Often, our conversations would turn around and we would be laughing by the end of them. Only best friends have that kind of power! It is really important to find people to have beside you in life. I can't recall all of these phone calls but she knew I needed them and she listened when I needed it most.

Part Three

Chapter 19

RUNNING FROM GRIEF

We demolish arguments and every pretension that sets itself up against the knowledge of God, and we take captive every thought to make it obedient to Christ.
2 Corinthians 10:5

The first year was the most difficult for us to get through. Reminders were seen everywhere we turned, conversations always lead back to the fact that Cameron was missing. Each holiday was the first without him, so there was strangeness and an adjustment that needed to be made. Should we hang his stocking at Christmas? Put out all of his tree ornaments? Continue the traditions we started with him? When the anniversary of his death rolled around, we struggled to know how to feel, but Cameron's birthday was definitely the toughest adjustment. We were reminded on that day of his birth, his first steps, his laugh, the things he liked and what he would have been looking forward to at his birthday party. The good news is that it got easier each year after as the freshness faded, but even now, years later we still visit these thoughts.

I (Natalie) have heard it over and over again that everyone grieves differently. There are stages of grief that have been studied over the years by doctors, and to tell you the truth, I don't know what they are. We never followed a plan or went to any grief support groups. We just pressed forward in the way we knew best and let time pass. We are not against counselling or support groups at all; for some reason I don't think we thought about them. I know a lot of people who have used those services and have been helped immensely in their grieving process. I grieved with my husband, but we also went through our own process apart from each other and our ways of grieving looked very different. If I expected Chris to feel like I was feeling, and vice versa, we would have felt unsupported by each other and drifted. We would have blamed each other for not understanding, become resentful and our marriage would have started to fall apart. We actually had to get to know each other in a different way than we had needed to in the past. We needed to realize each other's places of pain and what was hurting our hearts most. Sometimes, I would be having a better day and he would be struggling, and sometimes I would need to just lie in bed and cry and he would need to have grace for that. Our feelings can engulf us and make us look selfish and not care about the other person's needs, so communicating and listening is important. Divorce rates are very high amongst couples that have lost a child, so understanding the different ways people grieve is very important. Grieving solo is sometimes easier because you can ignore complicated emotions when the other one wants to talk about something painful and you don't have to risk being misunderstood. I have heard people say that writing is an easy way for them to communicate their feelings. Chris and

I didn't write to each other, we just cried with each other and talked. I think for people that can't bear to speak about things may find writing helpful. If we don't allow ourselves to focus on the living people in our lives and instead focus on the what-ifs, the what-could-have-beens, and the unanswerable question of why did this happen to me, we won't be able to move on. Moving on is hard; I am not denying that. It has been almost 11 years and I still think about it every day. Writing this story has brought up a lot of emotions for us to rework through.

During the immediate time following a death, whether expected or not, you can slip into a state of shock. You may need to talk yourself through every action you take. Some describe this as feeling like an out-of-body experience. It takes time for this new truth to be realized. After the initial shock begins to subside and you realize that life needs to continue, it becomes necessary to make some really important wise decisions. Some examples are: How will I choose to look at this? Will I find someone to blame? What will I do to help myself get through this? How am I going to fight the lies that I am going to be taunted with? How can I support my spouse, children, friends or anyone else involved? If these questions and decisions are something you missed while you were grieving, it is not too late to process them and start fresh. Life is good about giving us more chances. When we are purposeful about making wise decisions, it gives us something other than the darkness to focus on. The loss and sadness of death is extremely heavy and can easily keep us low for a long time, becoming our new identity and trapping us into a downward spiral. That being said, being sad and feeling your grief is important and has its place. Some people need to stay in that place longer than others and cry more often. However, a time should come, especially if you have children, when you will need to start focusing on finding happiness and joy again.

We are still sad at times, but know its okay to be joyful. At first, I struggled with allowing myself to be happy. I thought it was wrong to celebrate life when Cameron was dead, and I felt guilty because of it. Guilt is a direct lie from Satan and he is really convincing to us when we are weak. Cameron and most people who are deceased would not like to hear that since they passed the people who love them no longer chose to experience joy. There is definitely a time for sadness. However, if that is what our mind is focused on day in and day out it will be too heavy for us to carry and that is when destruction takes root. We are human and can only handle so much.

To numb the pain, many people cling to blame and anger to avert the real struggle, turn to drinking and drugs to help them get through another day, or engage in sinful behavior to try to create an "I don't care" mentality. Divorce is another high probability after the loss of a child. I don't think people intentionally choose to be lost and in such despair that the only solution is escaping from the pain in some form. I think it's because we don't have the capacity to handle and process all the pain and confusion. This is where a Savior comes in, someone who loves us no matter what and waits for us to draw from Him a kind of hope and peace only He can supply. It doesn't matter what kind of person you believe yourself to be, or what sins you have committed in the past or are now involved in. He died for your sins to be forgiven and is waiting for you to come to Him. We are all born with a sinning nature because of Adam and Eve. We all have the tendency at different times to want to sin and we all have sinned. Even Isaiah 64:6 says, *"All of us have become like one who is unclean, and all our righteous acts are like filthy rags; we all shrivel up like a leaf, and like the wind our sins sweep us away."* God frees us from this bondage and leads us on new paths that can bring vibrant life, even after crushing despair.

Chapter 20

GRACE

W alking through grief and trying to process with my family was not easy all the time. I (Natalie) needed God's grace to carry us through the most difficult times of my life. As a family, we had many good moments, but we also had our struggles. I found myself tiring from the constant reminders of needing to feel this sadness and needed something else to focus on. I had a pampering visit from a cousin of mine who worked for a direct selling company. She thought I would enjoy the friendships that came along with being a consultant with her, and the feeling of success in the small things. She told me there was a lot of laughing and celebrating, both of which sounded appealing. I signed up to be a consultant and had no idea what I was in for. See, when you focus yourself deeply into distractions whether it be a positive one or not, you are capable of climbing the highest mountain or digging the deepest valley. I quickly found myself chasing after every carrot the company had to offer. I was quickly forgetting about the sad things and started focusing on the exciting possibilities. In a short three months I had earned the use of a brand new career car. It was beautiful cherry red Pontiac Vibe. Chris and I had never driven a brand new car so we were very excited and feeling pampered. It took earning a brand new car for Chris to hit his first deer ever. The same night we picked it up from the dealership he or the deer decided it would be good to collide. Our initial time together as new car and new owner was short, but we would meet again after five weeks of repair time. It's funny how the timing of some things works out. It made for a good story and put my husband in a quick panic when he had to come home and tell me what happened. He paced at the foot of the bed and said, "Natalie, something bad has happened." I can only imagine how nervous he was on the rest of his ride home.

My new career proved to allow a lot of fun girlfriend time. I reached many of my goals and met a lot of wonderful people. It taught me that you truly can succeed if you put your mind to it, and that is what I was doing. I hit over $300,000 in career sales in less than two years and had added over 70 team members in a short time. To top it off I had even earned the use of a Pink Cadillac SUV! For those of you who know about them, they are not easy to come by. I had worked hard and was excited about the future of my business. It had all of my attention, and it kept me quite distracted.

After a small business trip, I was driving home and thinking about all that had happened over the past two years. There had been so many perks and rewards in belonging to this company, yet there was a sinking feeling in the pit of my stomach. I started to realize that when I was home, I was always on the phone and telling my sweet little children to wait. Me, the one who always dreamed of having children, homeschooling them and loving a large family was now delegating them at every chance I could. I was delegating everything that was non-income producing and that is what I had been trained to do in order to advance. It is important to do that when you are building a company for a time, but I was never in it to build a company. I was trying to get out once in awhile and have fun with ladies. I found myself now having someone clean my house weekly, do the laundry, make meals, organize inventory, watch our kids and buy groceries. I somehow got myself so busy and I couldn't manage to do any of those things. I busied myself with work so much mostly because I was scared I couldn't handle things at home anymore and it was easier to have someone else worry about them. As I started to rethink what my personal values were and had always been, I started to see clearly that I was not living my life according to them anymore. I realized that during these last two years I had not dealt with some of my grieving from losing Cameron. I was running from some heart issues that I tucked away and didn't have the energy to deal with. I was running from the hardness of life and my new identity masked that well.

On that drive home I had to pull over. I started to sob, and couldn't stop. It was one of those cries that you think may never stop, and the river came from holding it back for almost two years. I longed to hold my children and to understand the stages of life they were in. Caleb and Emma had grown to be best friends and after the first year of my new business we had another baby girl, two years out from the accident. We were so excited and knew how much of a blessing she would be. We decided on a name right away; she would be Grace Marie. God's grace was the reason we survived the death of Cameron, and God's grace was beautiful and present in our life. I found myself forgetting about God's grace because I had been so busy with my new life as a successful businesswoman. I was not very good at balancing everything like so many other women do.

Grace was grandma's girl right away because that is whom she spent most of her time with. When she would cry, grandma was the only one who could get her to stop. I wanted to be the one she wanted, but I was often not around, and the phone was stuck to my ear if I was. I cried for a good 15 minutes while pulled over on the side of the road, thinking about all the things I was missing out on with my kids. I know there are plenty of good moms out there who are also very successful businesswomen, but I couldn't juggle it and have always dreamed of staying home. I didn't sign on because I had to; I was doing it because I could. Successful businesswomen inspire me; however, I just needed to follow my heart on what I should be doing.

Once I gathered myself up well enough to drive, I couldn't get home fast enough. I wanted to hold my family all night. I felt everything in me was telling me to be radical. I needed to let the Cadillac go, put away the business suits, and not think about the money I would be kissing good-bye. I needed to face my real life and learn how to be happy with my family of five, without Cameron. I needed to be able to wake up and face my hardest job, being a full-time mom. So, I shocked everyone I had been working alongside of for the past two years and told them I needed to be done. I know myself, I love challenges and I tend to be an all-or-nothing kind of girl. If I would have stayed in, but worked less, I would feel the drive to do more. I prayed about it and talked to my husband and radical was the only way for me. Sometimes these decisions need to be made without too many other opinions so it doesn't create confusion. I know what I was being told and my heart was ready to take on the rest of the healing process. I disappointed some people who had put a lot of time into me, and my decision also affected other people's status in the company, so I didn't take it lightly. This was the hard part, because I tend to also be a people-pleaser and I did not want to disappoint the lovely ladies I had spent so much time with. However, we all have a different walk to walk and we need to do what is right for ourselves and our families.

I really wanted to share this part of our journey with you so you can see that we did not just choose joy one night and walk in freedom from that day forward. I avoided some major issues with my laser focus on success, but as I climbed the ladder to the Cadillac in record time, I also developed fears and feelings of inadequacy as a mother and wife. When I focused on success I was able to avoid facing those problems. I thought my broken heart and anxiety would get the best of me unless I was really busy and didn't have time to deal with the root cause. Allowing ourselves to feel the pain and not letting the pain become our new identity is hard. It almost becomes habit to wake up daily thinking you should be sad about something. There is an immediate darkness upon rising and if we don't take our thoughts captive day by day, they will take us captive. The apostle Paul wrote to the Corinthian church that, *we demolish arguments and every pretension that sets itself up against the knowledge of God, and we take captive every thought to make it obedient to Christ.* 2 Corinthians 10:5

Our minds are very powerful, so we need to be purposeful about what we decide to focus on. This business served its purpose in our life, and it showed us that we can achieve anything we set our minds to. It also helped me realize that there is opportunity out there for every woman who needs confidence and a like-minded family of friends. I am glad I chose a direct-sales company as something to put my energy toward, rather than drinking or other things that could have been more destructive. That day, in my car, I decided that I needed to be with our children and that is all there was to it. If something happened to one of them and I was not around, I would have a really hard time forgiving myself.

Since then, we have added another little boy to our family, Gavin Christopher. While I was pregnant with Gavin I prayed a lot that he would look just like Cameron so I could get a glimpse of him daily. I also prayed that this little baby would have some personality qualities that Cameron did. We laugh about it now because Gavin looks very similar to Cameron. In fact, Gavin thinks a lot of Cameron's pictures are of himself. Even his little teeth look just like Cameron's teeth did. Gavin has a huge love for candy and would do just about anything for a Tootsie Roll, which I should have prayed against. I also should have been more specific about the degree of strong willed and stubborn characteristics we would have liked Gavin to carry on. It may even take longer to convince Gavin to do something than it did Cameron. Either way, he's a blessing to our family and we couldn't imagine our household without him.

Chapter 21

LOOKING BACK,
MOVING FORWARD

One of the questions people ask is how it is for us on significant days, especially his birthday. We still sometimes get cards from friends on the anniversary of his death. What we have said is that it's not the anniversaries, but all the little moments that are tough. It's all the times when you wonder what might have been. Over the years, we have been fortunate to have been in contact with many of the families from Cameron's Early Childhood Family Education classes. I (Chris) have been very fortunate to get to know some of those very kids as they made their way through the high school; two are in my homeroom and I've had several in classes or study hall. I sometimes catch myself wondering if he would have been a runner, as I was in high school, or a soccer fan like his brother, or which batch of kids he would have hung out with in the lunchroom. I wonder if he would have given me or my colleagues some trouble or if he would have been able to teach me some of the math they're doing now.

Emma, Caleb, and I have traced some of the same route in the Boundary Waters I remember so fondly from that final trip with him the summer before he died. It has been good to remember the places and see some of the same sights with the other kids and to tell the stories of the past, but it's also been really important to make new memories, too. Too often, people get bogged down in recycling and rehashing tired old stories, failing to move on into the fullness of what life has for them now. I think there are actually too many monuments and statues of the heroes of the past, great men and women lost to history. It's an old desire of humanity to live, if not in reality, then in memory, forever. The problem with this is that most people don't or can't remember, and I would guess that after we get a generation or two away from the event or people monuments or memorials intend to memorialize, the less significant they become and the more annoying the space-taker becomes. They have their place(s), but what I'm against is getting stuck with them in that place. Remember, but don't live in the past. Grieve, but don't stop living. Cry, but know that life goes on, with or without you. Look to the future, a glorious, hopeful one.

Chapter 22

JOYFULNESS

You make known to me the path of life; you will fill me with joy in your presence, with eternal pleasures at your right hand.
Psalm 16:11

Even youths grow tired and weary, and young men stumble and fall; but those who hope in the Lord will renew their strength. They will soar on wings like eagles; they will run and not grow weary, they will walk and not be faint.
Isaiah 40:30-31

We still have bad days. We still have chaos and real life struggles. Our emotions still get the best of us, and yes, sometimes, medication is needed to help you get through the rough patches. We did not make the decision to choose joy once and then never struggle again. We struggle, and with four children and busy schedules we need to constantly fill ourselves up with positive thoughts, inspiring music and words to remind us to choose joy. Otherwise, our children would have a miserable existence seeing their parents suffer from all the lies that sneak in and try to cripple us. Choosing joy is a daily exercise and sometimes we start to give up and it slips away from us. Waking up with a constant dark cloud over your head can make life feel like it is not worth living and we know this is a reality for far too many. Don't let the world hold you down in a stagnant pool of shame, anger or guilt. There is freedom for you because Christ paid for it. He paid for your freedom and joy, you just need to receive it and ask Him to show you what to do. Choosing joy is an action that takes mental and physical work and reminders to rise above emotions that can overwhelm us and to claim the truth.

Numbness, bitterness, anger, vengeance, or generally being an awful person to be around is exhausting and defeating. We shudder to think where we would be as a family if we hadn't chosen joy on that darkest of days. We are a typical family, but we do have a big faith. After this death, and a series of events later, our faith has only grown stronger. The desire to share our journey also has grown over the years as we have watched it give hope to others. We want to help others find freedom after tragic situations, so they can still receive the fullness of joy God has for each of us. Over the past several years we have shared our experience with many people, and have realized that there is a whole lot of despair and hopelessness in our world. Our story may be what will help you rethink an angry heart, forgive someone who has hurt you or call on God again and trust his will for you.

We see a lot of people searching for happiness today and with all the options people try they get exhausted and hit dead ends. There is something to the mindful practices talked about today and living in the moment, because that is all we are guaranteed. The constant stress about what needs to get done, what tomorrow will look like or how we will pay for this or that expense keeps us in a state of anxiety and defeat. God knows all the answers and has things covered, so relax and trust him. That doesn't mean don't do anything, but we are instructed not to worry. I (Natalie), struggle with this one and I need to constantly meditate on this scripture to get me through. *Do not worry. Learn to pray about everything. Give thanks to God as you ask Him for what you need. The peace of God is much greater than the human mind can understand. This peace will keep your hearts and minds through Christ Jesus.* Philippians 4:6-7. God reminds us over and over again in the Bible that He is for us and without Him, we can get through things. There is a lot of negativity in our world, on our news, and everywhere on social media. We have to be on guard, protecting our heart and shielding our minds so we can fill it up with positivity. This is something that takes time and constant reminding, but little by little we can overcome and thrive. If you're going through difficulty, talk with others about what you're going through, be open to the possibility that someone might need to talk and then listen. We need to band together and encourage each other through the valleys in life and that is what we are attempting to do by sharing our story. Feel free to cry and rejoice with us.

Chapter 23

HEAVEN

*For while we are in this tent, we groan and are
burdened, because we do not wish to be unclothed but
to be clothed instead with our heavenly dwelling, so
that what is mortal may be swallowed up by life.
Now the one who has fashioned us for this very purpose is God, who
has given us the Spirit as a deposit, guaranteeing what is to come.*
2 Corinthians 5:4-5

*But in keeping with his promise we are looking forward to a
new heaven and a new earth, where righteousness dwells.*
2 Peter 3:13

*For God so loved the world that he gave his one and only Son, that
whoever believes in him shall not perish but have eternal life.*
John 3:16

Heaven, as we understand it, is a place where everything is good. People who were once broken are made whole again. There are no tears, sadness, bullying or depression. Beauty is immeasurable and joy is unending. Christians sing of dancing on streets that are golden and feasting at big tables. We believe in Heaven, so we are thrilled at the thought of such a glorious place. We have the Bible to use as a guide in life and it explains how to get to Heaven and have eternal life. For our family, this is very important because we want to be reunited with our loved ones that have passed. The reality of Heaven hit really close when Cameron died. We wanted to make sure we would get to see him again. *Jesus answered, I am the way and the truth and the life. No one comes to the Father except through me. John 14:6.* We need to know Jesus and follow him. *If you declare with your mouth, "Jesus is Lord," and believe in our heart that God raised him from the dead, you will be saved."* Romans 10:9. These are all directions for us so we can live eternally.

But it's not just about an exit strategy, though. It's about living with a security of the future, so we can live an abundant life now. We want to do things worth living for. Volunteering our time and helping others means more, and building good strong relationships is more of a priority. Doing good is more fulfilling because we know that this is just a temporary home.

For some, this might not come as easy as others, but a good start is having hope there is a Heaven. If you have been abused, hurt or lied to we understand that putting your trust in anything can be very difficult. However, you have choices: believe in God, or don't, in Christ or not, in Heaven or not. For us, the promise of Heaven and eternity with the people we love is what we hope for.

God's heart yearns for each and every person whether they have followed the wrong path or not. He loves us deeper than any of us can even understand, and it's an unconditional and forgiving love. *The Lord is not slow in keeping his promise, as some understand slowness. Instead he is patient with you, not wanting anyone to perish, but everyone to come to repentance.* 2 Peter 3:9. God wants the best for us and is giving us time to come to him. Take the lead. Find some others to come along. Worship God. You're worth it, so is He. *Suppose one of you has a hundred sheep and loses one of them. Doesn't he leave the ninety-nine in the open country and go after the lost sheep until he finds it?* Luke 15:4. God thinks that you are worth it and has time for you.

Sometimes when we have prayed through our doubts, it has sounded something like this: I am tired of the constant struggle in my life. I need a Savior who can carry me through these dark days and guide me. I want peacefulness and to know how to walk in this world. Help me in the relationships I am in to follow your lead and love others like you want me to. Pull me out of this rubble and clean me off so that I can see clearly. Jesus, I need you.

Chapter 24

UNSEEN SCARS

I t was really difficult for us to feel like our other children were safe and secure on the old farmstead after the accident. Losing Cameron made us feel helpless and vulnerable. After a tragedy, the natural tendency for most parents is to feel the need to tighten the grip on any other children, to pull back the reins, and avoid risk at all cost. The bricks from in and outside of what was to be the apartment were moved to piles on the other side of the barn, waiting for the manure pit to be cleared, so they could be used as fill and hurt no more. Rusty metal found in the long grass or outbuildings was piled in one place, off limits to play on or around. A small pond would be drained and a culvert replaced. A rickety shed toppled on our own terms. Nobody wanted to wonder about the safety of the kids, or be anxious for the next accident and its aftermath. We did all that we could to ensure as safe a place as we could. That said, life carries risks, and we didn't want to end up daily walking in fear.

Over the years, we have both seen our share of protective parents and the results that came from it. Neither of us wanted to hover constantly, making life miserable for our kids and us. It was especially hard for me (Natalie), because my body was responding as if I had some post-traumatic symptoms. Adrenaline is released into the body by the adrenal glands in order to produce what is needed to flee or fight stressors that cross our paths. We no longer have to get away from lions hiding in the grass, but I sometimes get a rush of adrenaline when kids linger too close to the edge at the top of the steps or when they are in a situation where they might get hurt. Rapid breathing, a racing heart and heightened senses are part of a God-given instinct to protect us and our loved ones from harm. Surely little bodies need to be protected, but as our kids started getting older, we needed help letting go a little. In fact, whenever each of our kids would get close to turning 5-years-old, we would get uneasy, and it would feel like we were over a hurdle every time we made it past that birthday. Our kids, like many, want to swim, ride skateboards, bikes and jump on trampolines. They climb trees and on big rocks, which makes us nervous. Kids do what kids do. We are watchful, but try to manage the risk and stress associated in a way that keeps the adrenaline at bay. Ultimately, we only get to control a tiny portion of our days and how they will unfold. We have worked to help our kids understand how precious they are and how to make good decisions about risks they take. We have to trust that they will be okay, turning them over to God's care again and again. We don't want our kids filled with fear and we want them to know how important it is for them to make decisions and mistakes in the best way they can. Many friends and family would say Natalie is still a bit nervous, but the truth is that we've both mellowed out quite nicely.

One time when Caleb was about 6, he fell off a trampoline and hit his nose on the bar. He was traumatized and panicked because blood was coming from his nose and mouth and that is what happened to Cameron. Caleb was almost 3 when the accident happened and he was right there next to Alex and Cameron. He didn't talk about things, but for a couple years, when the ambulance and police would sound the sirens at parades, his entire body would tremble.

Most adults struggle with this sort of loss, but when young kids lose a friend or loved one, the capacity to handle it is even less. Our nephew, Alex, withdrew a little as a result of the accident. He's been hard on himself over the years and is still reluctant to make close connections with other people. Even more heartbreaking for his parents was working through his survivor's guilt, a condition where people feel wrong for "making it" when others did not. He's as rowdy as any other teenage boy, but his parents are secretly thankful that he remains cautious to this day.

Another boy, one of Cameron's friends, JJ, would sometimes freeze with fear, traumatized if his circumstances were getting too stressful or if someone got hurt. The scars for young ones are often the hidden ones. They sometimes think that getting hurt may mean disappearing forever.

ACKNOWLEDGEMENTS

W ork on a project like this does not happen without assistance. We would like say a great big "Thank you" to:

- Our parents and extended families. All the support over the years has meant more to us than you can imagine. Your continued encouragement has lifted our spirits through some lousy days.
- Sarah, Chad, Alex and Bella Hamilton for carrying the memory of Cameron, sending positive messages and loving our kids like they are your own.
- WestBow Press for their patient guidance and help with the highs and lows of the self-publishing process and for taking us under their wings throughout the process.
- Tranette Stevens and Kayla Leville for their early insights and for moving us closer to doing more heavy-lifting on our own.
- Jill Pertler for her editing prowess.

- The Book Posse: Katie Cozzi, Joni Westlund, Rachel Willie, Sarah Vargo, Jennie Heikkila and Maija Colombe - thank you for all of your insights and for helping us when we needed it! We are not professionals and so your editorial work and suggestions along the way have been invaluable.
- All the wonderful people who supported the publication with their donations on our GoFundMe site; it was so good to have that vote of confidence and the freedom to focus on writing rather than finding money to make it happen. Without you, this wouldn't be possible, nor would we have drunk as much coffee in cheap hotel rooms away from the ruckus of regular life.
- The staff at CHS, and specifically the social studies department. I work with wonderful people and my department shouldered the burden of my absence during that last awful month of the school year back in 2004 and then later on during my leave to work on the railroad. Tim, Steve, Bret, Wendy and Steve have been a source of encouragement and support from the outset and I thank them for their continued excellence.
- Mr. John Langenbrunner, former school superintendent, for finding a way for me to take more than the contractually allotted leave after the loss of our son. I am forever grateful for your work to make it possible for me to be with my family during that difficult time.
- Cloquet High School students present and past. It has been really fun to hear from so many of you as we were fundraising and I am really grateful for all the times I doubted whether it was all worth it. I am especially thankful that you give me reason to laugh. Life is short and shouldn't be taken so seriously.
- Justin and Joy Hunt, Jim and Jennie Heikkala, Jason and Jeni Peterson, Bob and Lynn Hunt, Brandon and Bekah

Swanson have taken our children in while we spent long weekends holed up in front of computer screens. Writing takes time, and for us, time away. Without someone to watch our kids, it'd probably have taken another ten years.

- Coffee, you pulled us through many hours of putting this book together.

- Lastly, Caleb, Emma, Grace and Gavin. What most people may not really know is that this look at the past is really a message about the future for you and to you. You get to see us at our best and at our worst, and have lived through one of the most challenging seasons of our lives and so you can measure the words we have written against how we actually are with you. Like us, there may be times when you have doubts about what lies ahead or setbacks and challenges that keep you from everything you think should be yours. You'll make it. Keep fighting through. Remember how we have prayed with you and for you about embracing life. You have decisions to make about stepping into all He has for you. Choose joy.

ABOUT THE AUTHORS

C hris and Natalie Swanson have known each other since 5th grade and were married at the tender age of twenty. He teaches high school social studies and she takes care of the home front. They live with their four children, dog, goldfish, and a pet turtle in Cloquet, Minnesota. This is their first book.

CPSIA information can be obtained at www.ICGtesting.com
Printed in the USA
BVOW08s2113160116

433193BV00001B/56/P

UNITED NATIONS CONFERENCE ON TRADE AND DEVELOPMENT
Geneva

INTERNATIONAL ACCOUNTING and REPORTING ISSUES

2007 Review

Report by the Secretariat of the
United Nations Conference on Trade and Development

UNITED NATIONS
New York and Geneva, 2008

NOTE

Symbols of United Nations documents are composed of capital letters combined with figures. Mention of such a symbol indicates a reference to a United Nations document.

The designations employed and the presentation of the material in this publication do not imply the expression of any opinion whatsoever on the part of the Secretariat of the United Nations concerning the legal status of any country, territory, city or area, or of its authorities, or concerning the delimitation of its frontiers or boundaries.

PER
UNI
ST/CTC
I 51

UNCTAD/ITE/TEB/2007/5

UNITED NATIONS PUBLICATION
Sales No. E.08.II.D.2
ISBN 978-92-1-112732-4

Foreword

UNCTAD's Intergovernmental Working Group of Experts on International Standards of Accounting and Reporting (ISAR) has been contributing for over two decades to the global efforts geared towards promoting good practices in corporate financial and non-financial reporting. Reliable and comparable corporate financial and non-financial reporting plays an important role in fostering investor confidence and mobilizing domestic and international investment.

Since its establishment as a standing group of experts in 1982, ISAR has held twenty-four annual sessions. The twenty-fourth session of ISAR was held at the Palais des Nations in Geneva from 30 October to 1 November 2007. At its twenty-fourth session, ISAR considered several timely topics, including the practical implementation of International Financial Reporting Standards (IFRS), accounting by small and medium-sized enterprises, integration of corporate responsibility indicators into corporate annual reports, and corporate governance disclosure.

The utility of a principles-based, high-quality and enforceable set of global financial reporting standards, such as IFRS, for the efficient functioning and stability of the international financial system cannot be overemphasized. At its twenty-fourth session, ISAR continued to facilitate the exchange of views and experiences among member States on the practical implementation of IFRS. The contribution of such an exchange to the consistent implementation and interpretation of IFRS around the world is considerable.

In addition to financial information, investors and other stakeholders have been calling for concise and comparable reports on the contribution of enterprises to society. Over the last four years, ISAR has been working towards providing enterprises with voluntary practical guidance that will assist them in communicating to stakeholders their efforts to make positive contribution to society. The practical guidance was finalized at the twenty-fourth session of ISAR and it is indeed gratifying to witness the fruitful culmination of ISAR's deliberations on this topic in such a practical manner.

Corporate governance disclosure was also discussed at the twenty-fourth session, where participants reviewed three new reports prepared using ISAR's guidance on good practices in corporate governance disclosure. These reports provide useful information on the status of corporate governance disclosure in different markets, and further establish ISAR's guidance in this area as a practical international benchmark.

As an open and globally representative forum, ISAR has continued to play a positive role in facilitating the consistent implementation of internationally comparable standards of corporate reporting in the areas of accounting, corporate responsibility and corporate governance disclosure. It is my hope that this publication will provide policymakers, regulators, standard-setters, boards of directors, academics and others with timely and useful information.

Supachai Panitchpakdi

Secretary-General of UNCTAD
Geneva, December 2007

Executive Summary

The volume of the 2007 review of international accounting and reporting issues contains proceedings of the twenty-fourth session of the Intergovernmental Working Group of Experts on International Standards of Accounting and Reporting (ISAR). The main item on the agenda of the session was a review of practical implementation issues related to International Financial Reporting Standards (IFRS). Several other topics were also discussed under the item on "other business" segment of the session. These included draft guidance on corporate responsibility indicators in annual reports and the results of surveys on corporate governance disclosure.

Chapter I contains a review of recent trends towards convergence to IFRS and a summary of the main findings of three country case studies on Pakistan, South Africa and Turkey. The individual country case studies are contained in chapters II to IV and discuss issues that arise in the practical implementation of IFRS, focusing on institutional, enforcement and capacity-building aspects. Chapter V contains guidance on corporate responsibility indicators in annual reports, as finalized at the twenty-fourth session of ISAR. This guidance presents a methodology for compiling and reporting selected corporate responsibility indicators in corporate annual reports. Chapter V also contains a section that discusses the information needs of stakeholders and the selection criteria for the core indicators of corporate responsibility in annual reports.

The 2007 review of the implementation status of corporate governance disclosures is contained in chapter VI, and presents an inventory of disclosure requirements in 25 emerging markets, as well as an overview of recent developments and ongoing trends. Country case studies of Egypt and China on the implementation status of corporate governance disclosures are presented in chapters VII and VIII, respectively. The surveys on the implementation status of corporate governance disclosures are based on the *Guidance on Good Practices in Corporate Governance Disclosure* published by ISAR in 2006.

Introduction

The twenty-fourth session of UNCTAD's Intergovernmental Working Group of Experts on International Standards of Accounting and Reporting (ISAR) was held at the Palais des Nations in Geneva from 30 October to 1 November 2007. The session brought together 291 participants from 93 Member States. The main agenda item of the session was a review of practical implementation issues of International Financial Reporting Standards (IFRS). Several topics were also discussed under the "other business" segment of the session. These included, draft guidance on corporate responsibility indicators in annual reports and results of surveys on corporate governance disclosure.

Deliberations on the main agenda item featured three panels. The first panel discussion addressed various aspects of implementation of IFRS, including overall progress in practical implementation, implications of standards and interpretations that are in development, and the role of International Standards on Auditing in consistent implementation of IFRS. It also covered enforcement and convergence programmes. The second panel focused on country case studies with respect to practical implementation issues of IFRS. The county case studies covered Pakistan, the Republic of South Africa and Turkey. The presentations on the country case studies highlighted implementation challenges with respect to the regulatory framework of financial reporting, enforcement, and capacity building issues, including audit. Lessons learned in the implementation process were discussed. In addition to the country case studies, a report on the implementation of IFRS and the fair value directive in the European Union was also discussed. Implementation of IFRS in countries with economies in transition that focused on Ukraine was also presented during the second panel discussion. The third panel discussion facilitated deliberations on proposed revisions to the *Accounting and Financial Reporting Guidelines for Small and Medium-sized Enterprises* (SMEGA) Level 3 Guidance. Participants conducted extensive discussion on the proposed revisions on SMEGA Level 3. Delegates reiterated the importance of high quality global financial reporting standards for the efficient functioning of and stability of the international financial system. They requested UNCTAD to continue its work in the area of practical implementation of IFRS. They also requested further work on revising the SMEGA Level 3 guidance.

One of the main topics discussed under the "other business" segment of the session was draft guidance on corporate responsibility indicators in annual reports. The draft guidance contained a detailed methodology for compiling and reporting selected core indicators on corporate responsibility. The methodology included a background description of each indicator, definitions of technical terms required for standardizing preparation and reporting of each indicator, as well as instructions on compiling and presenting each indicator. The draft guidance was also supplemented by another document presenting the information needs of stakeholders and the selection criteria for the core indicators contained in the guidance. Many delegates commended the draft guidance and requested that it should be published and disseminated widely.

The discussion on corporate governance disclosure included a review of corporate governance disclosure requirements in 25 emerging markets as well as country level studies of the Peoples' Republic of China and Egypt. In the course of the panel discussion on this topic, panellists highlighted a number of corporate governance issues including: the role of corporate governance requirements in the development of stock exchanges and capital markets, the need for (and the challenges of) measuring the quality of corporate governance disclosures; the need for guidance for small and medium-sized enterprises on this subject; and the increasing integration of environmental and social issues in the broader corporate governance framework.

The UNCTAD Secretariat organized a technical workshop under the theme "Financial Reporting and Transparency in the Extractive Industries" that took place at the Palais des Nations in Geneva on the eve of the twenty-fourth session of ISAR, i.e., on 29 October 2007. The workshop addressed technical issues in relation to comparability of financial reporting by entities engaged in extractive activities. Participants also deliberated on how to effectively account for and manage potentially large revenues from the extraction of natural resources in developing countries and countries with economies in transition. Furthermore, at the beginning of the workshop, representatives from the International Accounting Standards Board (IASB) and the International Federation of Accountants presented technical updates on IFRS and International Standards on Auditing (ISAs), respectively. About 130 participants took part in the workshop. Almost all of these participants also attended the twenty-fourth session of ISAR.

At the opening of the twenty-fourth session of ISAR, delegates elected Mr. Ato Ghartey, President, Institute of Chartered Accountants of Ghana, as Chairperson and Ms. Tatiana Yefymenko, Deputy Minister of Finance, Ukraine, as Vice-chairperson-cum-rapporteur. UNCTAD appreciates the contributions of Mr. Ghartey and Ms. Yefymenko in leading the twenty-fourth session of ISAR to a fruitful conclusion. UNCTAD acknowledges with appreciation the contributions of Robin Jarvis, Nancy Kamp-Roelands, and Jackie Cook in their capacities as resource persons in the areas of accounting by SMEs, corporate responsibility reporting and corporate governance disclosure, respectively.

UNCTAD expresses its gratitude to panellists who spoke on practical implementation issues of IFRS. Members of the first panel were: Peter Clark, Senior Project Manager, IASB; Ulf Linder, Deputy Head, Accounting Unit, European Commission; Erik van der Plaats, Senior Financial Management Specialist, World Bank; and Jim Sylph, Executive Director, Professional Standards, IFAC. Panellists who spoke during the second panel were: Nazlı Hoşal Akman, Professor, Bilkent, Turkey; Robert Hodgkinson, Executive Director, Technical - Institute of Chartered Accountants in England and Wales; Ludmyla Lovinska, Chief, Accounting Methodology Division, Ministry of Finance, Ukraine; Ignatius Sehoole, Executive President, the South African Institute of Chartered Accountants; and Syed Asad Ali Shah, Council Member, Institute of Chartered Accountants, Pakistan. The following speakers facilitated the discussion on accounting by SMEs: Richard Martin, Head of Financial Reporting, Association of Chartered and Certified Accountants; Vickson Ncube, Chief Executive, ECSAFA; and Syed Asad Ali Shah, Council Member, Institute of Chartered Accountants, Pakistan. UNCTAD acknowledges with appreciation the contribution of the following in preparing country case studies on practical implementation of IFRS that were discussed at the twenty-fourth session of ISAR: the Institute of Chartered Accountants of Pakistan; the South African Institute of Chartered Accountants; Nazlı Hoşal Akman, Professor, Bilkent, Turkey and Can Simga-Mugan, Professor, Middle East Technical University, Turkey.

UNCTAD appreciates the contributions of the following experts to the panel discussion of corporate responsibility reporting: Burkhard Feldmann, Head of Environment, Ciba Specialty Chemicals, Switzerland; Nancy Kamp-Roelands, Head of Corporate Social Responsibility Services, Ernst & Young, The Netherlands; Michael Kelly, Director Corporate Social Responsibility, KPMG, United Kingdom; Mokhethi Moshoeshoe, President, CIVA Innovation Management, South Africa; and Ambreen Waheed, Executive Director, Responsible Business Initiative, Pakistan.

UNCTAD is also grateful to the following panellists for their contributions to the discussion of corporate governance disclosure: Anthony Kyereboah Coleman, Professor, University of Ghana Business School, Ghana; Khaled M. Dahawy, Professor, American University in Cairo, Egypt; Hans Hirt, Associate Director, Hermes Equity Ownership Services, United Kingdom; Mohammed Omran, Vice Chairman, Cairo & Alexandria Stock Exchanges, Egypt; Thiago Ribeiro, Issuers and Listings Development Analyst, BOVESPA, Brazil; and Li Weian, Professor, Nankai University, China.

UNCTAD acknowledges with appreciation the contributions of the following panellists who presented at the workshop on Financial Reporting and Transparency in the Extractive Industries that was held in Geneva on 29 October 2007: Peter Clark, Senior Project Manager, IASB; Angelica Ferreira, Manager of International Accounting Practices, PETROBRAS, Brazil; Torbjörn Fredriksson, DITE, UNCTAD; Arthur Fredrik, Counsellor, Permanent Mission of Norway in Geneva; Jan Bo Hansen, Professional Services Director, Deloitte, Denmark; Manuel Antonio Correia de Lemos, Director, Secretary of State for Natural Resources, Dili, Timor-Leste; Richard Martin, Head of Financial Reporting, Association of Chartered and Certified Accountants; Jim Obazee, Technical Director, Nigerian Accounting Standards Board; Francisco Paris, Extractive Industries Transparency Initiative Secretariat; Ignatius Sehoole, Executive President, the South African Institute of Chartered Accountants; Syed Asad Ali Shah, Institute of Chartered Accountants, Pakistan; Michael J. Stewart, PwC, London; Jim Sylph, Executive Director, Professional Standards, IFAC; André Foko Tomena, Secretary-General, Ministry of Finance, Democratic Republic of Congo; Geoffrey Townsend, Director, OAO, TMK; and Mark Walsh, Principal, Canadian Accounting Standards Board.

UNCTAD commends staff members for their dedication and contributions to the success of the twenty-fourth session of ISAR and the technical workshop on Financial Reporting and Transparency in the Extractive Industries. These are: Nazha Benabbes Taarji-Aschenbrenner, Officer-in-Charge, Enterprise Development Branch; Dezider Stefunko, Officer-in-Charge, Accounting and Insurance Section; Yoseph Asmelash, Head, Accounting Unit and Anthony Miller. Preparation of background documentation on corporate responsibility reporting and corporate governance disclosure and organization of the respective panels on these topics were conducted by Anthony Miller. Research support for the 2007 review of the implementation status of corporate governance disclosure was provided by Cheng Feng and Bo Zhao. Martha Cuadros Büchner provided critical administrative support.

CONTENTS

Chapter VIII. 2007 Review of the Implementation Status of Corporate Governance Disclosures: Case Study of China 167

Chapter I

Review of practical Implementation issues of International Financial Reporting Standards

Summary of discussions

The following is a summary of the discussions on the main agenda item of the twenty-fourth session of the Intergovernmental Working Group of Experts on International Standards of Accounting and Reporting (ISAR).

The Chairperson of the session invited the Officer-in-Charge of the Enterprise Development Branch to introduce the main agenda item of the session - review of practical implementation issues of International Financial Reporting Standards (IFRS). In introducing the agenda item, the Officer-in-Charge of the Enterprise Development Branch provided background information on prior work that ISAR conducted on the topic. She then drew participants' attention to documentation that the UNCTAD Secretariat prepared to facilitate deliberations on the agenda item. These included country case studies on practical implementation of IFRS covering Pakistan, the Republic of South Africa, and Turkey (TD/B/COM.2/ISAR/38 through 40, respectively) and a note containing recent developments in practical implementation of IFRS and a summary of the main practical implementation issues identified in the country case studies (TD/B/COM.2/37). Three panels presented various perspectives on the agenda item.

The first panel addressed various aspects of implementation of IFRS, including, overall progress, implications of standards and interpretations that are in development, the role of International Standards on Auditing in consistent implementation of IFRS, as well as enforcement and convergence programmes. The first panellist presented the perspectives of the European Commission on the topic. He noted that the transition to IFRS that occurred in 2005 reinvigorated the work of the European Commission as well as the deliberations at UNCTAD-ISAR. He described the endorsement mechanism through which IFRS are accepted in the European Union. He stated that some member States in the European Union were in a better footing than others with respect to implementation of IFRS. He highlighted various IFRS that were under consideration for endorsement at that time. He also noted an impact assessment that the European Commission conducted with respect to considerations for endorsement of IFRS 8, Segment Reporting. With respect to accounting by SMEs, the speaker stated that consultations were being conducted on the Exposure Draft of a Proposed IFRS for SMEs issued by the IASB.

The next panellist provided the views of an international development organization on practical implementation of IFRS. He said that his organization had assessed 75 countries on observance of international codes and standards on accounting and auditing. He highlighted several common practical implementation issues that were identified in the course of the assessments his organization conducted. These included: lack of conceptual thinking on general purpose financial reporting, inappropriate scope for use of IFRS, problems with consolidated accounts, incompatibility with supervisory reporting, lack of technical capacity, lack of current versions of IFRS and ISAs in languages other than English, weak audit function and enforcement, and poor enforcement of publication of financial statements. He also highlighted that in addition to proper accounting and auditing standards, a robust financial reporting infrastructure required several other pillars including statutory framework, monitoring and enforcement, education and training, and accounting profession and ethics.

The next speaker provided the perspectives of the International Accounting Standards Board (IASB). He discussed recent developments on adoption of IFRS in different regions of the world. He highlighted developments in the United States of America with respect to the proposal of the United States Securities and Exchange Commission (US SEC) to remove a requirement for foreign issuers to provide a reconciliation of their financial statements prepared under IFRS to United States Generally Accepted Accounting Principles. He also discussed a Concept Release by the US SEC on providing US domestic issuers with an option to prepare their financial statements in accordance with IFRS. He made reference to a hearing the United States Senate Subcommittee on Securities, Insurance and Investment conducted a few days earlier under the theme "International Accounting Standards: Opportunities, Challenges and Global Convergence Issues". The Chairman of the IASB and the Financial Accounting Standards Board (FASB) testified at the hearing. The panellist elaborated on some features of additional due process elements that the IASB had introduced. These included a two-year post implementation review, feedback statements and cost/benefit analysis.

The final speaker discussed the role of International Standards on Auditing (ISAs) in consistent implementation of IFRS. He underscored the importance of strengthening all aspects of the financial reporting supply chain, including IFRS and ISAs. He stated that the International Auditing and Assurance Standards Board (IAASB) had been undertaking a "Clarity Project". The objective of the project was to redraft ISAs in a new style that promotes consistent implementation by enhancing clarity and understandability of the standards and by eliminating any ambiguity about what is required of auditors. The project would be completed by the end of 2008 and the revised ISAs would be effective for financial reporting periods beginning on or after 15 December 2009. The implementation process of the revised ISAs envisaged a moratorium on issuing new ISAs for a period of two years. This was intended to provide entities that would be implementing the ISAs a stable-platform for the duration of the moratorium. The speaker invited delegates to respond to the IAASB's consultation paper on its strategy and work plan for 2009-2011.

After the presentations by the panel of speakers, delegates exchanged views on various aspects of practical implementation of IFRS. A delegate shared his observation that although about 100 countries were considered to be implementing IFRS, it was not clear whether these countries were requiring application of IFRS by all entities in their jurisdiction or the scope was limited to listed companies only. Delegates raised the need for making available to the public IASB publications, including IFRS, free of charge. Some delegates cited the publications of the International Federation of Accountants - including ISA that were available to the public free of charge. In this respect, the pressing needs of developing countries and countries with economies in transition were emphasized. To that end, some delegates suggested that development organizations such as the World Bank could contribute financial resources to the IASB. Some delegates also suggested that the IASB web site needed to be accessible in major languages other than English. It was noted that the Trustees of the International Accounting Standards Committee Foundation were working towards providing the IASB with more sustainable sources of funding which, among other things, might enable the IASB to make publications available in multiple languages and possibly, free of charge.

The next panel discussion focused mainly on country case studies with respect to practical implementation of IFRS. Panellists provided an overview of the state of implementation of IFRS in the respective countries they presented on. They also discussed the regulatory framework, enforcement, capacity building issues, including audit, as well as lessons learned in the implementation process. The speaker who discussed the case study of Pakistan stated that with the exception of a few standards IFRS had been adopted in the country. The exceptions were mainly due to time needed to reconcile the requirements of certain IFRS with national law. He also stated that the accounting framework of Pakistan was similar to the approach adopted by ISAR in developing the Accounting and Financial Reporting Guidelines for Small and Medium-sized Enterprises (SMEGAs). Listed companies and public interest entities were required to follow IFRS. Medium-sized entities were required to apply a standard similar to ISAR's SMEGA Level 2. Small-sized entities apply a standard similar to ISAR's SMEGA Level 3. The panellist highlighted a number of issues pertaining to enforcement, capacity-building as well as lessons learned in the implementation process. He highlighted adoption of IFRS rather than adapting them to specific circumstances of a country as a better long-term implementation strategy.

This was followed by a presentation on the case study of the Republic of South Africa. The panellist noted that South Africa was one of earliest countries that introduced International Accounting Standards into their national accounting framework. The Johannesburg Stock Exchange required listed companies to apply full IFRS for financial periods beginning 1 January 2005. It was also noted that South Africa had adopted as a transitional standard for limited interest companies the Exposure Draft IFRS for SMEs that was issued by the IASB in February 2007. The speaker elaborated on a number of issues that arose in the implementation process in South Africa. He expressed support for adopting IFRS in one move or "big bang" rather than taking a piecemeal approach. He also highlighted a need for allowing a reasonable time for transitioning to IFRS.

The next panellist presented her views on the practical implementation of IFRS in Turkey. She provided background information into some historical developments that influenced the evolution of the accounting system in Turkey. The panellist elaborated on various aspects of the regulatory framework for financial reporting in that country. The Turkish Accounting Standards Board was in the process of developing an accounting standard for SMEs. Some of the main challenges in the practical implementation of IFRS include, solving the multi-institutional structure of the accounting regulatory environment, establishing a public oversight board and enforcement of accounting standards.

The next presentation was on a report that the Institute of Chartered Accountants in England and Wales prepared for the European Commission. The title of the report was *European Union Implementation of IFRS and the Fair Value Directive*. The overall conclusion of the study was that implementing IFRS in the EU was challenging but successful, resulting in improvement in comparability and quality of financial reporting in the EU. The study included a review of 2005 financial statements of 200 companies listed in the European Union. The areas of financial reporting for which companies incurred significant costs were drafting of financial statements, derivatives, pensions, financial instruments, and revenue recognition. The study identified financial reporting by entities in the insurance and extractive industries sectors as needing further strengthening. The use of generic language or "boilerplating" in accounting policy disclosures was also another area needing further improvement.

The last speaker presented on application of IFRS in Ukraine. The speaker noted that the Government of Ukraine had only just recently passed a decree adopting a strategy for implementing IFRS in the country. The decree defined the scope of application of IFRS as well as the role of the State in the implementation process - including the Ministry of Finance. In Ukraine, the accounting reform process began in 1998. In accordance with the Ukrainian law on accounting and financial reporting, 32 national regulations were developed. The law required that national standards should not contradict international standards. The Methodological Council and the Accounting Methodology Department of the Ministry of Finance had been working on several aspects of a strategy for the development of accounting in Ukraine. The areas included improvement of state regulation, adaptation of an accounting legal and regulatory framework, accounting policy in the public sector entities, reform of accounting in government budgeting and accounting, improvement of management accounting, and accounting and financial reporting for small enterprises. The speaker noted that from 28 February to 1 March 2007, the Ministry of Finance held in Kiev, an international scientific and practical conference under the theme "International Accounting and Financial Reporting Standards: Experiences and Prospects of Implementation in Countries with Economies in Transition".

Following the panel presentations, the Chairperson opened the floor for discussion. Several delegates raised questions pertaining to the practical implementation of IFRS in the countries on which the case studies were conducted. One delegated sought clarification on what the auditors' report would state with respect to one of the case studies where one IFRS was not implemented. A panellist clarified that since IFRS were not adopted in full, the auditors report stated that the financial statements were prepared in accordance with "approved accounting standards" in that country and not IFRS. Other delegates raised questions about the implications for the independence of a professional accountancy organization if it was responsible for setting both accounting and auditing standards for a country. Clarification was provided with the explanation that the role of the professional accountancy body in question was more of a coordinating one, rather than setting standards per se. Experts also exchanged views on the enforcement role of professional accountancy bodies and the manner in which such bodies were empowered by law.

In concluding its deliberations on this issue, the twenty-fourth session of ISAR requested the UNCTAD secretariat to review practical implementation issues relating to IFRS and to prepare a publication that synthesizes the lessons learned in the practical implementation of IFRS by reviewing the country case studies discussed by ISAR at its twenty-third and twenty-fourth sessions, and to disseminate that publication as widely as possible. ISAR requested the UNCTAD secretariat to continue conducting studies on practical implementation issues relating to IFRS, including related topics such as implementation of International Standards on Auditing. It also requested the UNCTAD secretariat to disseminate its research in that area, and resources permitting, to organize related training workshops and conferences with a view to strengthening the accountancy profession in developing countries and countries with economies in transition.

The last segment of the discussion under the main agenda item focused on proposed revisions to the *Accounting and Financial Reporting Guidelines for Small and Medium-sized Enterprises (SMEGA) Level 3 Guidance* that ISAR issued in 2003. In introducing the agenda item, the UNCTAD Secretariat noted that in accordance with the agreement ISAR reached at its twenty-third session, a Consultative Group had been reconvened to propose revisions on SMEGA Level 3. The UNCTAD Secretariat indicated that during the intersession period, the Consultative Group had conducted consultations, including during its meeting in Geneva in early July 2007. With a view to facilitating deliberations on the topic at the session, the UNCTAD Secretariat had prepared a document (UNCTAD/NONE/2007/1) that contained proposed revisions on SMEGA Level 3.

Following an introduction by the UNCTAD Secretariat and brief commentaries by the Chairperson of the Consultative Group as well as two of its member, the Chairperson of the session opened the floor for discussion. In the course of the deliberations, delegates raised a number of issues. Some delegates sought clarification on criteria for categorizing enterprises into the three levels that ISAR had recommended. Certain delegates were of the view that the distinction between levels 2 and 3 was more difficult to understand. It was reaffirmed in the course of the deliberations that the decision as to how to categorize entities into the three levels was for each Member State to decide. There was general agreement on the need for providing further elaboration on the distinction between level 2 and 3 SMEs. Some experts wished to know whether SMEGA Level 2 would also be revised. It was recognized that SMEGA Level 2 would be revisited once the IASB's draft Standard for SMEs was completed.

Several experts requested clarification on "simple accruals" as used in SMEGA Level 3. Some experts wondered how such a basis differed from cash basis or accruals as used in full IFRS. Some asked whether a parallel could be drawn with the use of cash, modified cash, modified accruals and full accruals as used in the context of International Public Sector Accounting Standards (IPSASs). There was general understanding that as used in SMEGA Level 3, "simple accruals" would mean that certain complex accruals - for example, deferred taxes - would not be recognized in the financial statements of Level 3 entities.

The revised SMEGA Level 3 did not require SMEs in that category to prepare a cash-flow statement. A number of experts expressed divergent views on the issue. Some experts were of the view that a historical cash-flow statement was an essential component of the financial statements that SMEs would prepare. Thus, it should be required in the revised SMEGA Level 3. Other experts were of the view that a cash-flow statement would be too complex for SMEs to provide, particularly, if it were to be prepared using the direct-method. Other delegates were of the view that what would be useful for SMEs in Level 3 to prepare was a forecast or projection of the entities future cash flows - as opposed to a historical cash-flow statement. Such a statement would allow potential lenders to readily assess the entities ability to repay loans that they might consider lending it. A statement of this nature would also be useful for managing the entity more effectively. There was general understanding that this issued needed to be considered further.

Some experts were of the view that it would be useful to provide examples of explanatory notes that would accompany the balance sheet and income statement required by SMEGA Level 3. Others suggested that explanatory notes would be useful for describing risks and uncertainties. This could include contingent liabilities. Some experts thought that it would be useful to provide in the financial statements comparative figures of previous financial periods. One expert suggested that cash and bank accounts could be presented in a separate category outside of current assets. During the page-by-page review of the revised document, experts made a number of editorial and formatting suggestions. In concluding its deliberations on this topic, ISAR requested the UNCTAD Secretariat to incorporate into the document comments and suggestions received during the twenty-fourth session, as well as additional comments that interested delegations would submit within two weeks after the session. ISAR also requested the UNCTAD secretariat to reconvene a consultative group with a view to finalizing and distributing for comments an updated SMEGA Level 3 as soon as possible.

I. Introduction

The important role of the private sector in the economic development of member States has been recognized for a long time. Over the years, attracting financing needed for economic development has become more competitive. Economic resources have become more mobile across borders. Enterprises that provide potential investors with reliable and comparable financial statements are more likely to attract domestic and international investment. The United Nations has been providing an inclusive forum where member States exchange views and experiences on promoting reliable and comparable corporate reporting. In October 1982, the Economic and Social Council established the Intergovernmental Working Group of Experts on International Standards of Accounting and Reporting (ISAR).

At the tenth session of the conference (UNCTAD X), held in Bangkok, Thailand, in February 2000, member States requested UNCTAD to "promote increased transparency and disclosure by encouraging the use of internationally recognized accounting, reporting and auditing standards and improved corporate governance" (paragraph 122 of the Bangkok Plan of Action). Furthermore, at UNCTAD XI, held in São Paulo, Brazil in June 2004, member States reaffirmed the Bangkok Plan of Action and requested UNCTAD to "collect, analyze and disseminate data on best practices for stimulating enterprise development, and identify ways and means for enterprises, especially developing countries' SMEs, to meet international standards, including accounting standards" (paragraph 55 of the São Paulo Consensus).

ISAR has so far held 23 annual sessions. At the beginning of 2005, an unprecedented number of enterprises and countries around the world adopted International Financial Reporting Standards (IFRSs) issued by the International Accounting Standards Board (IASB) as their basis for preparing financial statements. In light of this development, at its twenty-second and twenty-third sessions, ISAR deliberated on practical implementation issues of IFRS. At its twenty-second session, ISAR reviewed trends in the IFRS convergence process and major practical implementation issues that were arising in the implementation of IFRS. These pertained to institutional development, enforcement and technical implementation capacity issues. At its twenty-third session, ISAR reviewed practical IFRS implementation issues, including case studies of Brazil (TD/B/COM.2/ISAR/33/Add.1), Germany (TD/B/COM.2/ISAR/33/Add.2), India (TD/B/COM.2/ISAR/33/Add.3), Jamaica (TD/B/COM.2/ISAR/33/Add.4) and Kenya (TD/B/COM.2/ISAR/33/Add.5).

At the conclusion of its twenty-third session, the group of experts reiterated the importance of principles-based, high-quality financial reporting standards, such as IFRS, for the coherent and efficient functioning of the international financial architecture, as well as the mobilization of financial resources for economic development. Participants at the session stressed the importance of a forum such as ISAR, where member States could share their views and experiences in this area, and identify best practices and guidance with a view to promoting harmonization, thereby facilitating the flow of investment.

At its twenty-third session, the group of experts recognized that – following the widespread adoption of IFRS in 2005 by a large number of countries and enterprises – various stakeholders, including regulators, preparers, users and auditors continue to encounter practical implementation challenges. In particular, the group of experts recognized that an effective regulatory regime, as well as an adequate audit system and professional education requirements, should be in place to facilitate the successful implementation of IFRS. The group also recognized that implementation is a long-term process and requires a defined strategy and appropriate mechanisms in order to build institutional and technical capacity supported by adequate resources.

In concluding its deliberations at the twenty-third session, the group of experts agreed to conduct additional studies and reviews to gain further insight into the challenges faced by developing countries and countries with economies in transition in meeting international requirements for high-quality and adequate standards with a view to developing guidance on good practices. Accordingly, three country case studies covering Pakistan, South Africa and Turkey have been prepared for consideration by the twenty-fourth session of ISAR. The objective of these case studies is to draw lessons learned in the practical implementation issues of IFRS and share these with member States that are either implementing IFRS or that intend to do so in the future. While a comprehensive review of practical implementation of IFRS requires a wider scope and analysis, the country cases have provided useful insights. The individual country case studies can be found in the following documents: Pakistan – TD/B/COM.2/ISAR/38; South Africa – TD/B/COM.2/ISAR/39; and Turkey – TD/B/COM.2/ISAR/40.

II.   Recent trends towards convergence to IFRS

During the inter-sessional period following the twenty-third session of ISAR, a number of developments indicating the growing convergence towards IFRS have occurred around the world. The chairman of IASB expects that in about five years, the number of countries that require or allow use of IFRS will probably have grown to 150. He also expects that countries that have converged to IFRS by then will face problems in attracting investment.[1]

In July 2007, further to the announcement by the Central Bank of Brazil in early 2006 of its decision to require all financial institutions in the country to apply IFRS by 2010 for preparing their consolidated financial statements, the Securities and Exchange Commission of Brazil issued rule number 457.[2]

In January 2007, the Minister of Finance and Economic Planning of Ghana formally launched the adoption of IFRS in his country. By December 2007, listed companies, government business enterprises, banks, insurance companies, securities brokers, pension and investment banks, and public utilities are expected to prepare their financial statements in accordance with IFRS.[3] In his address to participants at the launching, the minister referred to a Report on the Observance of Standards and Codes (ROSC) on Ghana that the World Bank issued in March 2006, and noted that the adoption of IFRS would address certain weaknesses the ROSC of Ghana has identified.[4]

Earlier this year, the Institute of Chartered Accountants of India formed an IFRS convergence task force to look into various convergence issues and prepare a road map for full convergence with IFRS.[5] At its 269th Council meeting in July 2007, the institute decided to bring Indian accounting standards fully in line with IFRS by 1 April 2011. Listed companies in India

---

[1] Sir David Tweedie in an interview with the *Journal of Accountancy* of the American Institute of Certified Public Accountants, July 2007: 36–39.

[2] *Gazeta Mercantil*, 16 July 2007.

[3] "Ghana adopts international reporting standards". *The Statesman*, 25 January 2007, Ghana.

[4] Speech by Minister Kwadwo–Baah Wiredu, Minister of Finance and Planning of Ghana on 23 January 2007 at the formal launching ceremony of IFRS in Ghana.

[5] *The Chartered Accountant*. May 2007: 1,695. Institute of Chartered Accountants of India.

will first be required to prepare their financial statements in accordance with IFRS. Other entities will be brought under the IFRS regime in a phased manner.[6]

In March 2007, the Financial Supervisory Commission and the Accounting Standards Board of the Republic of Korea announced that by 2009, all companies in the country, other than financial institutions, will be permitted to apply IFRS as adopted by the Republic of Korea. Use of IFRS will become mandatory starting in 2011.[7]

In response to a request from the Ministry of Finance of Ukraine, the UNCTAD secretariat co-organized a regional conference held in Kiev from 28 February to 1 March 2007 under the title "International financial reporting standards: Experiences and perspectives of implementation in countries with economies in transition". This event was particularly useful in identifying practical challenges and in sharing the experiences of those who have already undertaken practical steps in the implementation of IFRS that are of special relevance to countries with economies in transition.

At the conclusion of the Symposium on international convergence of accounting in emerging markets and transition economies, which took place in Beijing in mid-July 2007, participants launched the Beijing Initiative, which calls on emerging markets and transition economies to build up a clear concept about international convergence of accounting, and take action to develop a plan on convergence with IFRS. Participants proposed setting up an annual forum on international convergence of accounting in emerging markets and transition economies. They also proposed creating a regular exchange mechanism to improve and implement various suggestions participants proposed. The symposium was jointly hosted by IASB and the Ministry of Finance of China.[8]

In July 2006, IASB announced it would not require the application of new IFRSs under development or major amendments to existing standards before 1 January 2009.[9] This in effect provides four years of a stable platform for those entities that adopted IFRSs in 2005. At the same time, IASB also announced its intention to allow a minimum of one year between the date of the publication of wholly new IFRSs or major amendments to existing IFRSs and the date when implementation is required. This was in recognition of the time many countries require for translation and implementation of new standards into practice, and in certain circumstances where IFRSs are legally binding processing new standards through the legislative system.

One issue that often arises in the practical implementation of IFRS is whether small and medium-sized enterprises (SMEs) should be required to apply IFRS. Over the years, with the growing volume and complexity of IFRS, it has become more widely recognized that SMEs need a less burdensome set of standards. IASB has been working towards this goal. In February this year, IASB published for public comment an exposure draft of an IFRS for SMEs.[10] The proposed IFRS for SMEs is intended to provide a simplified, self-contained set of accounting principles that are appropriate for smaller, non-listed companies. It is based on full IFRS. Along with the 254-page exposure draft, IASB also issued implementation guidance consisting of illustrative financial statements and a disclosure checklist. The exposure draft has been translated into French, German and Spanish. Comments are due by 1 October 2007. According to the IASB work programme, a final version of the IFRS for SMEs is expected by the second half of 2008.

---

[6] "Indian accounting standards to match global norms by 2011". *Business Standard*. New Delhi. 22 July 2007.

[7] Press release of 16 March 2007. The Financial Supervisory Commission and Korea Accounting Institute.

[8] http://www.mof.gov.cn/news/20070713_1500_27121.htm

[9] "IASB takes steps to assist adoption of IFRS and reinforce consultation: No new IFRS effective until 2009". IASB press release. 24 July 2006.

[10] Exposure draft of a proposed IFRS for small and medium-sized entities. International Accounting Standards Board, London, February 2007.

In July 2007, the United States Securities and Exchange Commission (SEC) published for public comment a proposal to eliminate current requirements in the United States that foreign private issuers that file with the SEC their financial statements using IFRS as published by IASB also file a reconciliation of those financial statements to United States Generally Accepted Accounting Principles (GAAP). The proposal would enable foreign private issuers who prepare financial statements that comply with the English language version of IFRS as published by IASB to file those financial statements in their annual filings and registration statements without reconciliation with GAAP.[11] The commenting period on the SEC proposal is 75 days after it is published in the Federal Register.

Furthermore, the SEC unanimously voted to publish a concept release for public comment on allowing listed companies in the United States, including investment companies, to prepare their financial statements using IFRS as published by IASB. At present, United States listed companies are required to prepare their financial statements in accordance with GAAP.[12] Once the concept release is published in the Federal Register, the commenting period will run for 90 days.

Enforcement authorities in several jurisdictions are putting in the public domain their observations concerning IFRS-based financial statements they have reviewed. This is being done mainly with a view to promoting more consistent application of IFRS by entities in their respective jurisdictions. For example, in December 2006, the Financial Reporting Review Panel of the Financial Reporting Council of the United Kingdom published a preliminary report on implementation of IFRS.[13] Among other issues, the panel noted in its report that there was a tendency for companies to use generic language in describing the accounting policies they followed. In this respect, the panel encouraged companies to describe the accounting policies applied in practice, including information specific to their particular circumstances. Other areas the panel commented on include disclosure of judgments and estimates, possible impact of new standards and interpretations, sufficiency of disclosure with respect to impairment testing, related party disclosures, and presentation of financial statements.

Earlier this year, the Netherlands Authority for Financial Markets shared with companies listed in the Netherlands its observations on its review of 2005 IFRS-based financial statements.[14] The authority indicated that the "top five" IFRS financial reporting areas on which it raised questions with preparers who filed with it their 2005 financial statements were: (a) IAS32/39: financial instruments, including disclosure, presentation, recognition and valuation, the main questions in this area pertaining to equity versus liability classification in the balance sheet and omission of related disclosers; (b) IAS 12: income taxes, pertaining to deferred tax balances and effective tax rates; (c) IFRS 1: first-time adoption of IFRS, in relation to general level of transparency in this area and also differences between Dutch Generally Accepted Accounting Principles and IFRS; (d) IAS 1: presentation of financial statements; and (e) IAS 17 leases.

In a special issue of Standard & Poor's *CreditWeek* published at the beginning of the year, the credit rating agency indicated that IFRS generally enhanced the consistency of data used for comparative analysis in rating companies that implemented IFRS.[15] However, Standard & Poor's indicated that it found standard language (boilerplate) descriptions of accounting policy notes that contained little specific information on key transactions and corresponding policies uninformative

---

[11] United States Securities and Exchange Commission. Press Release No. 2007-128, 3 July 2007, Washington, DC.

[12] United States Securities and Exchange Commission. Press Release No. 2007-145, 25 July 2007, Washington, DC.

[13] *Preliminary Report on Implementation of IFRS*. Press Notice No. 98, Financial Reporting Review Panel, Financial Reporting Council, United Kingdom, 4 December, 2006.

[14] The Netherlands Authority for Financial Markets. Letter to companies, reference no. TFV-AJDe-07012880, 12 February 2007.

[15] Standard & Poor's, IFRS beyond transition. *CreditWeek* Volume 27, No. 5, 31 January, 2007.

and thus less useful for its purposes of credit rating. The company also indicated that various options in IFRS with respect to accounting policy, transition and presentation limit direct comparison of IFRS-based financial statements. Some of these options pertain to accounting for: borrowing costs, consolidation, valuation of property, plant and equipment, investment property, and inventories; pension and other defined benefit post-retirement obligations; and fair value in relation to financial assets and liabilities.

In April 2007, the Committee of European Securities Regulators (CESR) published extracts from its confidential database of enforcement decisions taken by European Union national enforcers of financial information. National enforcers are responsible for monitoring and reviewing financial statements filed by listed companies in their respective jurisdictions, and determining whether they comply with IFRS and other applicable requirements, including relevant national laws.[16] The extracts CESR published do not provide information about which listed company or country to which the enforcement decision relates. However, by sharing such extracts, CERS expects to inform market participants about which accounting treatment European Union national enforcers may consider as complying with IFRS, thereby contributing to consistent application of IFRS in the European Union.

The extracts contained enforcement decisions pertaining to business combinations, control of a subsidiary, capitalization of borrowing costs, restructuring plans, carrying value of a trade receivable, assessment of impairment loans, accounting for biological assets, forward purchases and sales of non-financial assets to be settled through physical inventory, redenomination of a foreign currency loan, and accounting treatment of a written puttable instrument on a minority interest.

In July 2007, the United States SEC released SEC staff observations of their reviews of annual reports for 2006 of more than 100 foreign private issuers that filed with the SEC for the first time financial statements that were prepared in accordance with IFRS.[17] The staff observations indicate that a vast majority of filers asserted that their financial statements were prepared in accordance with IFRS as adopted in a given jurisdiction. Most filers also asserted that their financial statements complied with IFRS as issued by IASB. Other staff observations include issues such as, among others: (a) variations in income statement formats; (b) classifications of items in cash flow statements; (c) accounting treatments for common control mergers, recapitalizations, reorganizations and acquisitions of minority interests; (d) disclosure on revenue recognition; (e) intangible assets and goodwill; (f) impairments and circumstances surrounding impairment reversals of long-lived assets; (g) leases; (h) contingent liabilities; (i) financial instruments, including derivatives; and (j) compliance of banks with International Accounting Standard (IAS) 39 in determining loan impairment. The staff observations also indicated substantial variations in accounting for insurance contracts and in the reporting of extractive industry exploration and evaluation activities.

With respect to sharing of decisions relating to the enforcement of IFRS at an international level, the final communiqué issued at the conclusion of the thirty-second annual conference of the International Organization of Securities Commissions (IOSCO) stated that, with respect to IFRS, the organization has been working toward convergence and consistent implementation of IFRS by creating an IOSCO database administered by the organization's secretary-general. The database, which was made fully operational in January 2007, is expected

---

[16] *Extracts from EECS's database of enforcement decisions.* The Committee of European Securities Regulators: 7–120, April, 2007.

[17] http://www.sec.gov/divisions/corpfin/ifrs_staffobservations.htm.

to facilitate sharing among securities regulators of decisions relating to the enforcement of IFRS, and also promote coordination and convergence.[18]

Most countries that either currently implement IFRS or intend to do so in the future are also implementing or considering implementing International Standards on Auditing (ISAs) issued by the International Auditing and Assurance Standards Board (IAASB).[19] At the end of October 2006, the World Federation of Exchanges (WFE) formally endorsed the process for establishing ISAs. WFE represents 57 securities and derivatives exchanges around the world which account for 97 per cent of world stock market capitalization.

In February 2007, the Transnational Auditors Committee of the Forum of Firms of the International Federation of Accountants published *Perspectives on the Global Application of IFRS: Good Practices in Promoting a Consistent Approach to International Financial Reporting Standards.*[20] The publication is intended to assist the networks of global accounting firms to avoid differences in how different companies and different teams of auditors in different countries interpret and apply IFRS. The good practices set out in the report are expected to enhance consistency. In the context of the international network of firms, good practices cover areas such as firm leadership for IFRS, organization of the technical function, developing a view on IFRS issues, training, accreditation of IFRS experts, review of IFRS financial statements, support tools for the practice and clients, and integration of IFRS in audit methodology and quality review.

III. Main practical implementation issues of IFRS

A. Overview of case studies

The country experiences presented in the case studies indicate that each country has initiated the introduction of IFRS into its financial reporting system at a different point in time. Pakistan started introducing IASs issued by the International Accounting Standards Committee (the processor of IASB) as early as the 1970s. South Africa initiated a similar process in 1993. In Turkey, the process began in 2003. Each country has a stock exchange. At present, the number of companies listed in the Karachi, Johannesburg and Istanbul stock exchanges are 660, 387 and 333, respectively.

The objectives the countries wished to achieve by implementing IFRS are similar in broad terms. Each country endeavoured to raise its financial reporting requirements to internationally recognized benchmarks. There is an additional factor in the case of Turkey. As a country that is negotiating membership with the European Union, implementing IFRS brings Turkey in line with financial reporting requirements in the European Union, thus facilitating economic integration on a regional basis.

The case studies of Pakistan and South Africa show the pioneering and leading roles of professional accountancy organizations in introducing IFRS into the economies of both countries.

---

[18] International Organization of Securities Commissions. Final Communiqué of the thirty-second annual conference, 12 April 2007.

[19] International Federation of Accountants. World Federation of Exchanges Endorses the IAASB's International Standard Setting Process. Press Release, 27 October 2006, New York.

[20] International Federation of Accountants, Forum of Firms, Transnational Auditors Committee. *Perspectives on the Global Application of IFRS: Good Practices in Promoting a Consistent Approach to International Financial Reporting Standards,* February 2007, New York.

On the other hand, the case study of Turkey indicates that the Capital Markets Board, and subsequently the Turkish Accounting Standards Board, led the IFRS implementation process.

Though a number of years have passed since IFRSs were introduced in the countries on which the case studies were conducted, none of them is currently in a position to assert that financial statements prepared by companies listed in its jurisdiction are in full compliance with IFRS as issued by IASB. In Pakistan, efforts are underway to accomplish this goal by 2009. In the case of South Africa, while IFRSs are adopted as issued by IASB, a national level due process is followed before an IFRS issued by IASB takes effect in the country. Although financial reporting standards applicable to companies whose shares are traded in Turkey are Turkish translations of IFRS, there are still certain differences between the two.

The case studies illustrate how different countries go about defining the scope of application of IFRS and catering to the needs of SMEs. In Pakistan, there is a three-tiered approach, similar to the one adopted by ISAR when it developed its guidance on accounting and financial reporting for SMEs. IFRSs adopted in Pakistan are applicable to listed companies only. The Institute of Chartered Accountants of Pakistan has developed separate guidance on accounting and financial reporting for SMEs.

In South Africa, IFRSs are applicable to listed companies whose shares are widely circulated. The country is considering recommending early adoption of the IFRS for SMEs as a transitional measure. As discussed above, IASB issued an exposure draft of the IFRS for SMEs earlier in 2007. In Turkey as well, IFRSs adopted in the country are applicable only to listed companies whose securities are widely held. The Turkish Accounting Standards Board has been working towards developing financial reporting guidance for SMEs which is expected to be in line with the exposure draft of the IFRS for SMEs issued by IASB.

B. Institutional issues

In each of the case studies, corporate financial reporting is governed and affected by a variety of laws enacted through legislative processes and various related rules and regulations. The foundations of financial reporting were formed in Pakistan by the Companies Ordinance of 1984, in South Africa by the 1973 Companies Act, and in Turkey by the Commercial Code of 1957. Obviously, these laws predate the time countries earnestly initiated IFRS. As a result, the regulatory requirements fail to provide clear legal backing for IFRS. For example, South Africa's 1973 Companies Act requires that financial statements of companies must comply with generally accepted accounting practice. In 1992, an amendment to the 1973 Companies Act introduced the concept of statements of generally accepted accounting principles approved by the Accounting Principles Board of the country as the basis for financial reporting.

However, currently each country is either in the early stages of implementing an amended corporate law or in the process of finalizing a draft law. In Pakistan, an example is the Finance Act of 2007, which amended Section 248 (2) of the Companies Ordinance of 1984. In South Africa, the Corporate Law Amendments Act of 2006, which was issued in April this year, is expected to be implemented in the near future. In Turkey, a new Commercial Code has been drafted and is awaiting enactment through the legislative process. Each of these legal reforms addresses aspects of IFRS in relation to the requirements of corporate financial reporting in the respective country.

As noted in previous case studies, the current case studies also demonstrate how fragmentation of regulatory authority over financial reporting by entities in a given jurisdiction impedes efficient introduction and effective implementation of IFRS. For example, in Pakistan, the Companies Ordinance of 1984 requires that surplus on revaluation of fixed assets be shown in the balance sheet after capital and reserves, whereas according to IAS 16 (property, plant and equipment), such surplus should be credited to equity under the heading of revaluation surplus.

In each of the countries covered in the case studies, prudential regulation of financial institutions and insurance companies is conducted through institutions and laws that are separate from those that govern the preparation of general-purpose financial statements. For example, in Turkey, the Bank Regulation and Supervision Agency regulates financial institutions. This agency issued accounting standards that financial institutions under its supervision should follow.

The case study of Pakistan provides an example where the regulatory agency for banks – the National Bank of Pakistan – prescribes formats for financial statements and other disclosures, which are not necessarily in conformity with IFRS. Similarly, in South Africa, prudential regulation of banks and insurance entities is conducted through laws that are distinct from the regulation of entities in other sectors. The practical implementation issue that arises in this context is the extent to which IFRS-based general-purpose financial statements could be used for prudential regulation. Such an arrangement would require clear understanding to be reached among the different regulators.

The introduction of IFRS in the countries included in the case studies has prompted the establishment new institutions or reinforcement of existing ones. For example, in South Africa, the case study shows that the country envisages the establishment of a Financial Reporting Investigation Panel, with a view to contributing to the reliability of financial reports by investigating alleged non-compliance with financial reporting standards and recommending measures for rectification or restitution. In the case of Pakistan, the Off-Site Supervision and Enforcement Department has been established to strengthen enforcement activities of the State Bank of Pakistan.

C.   Enforcement issues

The full benefits of a global set of financial reporting standards such as IFRS will be realized only when these standards are consistently enforced. Thus, IFRS consist of only one element of the financial reporting infrastructure. The institutions responsible for enforcing IFRS need to realize that, due to the growing globalization of financial markets, their enforcement efforts often protect both domestic and international investors.

The case studies illustrate various aspects of enforcing IFRS in the respective jurisdictions. In Pakistan, the Monitoring and Enforcement Department of the Securities and Exchange Commission of Pakistan (SECP) is responsible for enforcing compliance with IFRS through regular review of the quarterly and annual financial statements published and filed with the SECP by listed companies. In instances where it finds deficiencies or non-compliance with IFRS, it imposes fines and penalties on the preparers and their auditors.

In South Africa, the GAAP Monitoring Panel (GMP), which was created by a joint effort of the South African Institute of Chartered Accountants and the Johannesburg Stock Exchange in 2002, is responsible for ensuring compliance with financial reporting standards. Prior to this, there was no regulatory enforcement of financial reporting standards. In Turkey, the Capital Markets Board is responsible for monitoring and enforcing compliance with financial reporting standards by listed companies.

The case study of South Africa provides an example of how GMP dealt with cases of financial reporting that were referred to it. The decisions GMP took include withdrawal and re-issuing of financial statements, suspension of listing, and prospective application of amended accounting policies. Some cases were either pending or required no action.

Similar to the case studies discussed at the twenty-third session of ISAR, the case studies of Pakistan, South African and Turkey also show that each country is in the process of implementing ISAs issued by IAASB.

The case studies show the role of professional accountancy organizations in ensuring compliance with IFRS by their members. In Pakistan, the SECP refers to the Institute of Chartered Accountants of Pakistan (ICAP) chartered accountants the commission finds at fault. The case study indicated that the Investigations Committee of the ICAP received 20 disciplinary cases of its members and the committee dealt with 10 of them, including by suspending membership and referring to the courts. This shows that enforcement of IFRS is a collective effort that needs the cooperation of multiple institutions.

D. Technical issues

Practical implementation of IFRS requires adequate technical capacity among preparers, auditors, users and regulatory authorities. Countries that implement IFRS face a variety of capacity-related issues, depending on the approach they take. Pakistan and South Africa have been introducing IASs into their financial reporting systems for a number of years. In the case study of Turkey, within a period of about two years, the country decided to implement IFRS. Unlike in the case studies of Pakistan or South Africa, Turkish standards are translations of IFRS. One of the capacity requirements is therefore to translate IFRS into Turkish in a consistent and efficient manner. In general, while training on IFRS was needed in all countries covered by the case studies, the need appeared to be more pressing in the case of Turkey.

The practical application of fair value-based measurement requirements in IFRS presents technical challenges in all countries covered by the case studies. In Pakistan, due to capacity limitations in the banking sector, the implementation of IAS 39 (financial instruments: measurement and recognition) had to be done gradually. In South Africa, there are technical challenges in the application of fair value-based measurements to financial instruments for which there is no active market or where the market was illiquid, and in circumstances under which management's estimations are needed.

The case studies show that, due to the need for following due process at a national level or due to translation requirements, frequent amendments to IFRS create technical challenges. ICAP has adopted a policy that once an IFRS is adopted by the institute and endorsed by the SECP, any subsequent revisions or confirming amendments IASB makes on the standard are considered as adopted, unless otherwise specified.

The case studies of South Africa and Turkey illustrate certain technical challenges that are specific to a given economy. In South Africa, implementation of the Black Economic Empowerment initiative brought about a need for technical clarification of accounting for the discount on equity instruments granted to black South Africans or entities controlled by them. The issue of whether to capitalize as intangible asset or expense the amount of the discount granted was brought forward to the International Financial Reporting Interpretations Committee (IFRIC). The issue was resolved when IFRIC issued *IFRIC 8 – Scope of IFRS 2*. South African companies that encounter transactions of this nature now treat discounts (on equity instruments granted) as expenses.

In recent years, the Turkish economy has experienced significant inflation. When an economy undergoes hyper-inflationary situations, IAS 29 (financial reporting in hyper-inflationary economies) becomes applicable. However, in Turkey, the provisions of IAS 29 were not applied in full. Financial statements are prepared on historical cost basis, with the exception of revaluation of property, plant and equipment.

Another technical implementation challenge discussed in the case study of South Africa pertains to accounting for certain investments in shares of parent companies by subsidiaries in the insurance sector. In certain situations, subsidiaries of insurance companies invest in shares of their holding companies. Such arrangements create a situation where investments would be considered as liability in the financial statements of the parent company. At the same time, these would also be considered as treasury shares and would be deducted from equity.

Accounting for leases is another area where technical implementation difficulties are encountered. In the case study of Pakistan, ICAP decided to defer application of Interpretation 4 of IFRIC – determining whether an arrangement contains a lease – to 2009 due to concerns that application of IFRIC 4 would in effect convert Independent Power Producers (IPPs) in the country into leasing companies.

As the case study of South Africa shows, the computation of loan loss provisions for doubtful debts could create certain inconsistencies if appropriate clarification is not provided on how preparers should follow the requirements in IAS 39 as they transition form previous requirements such as schedules provided by a regulatory body, in this case the Central Bank.

The case study of South Africa illustrates yet another example of how national practice in the area of operating leases was amended to make it consistent with IFRS. Prior practice with respect to operating lease agreements with inflation escalations took into account the impact of inflation, and lease payments were computed and accounted for accordingly. After seeking the necessary clarification from IFRIC and realizing that what needed to be taken into account was not inflation but rather factors that impact on the physical usage of the asset leased, the South African Institute of Chartered Accountants issued a circular to bring national practice on par with IFRS.

IV. Lessons learned

The case studies illustrate different approaches that countries take to implementing IFRS. However, their objectives are more or less similar. The case studies once again confirm that member States see IFRS as an important means of integrating enterprises in their jurisdictions to the international economic system and also as a useful mechanism for fostering investor confidence and attracting foreign direct investment. In deciding when and how to implement IFRS, countries could benefit from the experiences of other countries with similar economic and financial reporting backgrounds that successfully embarked on the IFRS implementation process.

Consistent with findings of prior case studies, those of Pakistan, South Africa and Turkey show the need for creating a national coordination mechanism and engaging all stakeholders in the IFRS implementation process early. Preparers, users, regulators, professional accountancy bodies and educators need to be engaged in the planning as well as the implementation of IFRS. The impact of transitioning to IFRS on financial reporting should be communicated as early as possible to avoid any potential surprises.

As discussed earlier, the approaches the countries covered by the case studies have taken towards implementation of IFRS, including newly issued standards and interpretations or amendments, require either following due process at a national level or translation to a national language. These elements introduce discrepancies between the body of IFRS issued by IASB that are in effect at a certain time and IFRS required in the countries covered by the case studies. Users, particularly those outside the country, might find such discrepancies creating barriers to direct comparison of financial reports on a global basis. Thus, member States need to pay particular attention to the undesirable effects of any possible discrepancies that the approach they choose could introduce.

The case study of South Africa provides findings of surveys carried out in 2005 and 2006 by the accountancy firm Ernst & Young on the preparedness of entities to implement IFRS. The case study of Turkey also discusses findings of a similar survey. These surveys indicate that implementation of IFRS is a complex process that requires extensive preparations, including staff training and changes in information systems. Thus, an IFRS implementation plan needs to take into account the time and resources needed for efficient and effective implementation at the entity level.

The three case studies elaborate on the scope of application of IFRS in the respective country. An important aspect of the decision to implement IFRS in a jurisdiction is addressing the accounting and financial reporting needs of SMEs. This is particularly critical in situations where regulation that existed prior to implementation of IFRS does not specifically take into consideration the special needs of SMEs. As ISAR's work on the accounting and financial reporting needs of SMEs shows, IFRS could be burdensome for SMEs to implement. As discussed above, IASB has been working to address the needs of SMEs and it has issued an exposure draft of an IFRS for SMEs. Thus, this development needs to be taken into consideration when defining the scope of application of IFRS in a given economy.

The case study of South Africa illustrates how national accountancy firms could contribute to consistent application of IFRS, not only at the national level but also globally. The Technical Partners Forum of accountancy firms in the country identifies technical financial reporting issues that require clarification with a view to avoiding inconsistencies. Members of this forum benefit from their international networks. This approach facilitates technical dialogue among accountancy firms at the national as well as international level, and promotes consistent application of IFRS.

Transitioning from national financial reporting standards to IFRS has the potential to create a need for clarification or interpretation of the provisions of certain IFRSs. The case study of South Africa shows how such issues could be resolved by active engagement with IFRIC. While the majority of issues that require clarification or interpretation could pertain to situations that could be applicable to all jurisdictions, certain issues such as black economic empowerment are specific to a country. It is important to work closely with IFRIC rather than create a local interpretation which could lead to divergence of practice.

The case study of South Africa provides a good example of how the South African Accounting Practices Committee (APC) promotes participation of the stakeholders in the country in providing input into the IASB standard-setting process. An exposure draft issued by IASB is also issued in South Africa for comment by the APC simultaneously. The input received on the exposure draft issued in South Africa is considered by the South African Institute of Chartered Accountants when drafting its response on the exposure draft to IASB. Proactive engagement with IASB in the early stages of the standard setting process, particularly on practical implementation issues of IFRS, could contribute to reducing requests for clarifications or interpretations when issued.

The case studies once again demonstrate the critical role that professional accountancy organizations play in the implementation of IFRS. As discussed in the case studies of Pakistan and South Africa, one dimension of this role is facilitating communication between the national professional body and other stakeholders on the one hand, and IASB on the other. Another dimension of this role is how professional accountancy organizations contribute to promoting regulatory coherence on financial reporting by working closely with various national regulators and resolving practical implementation issues that arise in introducing IFRS.

Another important role professional accountancy organizations play is building technical capacity required for implementing IFRS in a sustainable manner. In the initial phase of implementation of IFRS, professional accountancy bodies contribute to technical capacity-building by providing training on IFRS to their members. As discussed in the case study of Pakistan, providing preparers with disclosure checklists on IFRS is an example of the positive roles that professional associations play. Furthermore, professional accountancy organizations also facilitate training geared towards keeping their members updated on new technical developments in the area of IFRS.

The case studies of Pakistan and South African provide good examples of how enforcement authorities such as securities and exchange commissions and financial reporting monitoring panels could contribute to more consistent application of IFRS by sharing their findings and enforcement decisions with a view to assisting preparers avoid wrong application of IFRS by learning from the experience of other preparers.

V.   Conclusion

In this chapter, the case studies of Pakistan, South Africa and Turkey are summarized. This chapter also discusses recent trends towards convergence with IFRS. The findings of the country case studies reiterate the findings of the country case studies that were discussed at the twenty-third session of ISAR. While these studies are of a limited scope and thus not comprehensive enough to draw conclusive views, they provide useful information on the different approaches that member States are taking to implementing IFRS.

The case studies provide useful insights into various practical challenges pertaining to institutional development, enforcement and technical issues that member States are facing in implementing IFRS. The country case studies also present various solutions that the respective countries are applying to resolve these challenges. The case studies show that implementation of IFRS is not a one-time process but rather an ongoing exercise that requires sustained efforts by all stakeholders.

During its deliberations at its twenty-fourth session, ISAR may wish to consider the following issues pertaining to the practical implementation of IFRS:

(a) What are some of the good practices for coping with new IFRS and major amendments on IFRS that will become effective by 2009? How useful has the extension of the period of "stable platform" been?

(b) IASB and the Financial Accounting Standards Board of the United States are in the process of developing a single converged conceptual framework. What are the implications of this project for countries that are implementing IFRS, particularly for those that are in the early stages of adopting IFRS?

(c) How could preparers of IFRS-based financial statement be encouraged to move away from "boilerplate" type descriptions of accounting policies and other disclosure, and provide more useful specific information that would provide users insights into the substance of transactions and figures on financial statements?

(d) How could the sharing of enforcement decisions pertaining to IFRS be enhanced so that such information is more widely available to a broader range of regulators? For instance, would it be useful to share such information during ISAR sessions?

(e) How could developing countries and countries with economies in transition join efforts and more actively participate in the IFRS standard-setting process?

(f) Would it be useful to assess practical implementation issues of International Standards on Auditing, which are increasingly complementing the implementation of IFRS?

(g) What are some good IFRS technical capacity-building practices that could be shared among member States?

Chapter II

Review of practical implementation issues of International Financial Reporting Standards: Case study of Pakistan*

I. Introduction

A.   Overview of economic indicators

With a population of about 160 million, Pakistan's economy delivered yet another year (2006/2007) of solid economic growth – 7 per cent, despite the continuing surge in oil prices that created adverse effects on its trade balance. Achieving gross domestic product (GDP) growth of around 7 per cent over the last five years indicates that Pakistan's upbeat momentum remains on track as it continues to maintain its position as one of the fastest growing economies in Asian region, along with China, India and Viet Nam.

Foreign direct investment in Pakistan is expected to reach $6 billion[1] in fiscal year 2007 compared to around $3 billion the previous year. International investors call for comparable financial information from countries competing for foreign investments. This requires that the corporate sector in Pakistan comply with internationally-acceptable standards on financial reporting. Pakistan, which currently has about 660 listed companies, has created a statutory framework to regulate business activities, including establishment of regulatory institutions for enforcing accounting and auditing standards. In order to ensure high-quality corporate financial reporting, appropriate enforcement mechanisms have been put in place.

B.   Requirements relating to IFRS implementation

With regard to compliance with IFRS, the SECP is empowered under Section 234 of the Companies Ordinance to prescribe the appropriate international accounting standards. SECP notifies the accounting standards based on the recommendation of ICAP.

IFRS considered appropriate to the local environment are adopted verbatim. Pakistan is amongst those few countries that started following the International Accounting Standards (IAS) regime early. The Council of ICAP has been adopting IAS since the 1970s and through its efforts 18 IAS were notified by SECP back in 1986.

---

[1]   Pakistan Economic and Strategic Outlook – Research conducted by Global Investment House.

C.   Accounting framework in Pakistan

The institute had issued the following revised statement to ensure compliance with the IAS/ IFRS, via its Circular 01/2003 dated Feb 24, 2003:

> "These financial statements have been prepared in accordance with approved accounting standards as applicable in Pakistan and the requirements of Companies Ordinance, 1984. Approved accounting standards comprise of such International Accounting Standards as notified under the provisions of the Companies Ordinance, 1984. Wherever the requirements of the Companies Ordinance, 1984 or directives issued by the Securities and Exchange Commission of Pakistan differ with the requirements of these standards, the requirements of Companies Ordinance, 1984 or the requirements of the said directives take precedence."

In some situations, Accounting Technical Releases are formulated where IFRS do not deal with a certain issue specific to the local environment or where additional guidance is required. These are mainly formulated in line with the principles underlined in IFRS. Departures from the requirements of IFRS are avoided to the maximum extent possible. Companies Ordinance, 1984 also prescribes presentation and disclosure requirements. Additionally, the State Bank of Pakistan, which regulates the commercial banks and development finance institutions, prescribes the recognition and measurement requirement in respect of loans, advances and investments.

D.   Due process for adoption of IFRS

ICAP, a statutory body established under the Chartered Accountants Ordinance, 1962 is the regulator of the accountancy profession in Pakistan. All public companies are required to have their financial statements audited by chartered accountants, who are members of ICAP. All members of ICAP are required to comply with the professional standards covering accounting, auditing and ethical pronouncements. ICAP has been adopting the IFRS issued by the International Accounting Standards Board (IASB), and International Standards on Auditing (ISAs) issued by the International Auditing and Assurance Boards for over 20 years. ICAP has also adopted the Code of Ethics issued by the Ethics Board under the aegis of the International Federation of Accountants (IFAC).

ICAP has established a due process of technical review and consultation by setting up various committees which review IFRS, disseminate the exposure drafts to the corporate sector and its members, and consult with the stakeholders and then recommend to the council adoption of a particular standard.

After completion of the due process, the Council of ICAP recommends to the SECP adoption of a particular standard. Thereafter, after undergoing its internal deliberations and review process, SECP notifies the adoption of such standards for listed companies.

It may be noted that, through the above process, Pakistan has been adopting the IFRS without making any amendments in such standards.

E.   Council's strategy for IFRS

While in the past, the Council of the ICAP and SECP have adopted most of the IASs so as to make Pakistan Generally Accepted Accounting Principles (GAAP) largely based on such international standards, the Council of ICAP has decided that ICAP will work together with SECP and the State Bank of Pakistan (SBP) to ensure that Pakistan GAAP becomes fully compliant with IFRS, as far as public interest entities are concerned, by the end of 2009. For this purpose, the Professional Standards and Technical Advisory Committee has formed a committee to carry out a detailed gap analysis, especially in terms of identifying inconsistencies between the prevailing law and the requirements of IFRS.

F.   Current status of adoption of IFRS

Pakistan has made significant progress in closing the gap between local requirements for corporate financial reporting and international standards by not only adopting IFRS but also by establishing mechanisms to ensure their enforcement. Over the past few years, this has contributed to significant improvement in corporate financial reporting.

At the time of the Reports on Observance of Standards and Codes review that was carried out by the Word Bank in 2005, all IASs had been adopted by ICAP and notified by SECP for listed companies except IAS 29 (financial reporting in hyperinflationary economies) and IAS 41 (agriculture), and IFRS 1 to 6. Subsequently, SECP, on the recommendation of ICAP, has notified IAS 41, IFRS 2, IFRS 3, IFRS 5 and IFRS 6.

In the case of the banking sector, on the recommendation of Pakistan Bank's Association and ICAP, SBP has suspended the application of IAS 39 and IAS 40. However, SBP has agreed in principle with ICAP that these standards, together with other IFRS, will also be adopted over the next two years, so as to ensure that banks and financial institutions' financial reporting becomes fully compliant with IFRS.

G.   Three-tiered structure and SME standards

The mandatory application of all IFRS for all companies tends to burden the small and medium-sized enterprise (SME). Given the substantial volume and complexities of IFRS, it is not possible for SMEs to ensure full compliance with all the requirements of IFRS. In reality, these SMEs do not have adequate technical capabilities and resources to ensure compliance with complicated reporting requirements.

While ICAP has been pursuing the objective of adoption and use of international standards for the preparation of general purpose financial statements over the years, it is also cognizant of the difficulties faced by SMEs in complying with the full set of IFRS that have been made applicable for listed companies.

In order to address the needs of the SMEs, the Council of ICAP initiated a project to develop a separate set of standards for such entities in line with similar work done in various other countries as well as the SME Guidelines on Accounting (SMEGA) issued by UNCTAD–ISAR in 2003. After several months of research on SME accounting standards by its committees, ICAP has developed two SME standards: Accounting and Financial Reporting Standard for

Medium-Sized Entities (MSEs) and Accounting and Financial Reporting Standard for Small-Sized Entities (SSEs). The Council has also laid down a three-tiered framework of accounting standards as described in paragraph 20 below.

While the Council of ICAP approved the aforementioned three-tiered structure as well as the two SME standards in its meeting on 28 July 2006, it is expected that SEPC will shortly notify these standards and three-tiered structure as part of the law, as such framework and the standards were developed in consultation with SECP, which has in principle agreed to incorporate these requirements as part of the statute applicable to all companies.

Pakistan's initiative for developing standards for SMEs was recognized by the South Asian Federation of Accountants (SAFA), comprising professional accounting bodies of India, Pakistan, Bangladesh, Sri Lanka and Nepal. SAFA has adopted these standards as SAFA standards/guidelines.

The institute has suggested the three-tiered structure as shown in table 1 for the applicability of these standards.

Table 1. Three-tiered structure for SME standards

Tier 1	Publicly Interest Entities (listed entities, entities that are considered large and entities that have public accountability)	The complete set of IFRS that is approved by the Council of ICAP and notified by SECP shall be applicable to these entities.
Tier 2	Medium-Sized Entities (entities that are neither Public Interest Entities nor SSEs)	The Accounting and Financial Reporting Framework and Standard for Medium-sized Entities issued by the Institute of Chartered Accountants of Pakistan are applicable to these entities.
Tier 3	Small-Sized Entities (small entities that have turnover and paid up capital below specified threshold)	The Accounting and Financial Reporting Framework and Standard for Small-Sized Entities issued by the Institute of Chartered Accountants of Pakistan are applicable to these entities.

H.   Impediments in implementing IFRS

While ICAP's Council is committed to complying with the full set of IFRS by 2009 so as to enable all public interest entities to give an unreserved compliance with all IFRS issued by IASB, there are various impediments and difficulties in achieving such compliance which are being addressed. These include the following:

Historically, there have remained some provisions in the Companies Ordinance, 1984 and other local laws that are inconsistent with the requirements of IFRS. ICAP has been working with the regulators to remove such inconsistencies, and has had reasonable success in recent years. Nevertheless, it takes significant time to reach agreement with regulators and also get the amendments incorporated through the legislative process.

Some of the IFRS – such as IAS 39, IAS 19, IFRS 3, etc. – are quite complex. Because of limited capacity available in Pakistan in terms of understanding, interpreting and training on the subject of such IFRS, the preparers require more time in implementing such standards.

Due to limited capacity available with the regulators, and frequent changes at key positions, it takes considerable time to persuade the regulators to adopt IFRS.

Although the State Bank of Pakistan has agreed to full implementation of IAS 39 and IAS 40, some of the preparers (some banks and financial institutions) are still not fully convinced of their adoption. Resistance from such stakeholders may further delay full implementation of IFRS.

There is a shortage of faculty for training and continuing education on IFRS.

I. Compliance gaps between IFRS and local statutes

At present, there are certain requirements of Companies Ordinance, 1984 and its Fourth Schedule (this contains disclosure requirements for listed companies) and SECP directives that are in conflict with the requirements of IFRS.

The developments in this regard include revision of the Fourth Schedule to the Companies Ordinance, 1984 issued by SECP on 5 July 2004, after which almost all the conflicting requirements and duplications have been eliminated.

Compliance gaps that still exist between IFRS and local statutes are summarized in table 2.

Table 2. Gaps between IFRS and local statutes

Companies Ordinance, 1984	IAS/IFRS
Surplus on revaluation of fixed assets shown in the balance sheet after capital and reserves.	Credited directly to equity under the heading of revaluation surplus (IAS 16.37).
Redeemable preference share classified as "Subscribed share capital". Redemption allowed only out of profits.	Classified as financial liability if it provides for mandatory redemption by the issuer for a fixed or determinable amount at a fixed or determinable future date, etc. (IAS 32.22).

SECP Directive	IAS/IFRS
To facilitate application of Revised Fourth Schedule, transitional relaxation has been granted by SECP to the listed companies for the following items:	

The listed companies carrying deferred cost as on 5 July 2004 are allowed to treat such cost as per superseded Fourth Schedule. However, after that date, any further deferral of costs will not be allowed.	The concept of deferred cost no longer exists in the IAS/IFRS.
The listed companies having outstanding liabilities for foreign currency loans as on 5 July 2004 are allowed to capitalize fluctuation of exchange gain/loss as per superseded Fourth Schedule up to 30 September 2007. Any exchange gain/loss on foreign currency loan contracted on or after 5 July 2004 will not be allowed to be capitalized.	The revised IAS 21 (the effects of changes in foreign exchange rates, effective 1 January 1 2005) has withdrawn the requirement of the old IAS 21, which allowed capitalization of exchange differences resulting from a severe devaluation or depreciation of currency.

In addition to the above, Prudential Regulations issued by the State Bank of Pakistan also include certain requirements that are in conflict with IAS 39. Some examples that constitute impediments to adoption of IAS 39 include:

Banks and development financial institutions are required to use age criteria (the number of days default/overdue mark-up/interest or principal) for the purpose of determining loan loss provisions) rather than estimating the expected cash flows in terms of IAS 39.

Unquoted securities are stated at cost.

Staff loans are recorded at the amount of cash disbursed and income on such loans is recorded at the subsidized rates.

Since many of the financial assets are required to be valued on a mark-to-market basis with changes in fair value being recognized in profit and loss, it results in recognition of unrealized gains and losses. Since recognition of unrealized gains could become taxable, banks and financial institutions are reluctant to adopt this standard. This is considered a major impediment to implementation of this standard.

ICAP, as part of its strategy, has been persuading both SECP and SBP to eliminate barriers in adoption of IAS/IFRS.

As discussed above, ICAP has developed and issued two separate sets of accounting and financial reporting standards for MSEs and SSEs. The standards await SECP notification for their applicability on SMEs.

In December 2006, SECP on the recommendation of ICAP, notified the following IAS / IFRS:

IAS 41 – Agriculture;

IFRS 2 – Share-based payments;

IFRS 3 – Business combinations;

IFRS 5 – Non-current assets held for sale and discontinued operations; and

IFRS 6 – Exploration for and evaluation of mineral resources.

To ensure effective implementation of SME standards, a revision of the Fifth Schedule to the Companies Ordinance, 1984 is in process (which prescribes presentation and disclosure requirements for non-listed public entities and private entities). Effort is being made to remove all such requirements from the schedule that are in conflict with the SME standards.

Regarding adoption of remaining IFRS/IAS (i.e. IFRS 1, 4, 7 and 8; and IAS 29 and IAS 41), the following strategies and action plans have been decided by ICAP:

IFRS 1 – It will be adopted once all other IAS/IFRS are adopted.

IFRS 4 – Previously, its adoption was deferred until finalization of phase II of IASB's Insurance Project, as it would necessitate some amendments to the Insurance Ordinance, 2000 and Regulations. However, it has recently been decided that, instead of waiting for the completion of Phase II of the project, ICAP will consider the standard for adoption. The Insurance Committee of ICAP is actively deliberating on the adoption of this standard.

IFRS 7 – ICAP has approved its adoption and SECP has been recommended by ICAP for its notification.

IFRS 8 – This standard is applicable for the accounting periods beginning on or after January 2009 and its adoption by ICAP is expected shortly as the standard supersedes IAS 14 (segment reporting) which was already adopted in the country.

IAS 29 – It was not previously adopted because it was not considered relevant in Pakistan's economic environment. However, the matter of adoption of IAS 29 is under active consideration by ICAP on the premise that there might be instances where a Pakistani company operates in or transacts with an entity of a hyperinflationary economy in which case the standard could become applicable.

IAS 39 – In the Finance Act 2007–2008, the taxation laws have been amended so that the adjustments that are made to the financial statements of the bank to comply with the requirements of IAS 39 (financial instruments: recognition and measurement) and IAS 40 (investment property) have been allowed to be excluded while calculating the taxable income of banks. These exclusions have been allowed to safeguard the bank from being taxed on unrealized gains as the above standards require measurement and recognition of financial instrument and investment property on the basis of their fair market value prevailing on the balance sheet date.

IAS 40 –The standard allows investment property to be measured either at cost or fair value. Therefore, if a bank/development financial institution chose the fair value model then it could distribute unrealized gains arising out of an upward revaluation of investment property, which is not considered appropriate by the regulator (SBP). This matter has been addressed through appropriate amendment introduced through Finance Act 2007 to the existing Section 248 (2) of the Companies Ordinance, 1984 by restricting all the corporate entities to pay dividends out of their realized profits only (as is the case with United Kingdom company law). It is expected that after this amendment, the deferment of IAS 40 by SBP will be eliminated.

At ICAP's request, SECP has also re-notified the IASs (only number and name) that were previously notified by reproducing the full text of the IAS. This step was taken to avoid lengthy process of adoption and notification each time an IAS is revised.

II.   Regulatory framework and enforcement

A.   Securities and Exchange Commission of Pakistan

The Securities and Exchange Commission of Pakistan (SECP) was set up in pursuance of the Securities and Exchange Commission of Pakistan Act, 1997 to succeed the Corporate Law Authority. This act institutionalized certain policy decisions relating to the constitution, structure, powers and functions of SECP, thereby giving it administrative authority and financial independence in carrying out its regulatory and statutory responsibilities.

SECP became operational in January 1999. It was initially concerned with the regulation of the corporate sector and capital market. Over time, its mandate has expanded to include supervision and regulation of insurance companies, non-banking finance companies and private pensions. SECP has also been entrusted with oversight of various external service providers to the corporate and financial sectors, including chartered accountants, credit rating agencies, corporate secretaries, brokers, surveyors, etc. The challenge for SECP has grown with the increase of its mandate.

B.   The Companies Ordinance, 1984

The Companies Ordinance, 1984 sets primary requirements for financial reporting of all companies incorporated in Pakistan. The Companies Ordinance requires the preparation, presentation and publication of financial statements, including disclosures and auditing of all companies incorporated in Pakistan. In addition to the various provisions pertaining to financial reporting, the Fourth Schedule of the Ordinance lays down the form, content and certain disclosure requirements for preparing financial statements for listed companies, while the Fifth Schedule outlines the same for non-listed companies. As discussed above, various provisions of the Companies Ordinance, including the Fourth Schedule, have already been revised in compliance with the requirements of IFRS.

It is mandatory for holding companies incorporated in Pakistan that have subsidiaries to prepare consolidated financial statements in accordance with requirements of the IFRS notified by SECP.

C.   The Insurance Ordinance of 2000

The Insurance Ordinance of 2000 regulates the financial reporting practices of insurance companies operating in Pakistan. The ordinance empowers SECP to monitor and enforce the applicable laws and standards, including the accounting and auditing for the insurance companies. The financial statements of all insurance companies are required to be audited by chartered accountants (members of ICAP). The auditor is appointed from the SECP-approved panel. The audited financial statements of insurance companies should be submitted to SECP within four months of the financial year end. As per the Insurance Ordinance, insurance companies are required to obtain actuarial certification that their reserves adequately meet all obligations to their respective policyholders.

D.   Non-Banking Financial Companies Department of SECP

The Non-Banking Financial Companies (NBFC) Department of SECP regulates the non-banking financial institutions in Pakistan, including their accounting and reporting. This department is responsible for regulating investment banks, leasing companies, discount houses, housing finance companies and venture capital companies.

The Enforcement and Monitoring and Department (EMD) of SECP is responsible for enforcing IFRS compliance, investigation, compliance with relevant laws and regulations by listed companies, and for prosecution (except in relation to specialized companies and insurance companies for which the SECP has specialized enforcement wings).

Listed companies are required to comply with SECP requirements with respect to financial reporting and disclosures. In pursuance of the authority granted under the Companies Ordinance (subsection (3), Section 234), SECP issues special regulatory orders prescribing mandatory IFRS application to listed companies.

EMD monitors the compliance with IFRS through regular review of the annual and quarterly financial statements published and filed with SECP by listed companies, NBFC and insurance companies. On identifying any disclosure deficiencies or other non-compliance of IFRS, EMD imposes fines and penalties on the preparers and their auditors. Over the last few years, EMD has penalized several companies, including nearly 25 firms of auditors. Further, EMD also refers the cases of defaulting auditors to ICAP for further disciplinary action through its investigation committee.

The NBFC Department of SECP is authorized to monitor and enforce the accounting and auditing requirements for the non-banking financial institutions as set by the Non-Banking Finance Company Rules 2003. The financial statements of the non-banking financial institutions must be audited by the ICAP members.

The Insurance Division of SECP is empowered to monitor and enforce the applicable laws and standards, including the accounting rules and regulations for the insurance companies.

E.   State Bank of Pakistan

The State Bank of Pakistan (SBP) is the central bank of Pakistan. While its constitution, as originally stated in the State Bank of Pakistan Order 1948, remained basically unchanged until 1 January 1974, when the banks were nationalized and the scope of its functions was considerably enlarged. The State Bank of Pakistan Act 1956, with subsequent amendments, forms the basis of its operations today.

Currently, over 50 financial institutions are supervised by SBP. These include banks, development finance institutions (DFIs), and microfinance banks/institutions. Banks operating in the country include public and private sector banks incorporated in Pakistan and branches of foreign banks.

F.   The Banking Companies Ordinance, 1962 and the role of SBP in the monitoring and enforcement of standards

The Banking Companies Ordinance empowers SBP to regulate and supervise commercial banks and financial institutions, including financial reporting by such institutions. The accounting and auditing requirements as outlined in the Banking Companies Ordinance are in addition to the requirements contained in the Companies Ordinance. SBP has prescribed formats for financial statements, including disclosure requirements that each bank must follow. Due to the exemption granted to financial institutions from the applicability of IAS 39 and IAS 40, these formats deviate from full compliance with IFRS. All banks and DFIs must publish audited annual financial statements and file those statements with SBP. The financial statements of all banks and DFIs are required to be audited by firms of chartered accountants, whose names are included in the panel/list of qualified auditors maintained by SBP. Exercising the authority conferred by Section 35(3) of the Banking Companies Ordinance, SBP issues guidelines for the auditors, primarily for the purpose of prudential regulations. Bank auditors are required to hold meetings with SBP inspectors before commencement of their on-site inspection. Also, inspectors are required to share their concerns with the respective auditors upon completion of the inspection. Furthermore, the auditors are required to send copies of the management letter and any other letters to bank management to the SBP within one week of issuance of such letters.

The Banking Inspection Department (BID) is one of the core departments at SBP. Its mission is to strive for soundness and stability of the financial system and to safeguard interest of stakeholders through proactive inspection, compatible with best international practices.

In order to assess a financial institution, BID conducts regular on-site inspection of all scheduled banks inclusive of the foreign banks and DFIs. The regular on-site inspection is conducted on the basis of the CAMELS (Capital, Asset Quality, Management, Earnings, Liquidity, Sensitivity and System and Controls) Framework. CAMELS is an effective rating system for evaluating the soundness of financial institutions on a uniform basis and for identifying those institutions requiring special attention or concern. The focus of inspection is generally on risk assessment policies and procedures of the banks and control environment to keep attached risks within acceptable limits and compliance with laws, regulations and supervisory directives. In continuation of the inspection process, discussions are held with external auditors to review banks' internal controls, compliance with legislation, prudential standards and adequacy of provisions. BID works in close coordination with the Off-Site Surveillance Desk at Banking Supervision Department and other departments in SBP.

The Off-Site Supervision and Enforcement Department (OSED) is one of the newly created departments emerging in the wake of the re-organization of the former Banking Supervision Department under recent SBP restructuring. OSED is responsible for off-site supervision of the financial institutions coming under regulatory purview of SBP. The department also ensures effective enforcement of regulatory and supervisory policies, monitors risk profiles, evaluates operating performance of individual banks/DFIs and takes necessary enforcement actions against institutions for their non-compliance (with laws of the land and regulations put in place by SBP) as identified by the inspection teams of BID during their on-site examinations, and/or by the supervisors of this department based on submitted returns, interaction with financial institutions and market information.

In recent years, SBP has inducted a number of chartered accountants and other professionals to strengthen its oversight on financial reporting by banks and other institutions.

SBP also works very closely with ICAP and seeks its input/advice on accounting and auditing matters.

G.   The Institute of Chartered of Accountants of Pakistan

ICAP is an autonomous statutory body established under the Chartered Accountants Ordinance, 1961 (CA Ordinance). It is governed by a council comprising 16 members that includes 12 elected members and four members nominated by the federal Government. The Government nominees include the Chairman of SECP, Chairman of the Federal Board of Revenue, Chairman of the National Tariff Commission and the Federal Secretary Privatization Commission. Under the CA Ordinance, the basic purpose of the institute is to regulate the profession of accountants. In order to discharge such responsibility, including reliable financial reporting by corporate entities, ICAP has been working together with government agencies and regulators such as SECP and SBP. For this purpose, there are joint committees of ICAP–SECP that usually meet on a quarterly basis.

ICAP is an active member of international and regional organizations, e.g. IFAC, Confederation of Asia Pacific Accountants and South Asian Federation of Accountants.

While ICAP has established robust regulatory mechanisms, the Government of Pakistan, on the recommendation of the Council of the Institute, has agreed to make necessary amendments in the CA Ordinance to further empower the council and to strengthen its disciplinary and regulatory processes

ICAP acts both as an examining body for awarding chartered accountancy qualifications and the licensing and disciplinary authority for members engaged in public practice. ICAP's aggregate membership in July 2006 was 3,864, of which about 15 per cent are engaged in public practice.

H.   ICAP's enforcement role as a regulator of the accountancy profession

Members of ICAP are required to follow the ICAP Code of Ethics for Chartered Accountants, which was revised in 2003 in line with the IFAC Code of Ethics for Professional Accountants, which was issued in November 2001. ICAP is currently deliberating adoption of the revised IFAC Code of Ethics issued in June 2005.

Members of ICAP are required to ensure compliance with IFRS: ICAP Council's directive TR 5 requires its members, who are auditors of the companies, to ensure that the financial statements they audit comply with the requirements of the IFRS (except IAS 29, and IFRS 1, 4, 7 and 8, which are being considered for adoption by ICAP).

ICAP's disciplinary process: The CA Ordinance has prescribed a procedure to deal with any breach of professional ethics and other instances of misconduct by the members. The Directorate of Corporate Affairs and Investigation works in conjunction with the Institutes Investigation Committee formed by the council to investigate such breaches. Under the CA

Ordinance, all complaints of misconduct against members of ICAP are required to be investigated by the Investigation Committee, which reports to the council for final decision.

During 2007, 20 cases were referred to the Investigation Committee and 10 cases were disposed off as follows:

Closed	3
Members reprimanded by name	2
Reprimanded by name + penalty Rs. 1000	1
Members reprimanded without name	2
Members cautioned	0
Membership suspended for six months	1
Reference made to High Court (for termination of membership above five years period)	1
Total	**10**

ICAP has the authority to penalize, reprimand or terminate the membership of the member who is found guilty of misconduct or negligent in performing his or her professional duties. The nature of the penalty depends on the nature and extent of misconduct by members.

I.   Quality Control Review

The Directorate of Professional Standards Compliance and Evaluation (DPSC&E) of ICAP carries out the Quality Control Reviews (QCR) of practicing firms that conduct audit of companies. The Quality Assurance Board (QAB) monitors the ICAP QCR programme, under which it examines audit working papers and identifies non-compliance with ISAs/IASs, etc. to the concerned auditors. If major departures or non-compliances are observed, then the case is forwarded to the Investigation Committee for further action against the member.

QCRs of the practicing firms are carried out with dual purposes. The primary objective is to determine whether a practicing firm has a satisfactory QCR rating (which is determined based on assessment of whether or not the audit work was done in accordance with the ISAs) to enable it to carry out audits of the listed companies. Secondly, it is ICAP's endeavour that the practicing firms that are not able to obtain satisfactory rating are helped and guided to develop an appropriate knowledge and skill base so that they can achieve the requisite standard.

J.   Quality Assurance Board

The Quality Assurance Board (QAB) of IPAC was formed in September 2005 to replace the Quality Control Committee, which used to monitor the quality assurance programme of ICAP up to that date. The board consists of various stakeholders, including representatives from SECP,

SBP, the Central Board of Revenue and the Karachi Stock Exchange. The chairman of the board is a non-practicing chartered accountant.

The QAB suggested revision in the QCR Framework, which was approved by the council on 12 September 2006. The salient features of the revised framework are as follows:

(a) QCR of a practicing firm will now be carried out after two and a half years instead of two years.

(b) A QCR must cover at least 25 per cent of audit partners of a practicing firm.

(c) The QCR report will be issued on a whole firm (instead of branch) basis.

(d) Additional files will be reviewed in case one file is assessed to be "not-in-accordance" with the ISA applicable in Pakistan.

(e) Files will be short-listed before the review has been done away with.

(f)

The QAB is currently in the process of incorporating International Standard on Quality Control 1 into the QCR programme of ICAP, taking into account the practical difficulties of small and medium practices.

III. Capacity-building: The role of ICAP in creating awareness of IFRS

A. Facilitating regulators

ICAP, at the request of regulators, holds separate seminars, workshops on IFRS and ISAs for their teams, i.e. Federal Board of Revenue (FBR), SECP, SBP, etc.

These programmes have in fact resulted in bridging the perception gap amongst ICAP and the regulators, and assisted in developing better understanding of standards by the regulators leading to smooth implementation and handling of IFRS-related issues.

B. Guidance

ICAP was closely monitoring changes in the IFRS and ISAs, and conducting seminars and workshops whenever a new IFRS or ISA issued by the standard setters for the guidance of its members. The Directorate of Technical Services (DTS) of ICAP caters to the needs of the members, especially in the practice. DTS issues guidance in the form of technical releases and circulars for the benefit of the members on local issues. ICAP is not authorized to issue interpretations, which can only be issued by the International Financial Reporting Interpretations Committee (IFRIC).

C.   Awareness programmes

Continuous awareness programmes have been organized by ICAP for improving the degree of compliance with IFRS requirements covering almost all the topics. In the First South Asian Accounting Summit, organized by ICAP, prominent scholars from widely recognized bodies such as IASB were invited to address different issues faced by the accounting profession globally and especially in the context of Pakistan.

D.   Members' information and education series

Considering the needs of its members, especially those in industry, ICAP has started a series of publications called "Members Information and Education Series". This initiative has been very much appreciated by the members.

E.   Disclosure checklist

ICAP also develops financial statement disclosure checklists to facilitate preparers and auditors in achieving compliance with disclosure requirements of IFRS as well as local regulatory requirements. The checklist seeks to provide guidance to the reporting companies and their auditors with regard to the disclosures to be made in the financial statements prepared in accordance with the approved accounting standards (IFRS notified by SECP) and the requirements of the Companies Ordinance, 1984.

F.   Training workshops for small and medium practices

In the year 2006, ICAP initiated a series of training workshops designed for the students of small and medium practices (SMPs). The response from SMPs was overwhelming and it was encouraging to note that they are keen to improve their procedures and practices, and have made efforts to bring them in line with the ISAs issued by the International Assurance and Auditing Standards Board (IAASB).

ICAP plans to continue such training programmes on a monthly basis all over Pakistan. It is hoped that these workshops will add value to the quality of audits and bring about a positive change in working of various practicing firms.

G.   Capacity-building measures

Capacity-building is imperative to consolidate the prior achievements, improve the knowledge base among auditors and the preparers of financial statements, and strengthen the monitoring and enforcement mechanisms for ensuring compliance with applicable standards and codes. This includes improving the capacity of regulators and professional bodies, upgrading accountancy education and training with focus on practical application of IFRS and ISA, issuing and disseminating implementation guidance on applicable standards, developing simplified SME reporting requirements, upgrading the licensing procedure of professional accountants and auditors, and enhancing the delivery of continuing professional education.

H.   Capacity-building at ICAP

ICAP is committed to IFAC's seven statements of membership obligations. In fact, the council has carried out a gap analysis with a view to achieving full compliance with such statements in the near future. While ICAP played an effective leadership role in the past for adoption and implementation of international accounting and auditing standards, it continues to make endeavours for further enhancing its capacity to fulfil its responsibility in the public interest of regulating the accounting profession in line with international best practices. ICAP has also proved itself to be an active member of IFAC, SAFA and CAPA, and participated actively in international events. The governance structure of ICAP is also considered to be in line with the best practices followed by other international bodies. Further, in recent years, ICAP has substantially increased the number of qualified people in its different departments. For instance, it has increased the number of CAs employed by ICAP to 25, compared to 17 in 2005.

I.   Upgrading the licensing procedure of professional accountants and auditors

ICAP is working towards upgrading the licensing procedure of professional accountants and auditors. This involves bringing changes in the by-laws to introduce more stringent licensing and renewal requirements and strengthening practical training aspects.

Audit of listed companies is only performed by the firm having a satisfactory QCR rating. Under the QCR framework, every firm of chartered accountants performing audit of listed companies is required to obtain a satisfactory QCR rating at least once every two and half years.

In order to strengthen practical training aspects, new training regulations have been introduced. These regulations cover the requirements as stipulated in the International Education Standard (IES) 5 – Practical Experience Requirement.

ICAP is currently developing guidelines for networking of audit firms. This will help SMPs in enhancing their resources, thus improving the quality of audits.

J.   Enhancing the delivery of continuing professional education

The Continuing Professional Development (CPD) Programme of ICAP is already in place, aimed at keeping the members abreast of the changes in the international accounting and auditing standards besides other relevant subjects. The CPD programme is in line with IES 7, and CPD committees and regional committees organize seminars and workshops on IFRS, ISAs and relevant local pronouncements on a regular basis. Members are required to gather a minimum number of 40 hours during the year by attending such seminars and workshops. The process is planned to be further strengthened and to make it available across the country.

To achieve this goal, ICAP organized the First South Asian Accounting Summit in 2006, bringing together senior representatives from the global standards setters, including the chairman of IASB Sir David Tweedie, office bearers of the major accounting bodies in the South Asian region and leading accounting professionals of the country.

K.   Developing simplified SME reporting tools

ICAP aspires to extend practical assistance to SMEs in implementing SME standards for which it is developing illustrative financial statements and disclosure checklists.

L.   Adoption of interpretations issued by IFRIC

All interpretations on IAS/IFRS that are issued by IFRIC (or its predecessor body SIC) are considered as adopted. ICAP does not formally adopt any of the interpretations issued by IFRIC for the reason that interpretations (issued by SIC or IFRIC) always relate to a particular standard (IAS/IFRS) and are presumed to be automatically adopted with the adoption of the relevant standard as are revisions to standards.

M.   Training regulations

Training regulations have been implemented with effect from April 2006. This will further strengthen various aspects of gaining practical experience. These regulations generally cover the requirements as stipulated in IES 5 – Practical Experience Requirement, issued by IFAC to ensure that future members acquire skills and values necessary for responding to the dynamics of the profession.

N. Board of Studies

In 2006, ICAP re-established the Board of Studies to be headed by a full-time chairman. The board shall perform functions including educational research and development, description of courses and development of their syllabi and course outlines, identifying books for recommended reading and development of study material.

An advisory committee with members from various professional fields and different stakeholders has been constituted to advise the Board of Studies on various matters.

O. Pakistan Accounting Research Foundation

In March 2006, the Council of ICAP approved in principle the formation of the trust Pakistan Accounting Research Foundation (PARF). The trust has been established for education, research and development of the accounting profession and allied services, and shall exist on a non-profit basis. The primary functions of PARF include:

(a) Forming a state-of-the-art university of accounting and finance;

(b) Providing assistance including financial and professional support to persons involved in research and development;

(c) Making endeavors to improve the standards of the accountancy profession;

(d) Arranging coordination between local and foreign students; and

(e) Arranging bilateral exchange of information, etc.

IV. Lessons learned

In Pakistan, the regulators of the corporate and financial sectors and ICAP that represent the accounting profession are of the firm view that financial reporting by public interest entities should be in conformity with the international financial reporting standards so as to generate high-quality financial information that is relevant, comparable, consistent and transparent so as to serve the needs of stakeholders. In this regard, ICAP's proactive leadership of the profession and collaborative approach of working together with the regulators has helped bring about significant improvement in the quality of financial reporting in line with international standards. Further, ICAP's strategy of adoption of IFRS over the last two decades, rather than adaptation, has also helped in acceptability, understanding and compliance with IFRS by the preparers as well as users of the financial statements. The process involved overcoming challenges such as limitations of technical resources, capacity issues, coordination and effective advocacy with the regulators, to ensure smooth implementation of IFRS in the country. The major lessons learned during the process are discussed below.

A.   Verbatim adoption of IFRS

From the very beginning, ICAP followed the approach of verbatim adoption of IAS/IFRS instead of making any changes to the text of standards to bring them in line with the local regulatory and business environment. The approach has been to bring the regulatory requirements in line with IFRS rather than the contrary. While this approach involved considerable difficulties at the initial adoption and implementation stage for which ICAP faced criticism, sometimes from its own members, in the long run this approach has served the interest of the profession and the country, as most people now agree that Pakistan has been able to develop high-quality financial reporting due to this approach. Also, Pakistan can achieve full IFRS compliance over the next two to three years, without too much difficulty.

B.   Staying at par with revisions/conforming amendments to IFRS

Revisions and conforming amendments to IAS/IFRS by IASB are a regular feature now, and keeping track of whether the individual revision/amendment has been adopted and notified has become all the more challenging.

ICAP as a matter of strategy decided that once a standard is adopted by ICAP and notified by SECP, any subsequent revision/conforming amendment made by IASB is considered as adopted unless otherwise specified.

This strategy has helped us stay at par with the latest developments in the standards which otherwise, with the limited availability of technical resources, would have become extremely difficult had we opted for adoption of each and every revision/amendment.

C.   Implementation of certain requirements of IFRS – a gradual process

Adopting IFRS is not just an accounting exercise. It is a transition that requires participation and support of all stakeholders, including preparers, auditors and users. While adopting and implementing IFRS, one should consider the fact that, in certain cases, it may cause undue hardship to the industry, at least to begin with. For instance, Pakistan's banking industry was not prepared to apply the provisions of IAS 39 immediately due to capacity and other related issues discussed earlier. Transitory measures had to be adopted, including providing them adequate time, for gradual implementation.

D.   Following an approach of working together with the regulators

Since its inception, ICAP has played a key role in adoption, creating awareness and education, and implementation of IFRS. A major factor in achieving this success was the collaborative approach adopted by ICAP of working together with the main corporate and financial regulators in public interest.

E.   Addressing differences in IFRS and law

As a recommending authority of financial reporting standards, ICAP has learned that where the accounting treatments prescribed in various IFRS are in conflict with the corresponding legal requirements, its role has become all the more important, acting in the best interest of the country and stakeholders at large, as well as balancing its responsibilities as a signatory to the membership obligations of IFAC. The approach adopted to deal with such issues varied with the nature and magnitude of the issue.

1.   Changes in law as per the accounting requirements

Since most of the commercial and corporate laws of the country have evolved from statutes drafted several decades ago, in most cases such laws are not consistent with the financial reporting needs of the corporate sector. Consequently, ICAP has in most cases worked to persuade the government officials and regulators of the need for making necessary amendments to bring them in conformity with international standards.

2.   Making a particular accounting requirement inapplicable to a sector of the economy

While in most cases laws and regulations are modified to make them consistent with IFRS, in certain cases immediate application of IFRS would be counterproductive, so ICAP has adopted a more pragmatic approach of either allowing more time or providing exemption to certain sectors. For instance, in the case of IAS 39, ICAP supported the banking sector's demand of providing them more time and deferral of the standard for a considerable period. Similarly, keeping in view the genuine difficulties faced by the Independent Power Producers on account of IFRIC-4, which would have converted all of these entities into leasing companies, ICAP supported the deferral of IFRIC-4 up to 2009.

F.   IFRS are not made to fit all entity sizes

ICAP realized that mandatory application of all IFRS to all companies is not practical and separate standards must be developed for SMEs before embarking on full IFRS compliance regime in the country.

Given the substantial increase and complexities of IFRS, it is not possible for SMEs to ensure full compliance with all their requirements. In reality, these SMEs lack adequate technical capabilities and resources to ensure compliance with complicated reporting requirements. Consequently, ICAP took the initiative of developing two separate financial reporting standards for MSEs and SSEs, which are expected to be notified by SECP soon.

G.   Involvement of stakeholders in the adoption and implementation process

In order to create awareness and ensure stakeholder participation, ICAP has been holding seminars, roundtables and workshops to get sufficient support from the stakeholders in the process of adoption and implementation of IFRS. This approach is considered essential for effective implementation.

H.   Role of QAB in improving standards of auditing and financial reporting

The QCR programme, in addition to ensuring compliance with the standards, is also educative in nature. Over the years, effective and regular quality assurance reviews conducted by ICAP's professional standards compliance department under the supervision of the Quality Assurance Board (previously Quality Control Committee) have helped in bringing about sustained improvements in the audit quality as well as compliance of IFRS.

I.   Investment in training and education in IFRS

An extensive and effective training and education programme is considered imperative for proper understanding and implementation of IFRS. More specifically, some of the complex accounting standards – such IAS 39, IAS 36, etc. – require significant effort in training and education for proper understanding and implementation. While ICAP has been pursuing a continuing education programme for its members and other stakeholders, there is a need for further investment in this area.

With the issuance of newer accounting standards or revision of existing ones on the basis of IFRS, various new concepts are being introduced (e.g. fair value concept) for which the preparers, auditors, analysts and other users need to be adequately trained and educated.

V.   Conclusions

With all three factors – i.e. implementation, regulatory framework and quality assurance – moving in the right direction, Pakistan is on track and not too far away in achieving full IFRS compliance in the next two to three years, in line with the IFRS strategy approved by the Council of ICAP.

The target date for achieving full IFRS compliance is December 2009, i.e. the financial statements prepared in Pakistan for the periods beginning on or after 1 January 2010 should be IFRS compliant so that all publicly accountable entities are able to give an unreserved compliance with IFRS.

The ICAP QCR programme is committed to a process of continuous and sustained improvement. The ultimate objective of this very important regulatory and educative programme is to maintain and enhance the reputation and image of this prestigious profession.

Chapter III

Review of practical implementation issues of International Financial Reporting Standards: Case study of South Africa*

I.   Introduction

South Africa is regarded as the economic powerhouse of Africa, with a gross domestic product (GDP) of four times that of its southern African neighbours and comprising around 25 per cent of the entire continent's GDP.[1] This positive picture of the South African economy is confirmed in the Chairman and CEO Statement of the Johannesburg Stock Exchange (JSE):

"The South African economy continues its strong performance, and translates into increased interest in the market from local and international investors, and trading volumes reach record levels…The building blocks for this success have been put in place by Government, and we must applaud its efforts in creating an environment in which the economy can thrive. A continued commitment to prudent macroeconomic policies builds confidence in South Africa as an investment destination, and boosts the image of the country as a whole. The JSE plays its role in providing an efficient, well-regulated exchange that makes the investment process as simple, low cost and transparent as possible, but the underlying investment decision is dependent upon perceptions of the future performance of South Africa as a whole."[2]

The Minister of Finance, Trevor A Manual, in summarizing the Government's efforts in the budget speech of 2007, said:

"As our young nation enters its 13th year, we have much to be proud of. We are building a society founded on principles of equality, non-racialism and non-sexism. We have built institutions of democracy, creating an open society founded on a rule of law. After stabilizing the economy and the public finance, we have created the conditions for rapid economic growth, job creation and the broadening of opportunities."[3]

The South African Institute of Chartered Accountants (SAICA), the JSE and the Accounting Practices Board (APB) of South Africa have recognized the need to be part of a global economy with respect to financial reporting.[4] Local accounting standards in South Africa have been harmonized with international accounting standards since 1993.[5] In February 2004, a decision was taken by APB to issue the text of International Financial Reporting Standards (IFRS) as South African Statements of Generally Accepted Accounting Practice (GAAP) without any amendments.[6] The reasons for the ongoing harmonizing and the issuing of the text of IFRS as South African Statements of GAAP were:

(a)   "For South African companies to attract foreign investment;

---

1   Available from http://www.southafrica.info/doing_ business/ economy/ econoverview.htm (accessed 25 June 2007).

2   JSE: Chairman and CEO Statement. Available from http://www.jse.co.za/chairmanceo.jsp (accessed 25 June 2007).

3   South African Government (2007). Budget Speech 2007 by Minister of Finance, Trevor A Manual, MP. 21 February 2007. Available from http://www.info.gov.za/speeches/2007/07022115261001.htm.

4   The Accounting Practices Board was established in 1973, the year in which the current Companies Act was enacted.

5   SAICA (2004). Preface to Statements of Generally Accepted Accounting Practice. August 2004; SAICA (2006). Circular 03/06 – Evaluation of Compliance with Statements of Generally Accepted Accounting Practice. March 2006.

6   Ibid.

(b) To provide credibility to the financial statements of South African companies in the global market; and

(c) To do away with the need for dual listed entities to prepare financial statements in accordance with more than one set of accounting standards."[7]

The main purpose of this case study is to set out South Africa's experience in the implementation of IFRS.[8] The case study starts in section II by providing a brief overview of the current financial reporting system in South Africa, including the development of the system and proposed reforms. The transition to IFRS in South Africa is integrated into this discussion. Thereafter, the South African experience in converting South African standards into IFRS is discussed, with a focus on issues of a more general nature (section III), and specific technical and application issues are presented in section IV.

II.   The South African financial reporting system

The legal framework for corporate reporting in South Africa is governed by the 1973 Companies Act, No. 61. However, the standard-setting process (discussed below) is developed in South Africa outside the scope of the Companies Act.

A.   Companies Act

The 1973 Companies Act requires that the financial statements of companies be in conformity with generally accepted accounting practice.[9] The concept of Statements of GAAP was introduced into the Companies Act with the introduction of paragraph 5 into Schedule 4in 1992.[10] It stated that if the directors of a company believe that there are reasons for departing from any of the accounting concepts in the Statements of GAAP approved by APB in preparing the company's financial statements in respect of any accounting period, they may do so, but particulars of the departure, the effects and the reasons for it shall be given.

Legal opinion was obtained by SAICA in September 1999 to interpret the effect of these provisions of the Companies Act.[11] The opinion merely confirmed that, to meet the requirements of the Companies Act, the financial statements should be prepared and presented in accordance with generally accepted accounting practice. However, the required disclosure needed to be provided if the financial statements materially departed from Statements of GAAP. Only additional disclosure was required. No true and fair view override, similar to IAS 1 (presentation of financial statements), was created by the Companies Act.

---

7 Ludolph S (2006). Why IFRS? Accounting SA, April: 19. Sue Ludolph is the SAICA Project Director – Accounting.

8 Except for different documents referred to in this report, the South African experience is obtained from discussions with representatives of companies such as Telkom, Sasol, the JSE and Standard Bank, and the auditors, Deloitte.

9 South Africa (1973). Companies Act No 61 of 1973, section 283(6). Pretoria: Government Printer.

10 SAICA (2005). Circular 8/99 – Compliance with Section 286(3) and Paragraph 5 of Schedule 4 to the Companies Act, 61 of 1973 and Statements of Generally Accepted Accounting Practice. June 1999.

11 *Ibid.*

The result is that the current Companies Act does not require companies to comply with South African Statements of GAAP. Thus, no statutory enforcement procedures for Statements of GAAP have been created by the Companies Act.

B. The standard-setting process in South Africa

Standard-setting in South Africa follows a two-level process. While APB approves and issues accounting standards, the Accounting Practices Committee (APC) serves as an advisory body to APB.

The objective of APC in this regard is firstly to propose to APB the issuing in South Africa of the international Statements of GAAP (AC 100 series) and Interpretations of Statements of GAAP (AC 400 series).[12] A second objective of APC is to develop South African pronouncements of Statements of GAAP and Interpretation (AC 500 series) in instances where issues are relevant to the South African context only. The AC 500 series developed by APC also undergoes a process of exposure and review of comments before being recommended to APB.

An exposure draft of a proposed IFRS, issued by the International Accounting Standards Board (IASB), is issued for comment by APC at the same time and for a period similar to IASB in South Africa.[13] Comments received on the South African version of the exposure draft are considered by APC in its process of drafting the comment letter submitted by SAICA to IASB. Once IASB issues an IFRS, APC reviews the IFRS to ensure that it is not in conflict with any South African legislation before recommending to APB that it is issued as a South African Statement of GAAP.

Since 1993, as stated above (see paragraph 3), South Africa has been harmonizing its Statements of GAAP with international standards, although the South African versions of the international standards have been issued as South African Statements of GAAP (AC 100 series) and Interpretation of Statements of GAAP (AC 400 series) after a due process. As a result, South African Statements of GAAP have been, in most respects, similar to IFRS. Minor differences have arisen as a result of different effective dates, and in some instances options permitted in IFRS have been removed from South African Statements of GAAP and additional disclosure requirements have been included.[14]

In February 2004, APB decided to issue the text of IFRS as South African Statements of GAAP without any amendments (see paragraph 3 above). From then on, each South African Statement of GAAP would be identical to each IFRS. However, transitional differences, such as implementation dates, could still exist, since a South African due process is still followed. To indicate the similarity between each IFRS and its corresponding South African Statement of GAAP, a dual numbering system is used to refer to both the IFRS number and the relevant Statement of GAAP number in the South African Statements of GAAP.[15]

If an entity applies South African Statements of GAAP, it cannot claim compliance with IFRS because of the transitional differences that still exist.

In respect to the public sector, Statements of Generally Recognized Accounting Practice (GRAP) are issued by APB in South Africa.[16] A key priority of APB is to develop a core set of standards of GRAP by 2009. These Statements of GRAP are drawn preliminary from the

---

12 SAICA (2004). Preface to Statement of Generally Accepted Accounting Practice. August 2004.

13 *Ibid.*

14 SAICA (2006). Circular 03/06 – Evaluation of Compliance with Statements of Generally Accepted Accounting Practice. March 2006.

15 *Ibid.*

16 Statements of GRAP are available at www.asb.co.za.

International Public Sector Accounting Standards (IPSAS) issued by the International Federation of Accountants' International Public Sector Accounting Standards Board (IPSASB).

C.   JSE Limited

The Johannesburg Stock Exchange (JSE) was originally established as the Johannesburg Stock Exchange in 1887. The name changed to JSE Securities Exchange South Africa on 8 November 2000, when it became a national exchange and expanded to other financial products. In 2005, JSE revised its corporate identity and changed its name to JSE Limited.[17]

JSE is among the 20 largest stock exchanges in the world and provides capital to large listed entities, with its Alternative Exchange offering access for small businesses, and its Social Responsibility Index supporting businesses that invest in socially, economically, and environmentally sustainable development. At the week ended 22 June 2007, the JSE Market Capitalization was 5, 814 billion Rand, an increase of 40.9 per cent from the corresponding week in 2006.[18]

Currently, just over 50 companies with dual listings are registered on JSE, of which more than half are primarily listed in South Africa.[19] This demonstrates that most of these companies originated in South Africa. However, some companies with dual listings, such as SABMiller and BHP Billiton, have been created through international mergers and takeovers. Only five of these companies are listed on the New York Stock Exchange and will benefit if the United States GAAP reconciliation is abolished.

As of October 2000 JSE required listed companies to prepare their annual financial statements in accordance with the national law applicable to listed companies (the Companies Act) and to apply either South African Statements of GAAP or International Accounting Standards.[20] The reason for allowing the choice was to assist companies with dual listings on overseas stock exchanges and overseas companies listed on JSE.

Further revised listing requirements called for listed companies to comply with IFRS for financial periods commencing on or after 1 January 2005.[21] In the light of the above, APC took a decision to issue the text of IFRS in South Africa without any amendments in February 2004.[22]

D.   Developed practice

Although the Companies Act does not explicitly require companies to apply South African Standards of GAAP, such a practice has developed in South Africa. This practice is also

---

17 JSE (2007). Our history. Available from http://www.jse.co.za/our_history.jsp (accessed 23 April 2007).

18 JSE (2007). Weekly Statistics: Week ended 22 June 2007.

19 JSE (2007). Dual Listed Company Information. Available from: http://www.jse.co.za/dual_listrd.jsp (accessed 25 June 2006).

20 Section 8.62(b) of the then JSE Listing Requirements.

21 Section 8.3 of the JSE limited Listing Requirements.

22 SAICA (2006). Circular 03/06 – Evaluation of Compliance with Statements of Generally Accepted Accounting Practice, March 2006.

confirmed by the audit practice in South Africa, which does not recognize generally accepted accounting practice as a financial reporting framework for audit assurance purposes.[23]

To confirm this practice, and taking into account the JSE requirements discussed above, SAICA issued a circular in 2006 stating that:[24]

(a)   Companies listed on JSE must prepare financial statements in terms of IFRS, and unlisted companies are permitted to do so.

(b)   Unlisted companies that choose not to follow IFRS must prepare financial statements in terms of South African Statements of GAAP. Where there is a departure from such statements, the departure, its particulars, the reason for the departure and its effect on the financial statements must be disclosed.

(c)   If unlisted companies choose to adopt IFRS by way of an explicit and unreserved statement of compliance with IFRS, IFRS 1 must be applied in the preparation of their first set of IFRS financial statements. Unlisted companies that comply with Statements of GAAP are not permitted to use the IFRS 1 (AC 138) [25] option.

This circular issued by SAICA does not create any regulating authority on unlisted companies. It is foreseen that corporate law reform will legislate this practice in South Africa. Further, no relief is currently available for small and medium-sized enterprises (SMEs) in South Africa.

E.   Corporate Law Amendment Act

The Corporate Law Amendment Act, 2006, was issued on 17 April 2007 as the first official document in the process of the reform of the Companies Act, but at the time of writing (July 2007) does not have an effective date. It has been seen as the first phase of the reform process. The second phase entails a complete review of the Companies Act.[26]

The Corporate Law Amendment Act provides for differential accounting in South Africa by identifying two types of companies: a widely held company and a limited interest company. The Amendment Act specifically declares that financial reporting standards for widely held companies shall be in accordance with IFRS.[27] A company will be classified as widely held if its articles provide for unrestricted transfer of its shares, if it is permitted by its articles (or by special resolution) to offer shares to the public, or if it is a subsidiary of a widely held company.

Once the Corporate Law Amendment Act is effective, relief will be granted to limited interest companies in that they will not have to comply with the stringent requirements of IFRS or South African Statements of GAAP. However, the financial reporting standards for limited interest companies still need to be developed. As an interim measure, limited interest companies are required to prepare their financial statements in terms of accounting policies adopted, which must comply with the framework for the preparation and presentation of financial statements (AC

---

23 Public Accountants and Auditors Board (PAAB) (2005). South African Auditing Practice Statement (SAAPS 2) – Financial reporting frameworks and audit opinions, July 2005.

24 SAICA (2006). Circular 03/06 – Evaluation of Compliance with Statements of Generally Accepted Accounting Practice, March 2006.

25 SAICA (2006). IFRS 1 (AC 138) – First-time Adoption of International Financial Reporting Standards, the South African equivalent to IFRS 1.

26 SAICA (2007). Summary of the main features of the Corporate Laws Amendment Bill. Johannesburg: SAICA.

27 Section 440S(2) of the Corporate Law Amendment Act, 2006.

000 in the South African context, which is identical to IASB's conceptual framework).[28] In anticipation of this relief for limited interest companies, APC will recommend to APB an early adoption of IASB's ED 222 (IFRS for SMEs) as a transitional measure.[29]

A further initiative of the Corporate Law Amendment Act is the establishment of a statutory Financial Reporting Standards Council (FRSC), which will take over the function of APB as the non-statutory standard setter in South Africa. Until the FRSC is established, APB will continue its function as the South African standard-setting body. The objective of the FRSC will be to establish financial reporting standards that promote sound and consistent accounting practices.[30] The functions of the FRSC will be to:

(a)   Establish financial reporting standards for widely held companies in accordance with IFRS; and

(b)   Develop separate reporting standards for SMEs in South Africa.[31]

F.   Enforcement

Currently, the Companies Act does not create any procedures for the enforcement of financial reporting in South Africa.

As an interim phase, in 2002 JSE, in partnership with SAICA, established the GAAP Monitoring Panel (GMP) (see paragraphs 6 and 10 above) in response to the need to create an oversight body that would enhance compliance with accounting standards.[32] The results of investigations by GMP are reported to JSE, which takes action against any company guilty of non-compliance. (This is discussed further in chapter III below.)

The Corporate Law Amendment Act also creates initiatives for the monitoring and enforcement of financial reporting standards. For monitoring purposes the act proposes that a suitably qualified officer may be appointed to monitor the financial reports and accounting practices of certain widely held companies in order to detect non-compliance with financial reporting standards that may prejudice users.[33]

To enhance enforcement, the Corporate Law Amendment Act proposes that a Financial Reporting Investigation Panel (FRIP) be created to replace GMP. The objective of FRIP will be to contribute to the reliability of financial reports by investigating alleged non-compliance with financial reporting standards and recommending measures for rectification or restitution.[34] Any person, whether or not a shareholder, who has reason to believe that the financial report of a widely held company has failed to comply with a financial reporting standard may refer the matter to FRIP for investigation. FRIP will have much wider powers than GMP. Once FRIP is established and fully operational, it is the intention of SAICA and JSE to dissolve GMP.[35]

---

28 Section 56(3) of the Fourth Schedule of the Corporate Law Amendment Act, 2006.

29 SAICA issued ED 225 – Financial Reporting for Small And Medium-Sized Entities (SMEs) – Proposed Process in May 2007 to invite the South African accounting practice to comment on the process leading to the early adoption of the IFRS for SMEs in South Africa.

30 Section 440P(1) of the Corporate Law Amendment Act, 2006.

31 Section 440S(1) of the Corporate Law Amendment Act, 2006.

32 SAICA (2006). GAAP Monitoring Panel has taken a closer look at 30 listed companies. Press release, 29 November 2006.

33 Section 440V of the Corporate Law Amendment Act, 2006.

34 Section 440W of the Corporate Law Amendment Act, 2006.

35 SAICA (2007). Summary of the main features of the Corporate Law Amendment Bill. Johannesburg: SAICA.

III. Implementation issues of a general nature

The major implementation issues of a general nature encountered in South Africa with the transition to IFRS are discussed in this chapter. Although both SAICA and JSE were instrumental in publicizing the decision to implement IFRS in South Africa (SAICA and JSE communicated the nature of the IFRS implementation decision through press releases and circulars), they were not involved in developing the strategy to implement IFRS. Each company had to adopt its own strategy as is explained below.

A.　Transition to IFRS

As stated earlier, JSE required that all listed companies comply with IFRS for financial periods commencing on or after 1 January 2005. Two groups of listed companies existed in South Africa in 2005: those that had already adopted IFRS before 2005 by voluntarily electing to convert, and those that had converted in 2005. Some of the companies in the first group had adopted IFRS before 2005 as they were dual listed on other security exchanges and IFRS was more internationally recognized.

Many companies in South Africa, especially in the banking industry, saw the implementation of IFRS as a two-step process. Firstly, under South African Statements of GAAP, the principles of IAS 39 (financial instruments: recognition and measurement) were adopted in 2001/2002.[36] Secondly, the full adoption of IFRS occurred in 2005. IFRS 3 (business combinations) and the consequent amendments to IAS 36 (impairment to assets) and IAS 38 (intangible assets) were applicable under SA Statements of GAAP from 2004.[37] This could create the impression that transition to IFRS in South Africa during 2005 was not a burdensome process. However, two surveys conducted by Ernst and Young in South Africa demonstrated that South Africa's transition to IFRS in 2005 was still a significant and costly exercise for most companies.

Ernst and Young carried out a survey of 46 JSE-listed companies in the first quarter of 2005 to investigate the IFRS implementation status of companies in South Africa.[38] The survey indicated that 96 per cent of the companies surveyed were not on track for reporting IFRS 2005 interim results and that only 33 per cent were on track with the overall progress of the IFRS 2005 implementation. This clearly indicates that many South African companies underestimated the transition to IFRS.

In 2006, Ernst and Young conducted a follow-up survey to assess the implications and impact of the IFRS transition both for first-time adopters (IFRS Conversion) and previous adopters (the effect of the improvements project).[39] The survey highlighted the challenges South African companies faced with the adoption of IFRS, which included greater complexity than

---

36　AC 133, the South African equivalent of IAS 39, was applicable for financial years starting from 1 January 2001.

37　IFRS 3 (AC 140) – Business Combinations was applicable to all business combinations with an agreement date on or after 31 March 2004.

38　Ernst and Young (2005). IFRS readiness amongst South African companies – a survey. April 2005.

39　Ernst and Young (2006). Transition to IFRS – the final analysis results. No date.

anticipated, high costs in some cases, poor understanding of the reasoning behind the transition, and potential confusion about company performance information.[40]

The survey indicated that almost two thirds of the respondents surveyed made use of a steering committee for their IFRS projects and held regular meetings to assess progress and discuss issues. Nearly all of the companies implemented IFRS in-house, but over 80 per cent indicated that they were assisted by their external auditors and/or other external consultants (including other auditing firms). What mostly occurred was that the external consultants presented their findings, and the companies' auditors were involved in verifying the choices made and policies implemented by the companies. Consistency and control procedures were created through such a review process.

The transition to IFRS also placed a burden on company staff. Training of staff was deemed necessary and, in response to the survey, approximately a third of the companies indicated that they had had to employ staff on a permanent basis to take responsibility for compliance with accounting standards and disclosure requirements. Some respondents had employed staff from the inception of the IFRS project, while others were still looking for additional staff to assist with the accounting function. In practice, because South Africa was one of the first countries to harmonize its accounting standards with IFRS, its experience is sought after by other countries. Experienced accountants with relevant skills in IFRS are leaving South Africa to work in other countries. This has occurred particularly in relation to the implementation of the financial instrument standards (IAS 32 and 39).

At present, 5,942 of the 26,222 SAICA members (26.6 percent) who hold the South African chartered accountant designation are based outside South Africa.[41] To date, SAICA has focused its attention on the education and training of chartered accountants. SAICA has also identified the need to better assess the supply of and demand for accounting and financial expertise at all levels in South Africa. To understand the nature and extent of the current shortage in financial management, accounting and auditing skills, and nature and extent of the retention of trainee accountants, SAICA launched two research projects during June 2007.[42] These projects are a first step toward resolving the skills shortage in the accounting field in South Africa.

The 2006 survey also indicated enormous cost and time constraints for certain companies in the adoption of IFRS. One third of the respondents had taken more than a year to implement the changes, while only a small group (16 per cent) had taken less than six months. More than half the respondents indicated that the IFRS implementation had cost them more than R1 million and more than 10 per cent believed that the cost had exceeded R5 million.

In the survey, most of the respondents (66 per cent) indicated that the IFRS changes had resulted in more meaningful information being provided to shareholders. However, they also indicated that the adoption of IFRS brought with it increased intricacies and complexities.

Interestingly, the survey pointed to a mixed impact on the bottom-line profit being reported. Almost 66 per cent of the respondents indicated an adverse effect, while approximately one third reported a positive effect.

One of the most significant findings of the survey concerned the impact on the recording and maintenance of financial information. Information and communication technology (ICT) systems were reported to be unable to supply information in all instances and workarounds were

---

40 Ernst and Young (2006). Facing the challenges of IFRS adoption. 27 July 2006.

41 SAICA (2007). CA(SA) qualification results reflect blossoming transformation in accountancy profession. Press release, 22 June 2007.

42 SAICA (2007). Request for proposal: research into the financial management, accounting and auditing skills shortage, and request for proposal: research into the attrition and retention of trainee accountants.

reported to be required to achieve compliance with IFRS, which suggests that more ICT system changes will be seen in the future. Concerns were expressed mostly in the following areas:

(a)   Maintenance of information relating to property, plant and equipment, such as updating of the fixed asset register and recording and updating of the residual values and useful lives: In the transition to IFRS in 2005, the improvements to IAS 16 (property, plant and equipment) were seen as the most burdensome task. Many companies applied the deemed cost approach in IFRS 1 to eliminate retrospective adjustments. However, uncertainty about the level of application of the component approach to depreciation remained a challenge.

(b)   Financial-instrument valuation and recording, including risk-management disclosures, complying with de-recognition principles and splitting financial instruments: Currently, under IFRS 7 (financial instruments: disclosure), companies trading in different countries with different functional currencies experience difficulty in completing sensitivity analyses.

(c)   Processes around doubtful debt provisions and accounting for employee and management/executive compensation: The South African experiences surrounding doubtful debt provisions are discussed in greater detail below.

B.   Local technical committee

With the adoption of IFRS, the question could be raised whether a local technical committee, such as the South African APC, is indeed still needed. The South African experience confirms a positive need for such a committee.

The first need for such a committee is to achieve the involvement of the local accounting community in the due process of standard setting by IASB and the International Financial Reporting Interpretations Committee (IFRIC) through commenting on exposure drafts and discussion papers. Firstly, APC is regarded as being representative of the South African corporate world in that members of the committee represent commerce and industry, users, auditors, JSE and academics. Further, by creating a separate technical subcommittee for each new exposure draft or discussion paper, APC invites the local accounting community and industry experts to be involved in its comment process should this be necessary.

The second need for such a committee is the role it plays in education. APC assumes the role of educating the local accounting community on new developments in the accounting field. Road shows (sometimes involving IASB staff) and other opportunities for discussion are held when the need is identified. SAICA, through its continued education process, also provides training seminars to its members on pre-identified topics.

The last, and maybe the most important, need for a committee such as APC is that such a committee should consider the correct treatment of accounting issues for which there is currently insufficient guidance in IFRS, including also instances where diversity in practice is detected. Such issues to be discussed and resolved by APC are obtained through the following role players:

(a)   The APC members themselves;

(b)   Other SAICA committees;

(c)   Industry committees;

(d)   The technical partners' forum;

(e)   JSE;

(f)   The top 40 CFO forum; and

(g)   Members of SAICA.

C.   Local issues and diversity in practice

The experience in South Africa is that diversity exists in practice. However, one of the main advantages of converting to IFRS is that, through this conversion, many of these divergent practices have been eliminated. By adopting IFRS, companies have had to evaluate their existing accounting policies and procedures. The involvement of external consultants and the review process of the internal auditors have created a move toward consistency in implementation. Consistency has been strengthened by industry experts coming together and resolving related issues. In this regard, the technical partners' forum plays a vital role in resolving issues and creating consistency. Each of these technical partners also has the support of their international technical desk.

Local issues and diversity in practice that cannot be resolved through the above structures are channeled to APC. The task of APC is then to determine the appropriate means of resolving these issues. The first question APC asks is whether the issues are widespread and significantly divergent to send a request to IFRIC. Issues such as operating leases and Black Economic Empowerment (BEE) transactions (discussed further in chapter IV below) are examples of South African requests that have been referred to IFRIC.

If the decision is made not to refer an issue to IFRIC for a number of valid reasons (e.g. the issue is considered to be only a local one), the alternatives are to release a local standard, a circular or a guide, or to use other communication methods of announcing how the issue has been resolved. APC recommends the issuing of such South African pronouncements to the appropriate authoritative body.

Where appropriate, a local standard (one of the AC 500 series of Statements of GAAP) is issued by APB to interpret specific accounting aspects, transactions or other issues that occur only in the South African context, where such aspects, transactions or other issues are not specifically or clearly addressed in IFRS.[43] The AC 500 series has the same authority as the AC 100 series of Statements of GAAP, and must be adhered to by South African companies even if they prepare the financial statements in accordance with IFRS.[44] A company which claimed compliance with IFRS and which also complied with the AC 500 series would not be in contravention of IFRS, as these local standards are merely local interpretations of IFRS. These companies would not need to also claim compliance with South African Statements of GAAP, and in fact would not be able to as they would have applied IFRS 1 (which is not part of South African Statements of GAAP).

---

43 SAICA (2005). Circular 8/05 – Status of Professional Announcements. August 2005.

44 JSE (2005). Compliance with the AC 500 Series of Standards. JSE's Listing Division's letter, 12 May 2003.

The guides issued by SAICA are not regarded as having the same status as Statements of GAAP.[45] Members or associates that are responsible for preparing financial statements and that do not comply with a guide could be called upon by SAICA to explain why they did not do so. Most of the guides are issued to resolve industry-specific issues.

Circulars issued by SAICA communicate relevant issues to members, but never interpret issues. Where communication is provided on accounting issues, circulars have the same status as the accounting guides referred to above.[46]

The more significant of these pronouncements are discussed under specific issues in section IV below.

D.   Monitoring and enforcement

The formation of GMP has also contributed to consistency in accounting application in South Africa. On the advice of GMP, the Listing Division of JSE has issued guidance to listed companies in respect of the correct accounting treatment of certain transactions or events identified by GMP. This includes the following:

(a) Insurance companies should not include smoothing adjustments relating to long-term investment returns in their income statements.[47]

(b) Concerning the correct presentation in the income statement, it is inappropriate to end the income statement with the line item "headline earnings" or with any figure other than net income attributable to ordinary shareholders (the previous format of the income statement).[48]

(c) A statement that "certain comparative figures have been restated to comply with current year classification" should be supported by full disclosure on a line-by-line basis of all reclassifications.[49]

(d) Companies should review their accounting treatment of their share trusts to ensure that they comply with consolidation principles.[50]

(e) Compliance with IFRS also includes compliance with the AC 500 standards.[51]

Currently, 28 companies have been referred to GMP for review. Nine of these have required a review of the total financial statements, and 18 have required reviews of specific policies or line items in the interim or annual financial statements.[52] The results of the recommendations and actions taken by JSE are presented in table 1.

Table 1. Decisions on cases referred to the GAAP Monitoring Panel

---

45 SAICA (2005). Circular 8/05 – Status of Professional Announcements. August 2005.

46 *Ibid.*

47 JSE (2003). Long-term investment return adjustment to income statement. JSE's Listing Division's letter, 21 February 2003.

48 JSE (2003). Income statement presentation. JSE's Listing Division's letter, 12 May 2003.

49 JSE (2003). Listing Division of the JSE. Restatement of comparative financial information. JSE's Listing Division's letters, 22 October 2003 and 29 December 2003.

50 JSE (2004). Consolidation of share incentive scheme trusts. JSE's Listing Division's letter, 16 February 2004.

51 JSE (2005). JSE. Compliance with the AC 500 series of standards. JSE's Listing Division's letter, 24 January 2005.

52 SAICA (2007). Summary of matters. Available from http://www.saica.co.za/documents/summary_of_matters. (accessed 23 April 2007).

Recommendations or actions	Number
Annual financial statements withdrawn and re-issued	3
Companies suspended (other JSE problems also present)	2
Accounting policy changed for future financial reports/other companies also adopting the policy advised to comply in the future/draft publication of the results changed before final publication of the results	7
Revised results announcement made	9
Reference to issues identified by GMP made in next interim results and full disclosure made in annual report	2
Correct headline earnings per share re-published on Security Exchange News Service and in annual report before distribution	1
Results revised before distribution to shareholders	2
No action required	1
Pending	1
Total	**28**

Source: SAICA (2007). *Summary of matters.* Available from http://www.saica.co.za/documents/summary.

The South African history of a lack of legal enforcement of financial reporting standards has created the opportunity for different interpretations and applications in practice, sometimes even for accounting manipulation. The lesson learned is that if South Africa truly wants to be a player in the global market, monitoring and enforcement must be a cornerstone of the financial reporting system. IASB is not responsible for monitoring and enforcement of IFRS. These tasks are the responsibility of national regulators. South African regulators are committed to carrying rigorous monitoring and enforcement. In this respect, efforts so far have proved to be successful in ensuring compliance. Professor Harvey Wainer, chairman of GMP, stresses the urgency and seriousness with which GMP views its task as advisor to JSE in the achievement of this compliance.[53]

E.   Involvement of local firms

The technical partners' forum in South Africa plays an important role in identifying different practices and applications of financial reporting standards. This technical partners' forum represents a network of technical partners in South Africa. This could be seen as a first step in the process of creating consistency in the application of financial reporting standards in South Africa. Through their international networks, these partners also obtain knowledge of international practices to resolve identified issues. In the sustainability of consistent global reporting practices, this networking is seen to be crucial.

---

[53] SIACA (2006). GAAP Monitoring Panel has taken a closer look at 30 listed companies. Press release, 29 November 2006; only 28 of the 30 companies have been actioned.

Local auditing firms are also required to refer accounting issues to their international desks in order to create consistency in practice. The downside, however, is increased cost and increased turn-around time, which has frustrated auditors and clients in practice.

IV. Technical and application issues

The major technical and application issues encountered in the transition to IFRS in South Africa are highlighted in this chapter. These issues have been identified through a review of the formal process of APC and discussions with industry leaders.

A. Impairment of debtors' book

Processes to create provisions for doubtful debts were identified as an implementation issue in the second Ernst and Young survey (discussed above). The issue started in the banking industry with the adoption of the South African version of the original IAS 39 in 2001/2002.[54] At that stage, the South African Reserve Bank (the regulator of South African banks) required banks to calculate the impairment on loans and receivables on the basis of a provision matrix. This matrix did not explicitly consider a discounted cash-flow model based on expected cash flows, as required by the original IAS 39. The practical question raised at that stage was whether any adjustments to the expected cash-flow model should be made to the opening balance of retained earnings. SAICA's response was that the transitional provisions provided for an adjustment to the opening balance of retained earnings if the provisioning matrix did not explicitly consider the amount or timing of underlying cash flows.[55]

This clearly demonstrates that the adoption of IFRS for financial statement purposes is a move away from any requirements prescribed by a local regulatory body.

The second issue with the impairment of the debtors' book arose with the revision of IAS 39, through which the "expected cash-flow model" was replaced by an "incurred-loss model". The critical question was how to apply the historical loss experience test in collective assessments. The banking sector started its discussions before the IAS 39 amendment to the "incurred-loss model" was implemented and through the banking association corresponded with IFRIC. The banking sector's concerns were incorporated in the "incurred-loss model" amendment, which resulted in the sector accepting the change to the "incurred-loss model".[56]

B. Operating leases

In respect of the straight-lining of operating leases, the South African practice differed from international practice. The South African practice was that operating lease agreements with inflation escalations should not be straight-lined. It was believed that inflation escalations were "another systematic basis" from which to spread the lease payments over the term of the lease. This issue was referred to IFRIC, but the body rejected the issue on the grounds that the standard

---

54 SAICA (2001). AC 133 – Financial Instruments: Recognition and Measurement. April 2001.

55 SAICA (2003). Circular 6/03 – Implementation Guidance for AC 133 – Financial Instruments: Recognition and Measurement. November 2003.

56 Information obtained from discussions held with the banking sector.

is clear: IAS 17 (leases) refers to "another systematic basis" that is "more representative of the time pattern of the user's benefit". The time pattern of the user's benefit should only be affected by factors that impact on the physical usage of the asset, which does not include inflation.

SAICA issued two circulars to announce the conversion of the South African practice to the international practice.[57] In spite of many negative reactions by preparers, this diverse practice has been amended in South Africa.

C.   South African dividends tax

A dual tax system for companies was introduced by the South African Income Tax Act, 1993, comprising a normal tax levied on taxable income and a secondary tax on companies (STC). STC is a tax levied on dividends declared by South African companies and is based on the amount by which a declared dividend exceeds dividends previously received. Since this is a South African-specific issue, APB issued South African GAAP Standard AC 501 (secondary tax on companies) to clarify the accounting treatment of STC on the basis of the principles of IAS 12 (income taxes).[58]

The main question raised by AC 501 is whether STC should be included in the income-tax line in the income statement. The consensus reached was that STC is a tax on income since STC is a tax on companies and not a withholding tax. AC 501 links the recognition of the STC liability to the recognition of the liability for the dividend declared. The STC liability should be recognized when the liability for the dividend declared is recognized. AC 501 also adopted the principles of the creation of deferred assets in IAS 12. Deferred tax for an STC credit (instances where dividends received exceed dividends paid) may only be recognized to the extent that it is probable that the company would declare dividends in the future to use the STC credit.

This issue demonstrated that legislation could cover local issues not specifically covered by IFRS.

D.   Black Economic Empowerment

Black Economic Empowerment (BEE) is a formal process followed in South Africa to uplift black South Africans.[59] The accounting issue in South Africa deals with the situation where entities issue equity instruments to black South Africans or entities controlled by black South Africans at a discount to fair value to achieve targets for the empowerment of black people. In terms of guidance in IFRIC 8 (scope of IFRS 2) it is clear that IFRS 2 (share-based payment) applies to such BEE transactions where the fair value of cash and other assets received from BEE partners is less than the fair value of equity instruments granted to the BEE partner, i.e. the BEE equity credential element.

---

57 SAICA (2005). Circular 7/05 – Operation Leases; and SIACA 2006: Circular 12/06 – Operating Leases. August 2006.

58 AC 501 was effective from financial years starting on 1 January 2004.

59 The South African Government has issued various BEE documents, including the Broad Based Black Economic Empowerment Act, Act no. 53 of 2003. The act empowers the Minister of Trade and Industry to issue codes of good practice, which are applied to determine an entity's BEE credentials.

APB issued AC 503 (accounting for BEE) transactions to clarify whether a BEE equity credential should be recognized as an intangible asset or as an expense.[60] The conclusion reached is that BEE equity credentials should be expensed, except where the cost of the BEE equity credentials is directly attributable to the acquisition of another intangible asset. The main reason for expensing the BEE equity credentials, based on the principles of IAS 38 (intangible assets), is that the BEE equity credentials are not controlled by the entity because the entity is not able to demonstrate that it has the power to obtain the future economic benefits flowing from the underlying resource, either through legal rights or exchange transactions.

This issue regarding BEE transactions, although South African-specific, was referred to IFRIC for clarity and IFRIC issued IFRIC 8 (scope of IFRS 2) in response.

E.   Divergence due to IFRIC rejecting items

Sometimes IFRIC rejects items submitted to it for consideration on the grounds that it considers the appropriate accounting treatment to be clear. However, the South African experience is that IFRIC's reasoning in such cases could identify divergence of practice in South Africa. SAICA's Circular 09/06, which relates to cash discounts, settlement discounts, other rebates and extended payment terms, contains examples where such divergence has been identified.[61]

(a) Cash discounts: IFRIC's view is that IAS 2 (inventory) provides adequate guidance. Cash discounts received should be deducted from the cost of the goods purchased. In contrast, many South African entities account for cash discounts received as "other income", thus creating divergence. Similarly, Circular 9/06 clarifies that cash discounts granted to customers should reduce the amount of revenue recognized on the date of sale.

(b) Settlement discounts: In rejecting the issue regarding settlement discounts, IFRIC agreed that settlement discounts allowed should be estimated at the time of sale and presented as a reduction in revenue. Settlement discounts received should similarly be deducted from the cost of inventory. The practice of many South African entities at the time was to account for settlement discounts allowed to customers as "operating expenses" and settlement discounts received as "other income".

(c) Other rebates: Many South African entities account for rebates received as "other income". However, IFRIC agreed that in terms of IAS 2 (inventory), those rebates that have been received as a reduction in the purchase price of inventories should be taken into account in the measurement of the cost of inventory. Rebates specifically related to selling expenses would not be deducted from the cost of inventory.

---

60 Issued in 2006

61 SAICA (2006). Circular 09/06 – Transactions giving rise to Adjustments to Revenue/Purchases. May 2006.

(d) Extended payment terms: There continues to be diversity in practice on the treatment of extended payment terms. This issue remains unresolved, as more than one standard deals with principles on deferred settlements, and different preparers interpret the requirements differently. IAS 2 (inventory) states that, when the arrangement effectively contains a financing element, that element must be recognized as interest over the period of the finance. IAS 18 makes a similar reference in respect of the recognition of revenue. The IFRIC reasons for rejecting an interpretation are that the accounting treatment for extended payment terms such as six-month's interest-free credit is clear: the time value of money should be reflected when it is material. The diversity has arisen with regard to the interpretation of extended credit (and therefore the necessity to present value the amounts in terms of IAS 39 (financial instruments: recognition and measurement)). Some auditors and users interpret extended credit as payment after the transaction date (i.e. that credit has been extended) and others have interpreted it as credit being extended for a period that is longer than normal for that industry. In addition, some preparers contend that when cash sales are concluded at the same selling price as those with extended payment terms, the sales revenue to be recognized must be the same.

F.   Insurance industry: anomalies relating to treasury shares

Prior to the adoption of IFRS, the insurance industry applied a local standard, which had the effect of ring-fencing the results of insurance businesses.[62] Assets and liabilities relating to insurance business were disclosed separately from other business in the financial statements. The move to IFRS and also the application of IFRS 4 (insurance contracts) has resulted in assets being disclosed by their nature. For instance, financial assets held to manage the insurance business are not disclosed separately from other assets.

The main result of the abolishment of the ring-fencing principle is the effect of treasury shares. Certain insurance divisions (subsidiaries) invest in equity shares of the entity (holding company). For instance, insurance operations offer products that are linked to equity performance, and, as a result, they often invest in shares of their holding companies.[63] These shares could also be bought for the purpose of linked investments (investments linked to the performance of a basket of shares) or to generate a direct return for policyholders. The main anomaly is that the value of these shares would be considered in the value of the insurance liability, but that the effect on the asset side is eliminated through the deduction of such shares as treasury shares from equity. The treasury shares are also deducted from the weighted number of shares in issue for the earnings per share calculation, which could potentially inflate the earnings per share number on an IFRS basis.

The issue of treasury shares was discussed with Sir David Tweedie, chairman of IASB, when he visited South Africa in November 2006. His response was that IASB had discussed the

---

62 AC 121 – Disclosure in the Financial Statements of Long-term Insurers was abolished during 2004.

63 SAICA (2006). Minutes of the meeting of the APC, 30 November 2006 (the meeting where the visit of Sir David Tweedie was documented).

topic at various board meetings and had not been able to arrive at an acceptable solution without creating an exception for an industry.[64]

G.   Fair value measurement considerations

Another concern raised by APB and the APC at their meeting with Sir David Tweedie was the application of fair value measurement applied to financial instruments in cases where there was no active market or where the market was illiquid.[65] The concern especially relates to instances where fair value measurement is based on management's estimates.

Tweedie's response was that an evaluation of the discussion paper on fair value measurement guidance was needed, which would contain a hierarchy for fair value measurement. This evaluation would be the process needed to resolve the fair value measurement concerns. The progress on this project is being closely monitored in South Africa.

H.   Separate financial statements

In South Africa, holding companies were always required to prepare separate financial statements on the basis of the South African Statements of GAAP. While IFRS are not explicitly written for consolidated financial statements only, there is almost an implicit focus on the consolidated position rather than the separate financial statements.[66]

Some of the challenges facing preparers of financial statements stem from the uncertainty of applying the concept of substance over legal form. In respect of special purpose entities, the question is to what extent a "look-through" approach should be applied in the separate financial statements to reflect the economic substance rather than the legal form on the basis that the special purpose entity was effectively just a conduit or a warehousing vehicle. Similarly, in respect of transactions with other related parties, the question is to what extent the economic substance, and not merely the legal form, should be analyzed and reflected, particularly where the transactions might not be on an arm's-length basis.

Sir David Tweedie's response in this regard was that IASB was aware of these issues and had been debating them, and that the preference at this stage was for the look-through approach to be applied.[67]

---

64 *Ibid.*

65 *Ibid.*

66 *Ibid.*

[67] *Ibid.*

V.   Conclusion

The adoption of IFRS has clearly increased South Africa's role as a global player in the accounting field and has strengthened uniformity in the application of IFRS in South Africa. Listed companies and the accounting practice have tackled the task of implementing IFRS diligently and have achieved great successes. Clearly, many teething problems have been resolved.

The adoption of IFRS has enhanced consistency of the application of IFRS and has further confirmed the need for a local technical body that will contribute to IASB's due process and resolve specific local issues and divergence in practice.

The country has witnessed a significant growth in the technical accounting departments of audit firms to cope with the increased technical demand. However, many accounting specialists trained in South Africa have left the country because of global demand for their skills.

The challenges facing South Africa are to create a process of legal backing for accounting standards by proper monitoring and enforcement structures and to implement a system of differential reporting.

Chapter IV

Review of practical implementation Issues of International Financial Reporting Standards: Case study of Turkey[*]

I.   Introduction

As a developing country with an emerging capital market, Turkey closely follows developments in international financial reporting and auditing. This report presents the historical development of accounting and financial reporting in the country and discusses the recent regulatory developments following the attempts at convergence with the global set of financial reporting standards that are referred to as the International Financial Reporting Standards (IFRS). In doing so, this report conveys the Turkish experience in adapting to IFRS as well as lessons learned in the implementation process.

Turkey has been attracting foreign direct investment (FDI) at various levels since the establishment of the Turkish Republic in 1923. Turkish companies started to invest in other countries in the late 1990s. The amount of FDI flowing into Turkey between 2002 and 2005 was $15.4 billion, whereas FDI flowing out of Turkey during the same period was $2.6 billion.[89] As of 31 December 2006, there were 14,932 companies in Turkey with foreign capital. Five percent of these companies received investments from the United States, and 56 per cent received investments from European Union-based companies.[90] Turkish companies, on the other hand, had most of their investments in the European Union and in the Commonwealth of the Independent States.

Turkey was hit by a severe economic crisis in November 2000 that continued through February 2001. There was a 7.5 per cent contraction in gross domestic product (GDP) and inflation jumped, with an annual increase in the consumer price index of 68.5 per cent. Economic growth recovered in the following years and inflation fell below 10 per cent starting in 2004. The GDP growth rate for 2006 was 6.1 per cent, reaching $400 billion.[91]

Turkey applied for membership in the European Union in 1999, and currently is a candidate country. With the resolution adopted by the European Parliament on 15 December 2004, negotiations for full membership started on 3 October 2005. Among many other legislative issues, the relations with the European Union require Turkey to adapt its financial reporting system to European Union legislation.

---

89   http://www.unctad.org/sections/dite_dir/docs/wir06_fs_tr_en.pdf April 12, 2007

90   http://www.hazine.gov.tr/ybs _firmalar listesi.xls

91   http://siteresources.worldbank.org/INTTURKEY/Resources/361616-1121189119378/turkey,_cem_report_chapter1.pdf,
      http://www.turkstat.gov.tr/PreHaberBultenleri.do?id=473, http://www.turkisheconomy.org.uk/economy/output.htm.

A brief history of accounting in Turkey[92]

The development of accounting practices in Turkey is heavily influenced by the practices of a number of Western countries as a result of the economic and political ties in a specific period. The first Commercial Code of 1850 was a translation of the French Commercial Code and reflected the French influence of the era. The end of the 19th century and the beginning of the 20th century mark the increased trade relations between Turkey and Europe, especially Germany.

These historical and political developments – and the fact that most foreign manufacturing businesses had been operated by Germans at the start of the Turkish Republic – led to strong German influence on the economic development of the emerging State. Following the establishment of the Turkish Republic in 1923, a second Commercial Code was enacted in 1926 (Law Number 826). This code was based on the German commerce and company laws that controlled the accounting rules.

Due to the lack of private enterprises and private capital at the beginning of the republic, the State took the responsibility to set up heavy industry and several manufacturing companies. These state-founded and operated companies are called State Economic Enterprises (SEEs), and Sümerbank (mine and textile products) was founded as the first SEE in 1933. It was originally entrusted with the operation of principal mines that were acquired through nationalization from German companies. Therefore, it is not surprising to see that Sümerbank's and other SEEs' accounting systems were developed by experts from Germany. Hence, through these enterprises the German influence was carried to the private sector as well. Furthermore, in the late 1930s, Turkey welcomed German academics of various fields in Turkish universities.

The decade of 1950–1960 marks the first attempts towards a more liberal economy. The current Commercial Code of 1956 came into effect on 1 January 1957, following contemporary economic developments.

After the Second World War, developments in the world economy such as the Bretton Woods economic conference affected the Turkish economy. In 1950, the Turkish Industrial Development Bank was founded with support from the World Bank to foster and finance private industrial investments. In the early 1950s, the country enjoyed unprecedented economic growth. The economic boom ended in the mid-1950s, and was followed by a period of economic crisis. A major outcome of the crisis was the need for foreign loans that eventually led to an International Monetary Fund (IMF)-led stabilization program in 1958[93].

During the 1950s, incentives were provided for the private sector and foreign investments. Since the second half of that decade, American expertise has been utilized, and the Turkish economic system has thus been heavily influenced by the American system. Successful individuals in various fields have been trained, and have pursued graduate degrees in foreign countries, especially in the United States, starting in the late 1950s. Since the return of the first of these graduates in the early 1960s, the accounting system has been heavily influenced by the American system. Furthermore, the American influence was also felt in the curriculum of business schools, especially in the fields of management and accounting.

The decade of 1970–1980 was an era of political instability which, together with the oil crises in 1973 and 1974, had adverse effects on the Turkish economy. From 1977 onwards,

---

92 This section is heavily adapted from the article: Simga-Mugan C and Hosal-Akman N (2005). Convergence to international financial reporting standards: The case of Turkey. *International Journal of Accounting, Auditing and Performance Evaluation*. Vol. 2, No. 1/2, 12–139

93 Ceyhun F (1992). Turkey's debt crises in historical perspective: A critical analysis. *METU Studies in Development*, vol.19, no.1: 9–49.

Turkey faced great difficulties in meeting foreign debt payments and encountered import bottlenecks. The increase in the wholesale price index reached 63.9 per cent per annum in 1979 and 107.2 per cent per annum in 1980[94].

In January 1980, a series of economic decisions following the IMF's recommendations were taken to reduce the inflation rate, increase production, and support importing activities. In the reconstruction period starting in the early 1980s, Law Number 2499 was put into effect in 1981 by the parliament to prepare the grounds for establishing the Capital Markets Board (CMB) and was amended in 2002. The Istanbul Stock Exchange (ISE) law was adopted in 1984, but full operations did not start until 1986. It is still the only stock exchange in Turkey. FDI rules were eased in 1988 and 1989.

Foundation of the CMB, ISE and the increase in foreign investments promoted the development of accounting and auditing standards. Increases in joint ventures and foreign trade led to the establishment of offices by the then "Big Eight" accounting firms in Turkey. As a result of these developments, large private enterprises started to report their financial statements in accordance with the International Accounting Standards (IASs) in addition to national reporting requirements. During this decade, Turkey enjoyed economic growth.

Turkey started the 1990s on a sound economic footing. However, altogether it was an economically unstable decade. The first major crisis was in 1994. This was followed by further crises in 1997, 1998 and 1999. During this decade, the inflation rate surpassed 100 per cent. As a result of the instability and high inflation rates, historical financial statements lost their information value. Although the IASs were translated into Turkish since the beginning of 1980s by the Turkish Expert Accountants' Association, they were not enforced by any authority.[95] Companies did not use inflation accounting. The subsidiaries of multinational companies and joint venture companies were applying inflation accounting either voluntarily or when it was required by the headquarters of the parent company.

In line with European Union requirements, CMB issued the IFRS-based standard Communiqué Serial: XI, No. 25, entitled "Accounting Standards in Capital Markets" on 15 November 2003 (from then on the new CMB rules) and required publicly-owned and traded companies to use the new rules starting January 2005 while encouraging early adoption. Currently, there are 333 companies traded on the Istanbul Stock Exchange (ISE), while 65 companies are traded on foreign stock exchanges, including Frankfurt, London, and New York.[96] For companies traded on European Union stock exchanges, IFRS-based statements are required, which is also allowed by the CMB. However, at present, there are no foreign companies listed on the Istanbul Stock Exchange.

II.   Regulatory framework

A.   Non-bank private entities

Until the establishment of the CMB and the Istanbul Stock Exchange, legal requirements were the main influence on the financial accounting system. Consequently, the Procedural Tax Code heavily influenced the accounting practice in Turkey.

---

94 Simga-Mugan C (1995). Accounting in Turkey. *The European Accounting Review*, Vol.4, No.2: 351–371.

95 http://www.tmud.org.tr/default.asp

96 www.reuters.com (found under TRSTOKS)

The first set of financial accounting standards was developed in January 1989 by the CMB to be in effect for the fiscal years that started on or after 1 January 1989 (Serial X, No:11).[97]

As mentioned above, the environment surrounding the accounting practice in Turkey went through several transformations. However, accounting principles did not show such a development, and accounting was, and to some extent still is, treated as identical to tax accounting. Moreover, although there have been several attempts to form an accounting body since the 1940s, until recently there was no effort to pursue the establishment of standards. The main reason for this delay is the lack of pressure on Turkish companies to make publicly available comparable financial statements, because most of the businesses are family owned. The accountants in such companies are responsible for (a) bookkeeping for tax purposes (i.e. following procedural tax code); (b) cash management; (c) budgeting; (d) preparation of tax returns and financial statements required by the tax codes; and (e) very limited internal auditing.

In 1992, the Ministry of Finance organized a committee to establish accounting principles and a uniform chart of accounts that would be used by all companies. The ministry published the committee's report in a communiqué on 26 December 1992 establishing the principles and the Turkish Uniform Chart of Accounts (TUCA) to take effect 1 January 1994. All companies except banks, brokerage firms and insurance companies are required to conform to the guidelines stated in the communiqué.

According to the requirements of the 1992 communiqué, financial statements prepared in Turkey include a balance sheet, an income statement, a statement of cost of goods sold, a funds flow statement, a cash flow statement, a profit distribution statement and a statement of owners' equity, as well as notes to these statements. The balance sheet, income statement and notes to these statements constitute the fundamental statements, and the others are supplementary statements. The Ministry of Finance communiqué of September 1994 states that small companies are required to submit the fundamental statements only. Tax rules, on the other hand, require a balance sheet and an income statement from all first-class merchants. Financial statements have to be prepared within the three months following the end of an accounting period, which is usually the year end.

The Code of Obligations and the Commercial Code regulate the formation and activities of the businesses. The Code of Obligations controls ordinary partnerships which lack the status of legal entity. The Commercial Code, on the other hand, specifies the following types of legal entities:

(a) General and special partnerships;

(b) Limited partnerships;

(c) Partnerships limited by shares; and

(d) Corporations.

As mentioned above, the CMB issued the first financial accounting standards for publicly-owned companies in 1989, following the inauguration of ISE in 1986. This set of CMB standards was comparable to IASs, including the assumptions of going concern, consistency, time period, unit of measure and the basic principles such as, cost, matching, conservatism, materiality, objectivity and full disclosure. However, there were very significant differences in measurement and disclosure issues. The significant differences, among others, were accounting for the effects

---

[97] www.spk.gov.tr

of inflation under hyperinflationary economies, and also accounting for long-term investments. Although Turkey had been experiencing considerable rates of inflation since 1984, financial statements were prepared at historical cost except for the revaluation of property, plant and equipment. Furthermore, long-term investments including subsidiaries and equity participations were carried at cost.

If the number of shareholders of a corporation exceeds 250, then that corporation is categorized as a publicly-owned company and is subject to CMB regulations. Currently, there are 274 publicly-owned companies whose securities are not publicly traded. Serial X, No: 11 standards (old CMB rules) are still in effect to regulate financial reporting of such entities. Publicly-owned companies whose shares are traded in the stock exchange are subject to the new CMB rules (Serial X, No: 25) that are based on IFRS.

There are some major issues that are covered in IFRS/IAS but not in the old CMB rules. These can be summarized as follows:

(a) Impairment of assets (IAS 36);

(b) The de-recognition of financial assets (IAS 39);

(c) Provision for employee benefits other than lump-sum termination indemnities (IAS 19);

(d) Segment reporting (IAS 14);

(e) Provisions, contingent liabilities and contingent assets (IAS 37);

(f) Deferred taxes (IAS 12);

(g) Treasury shares (IAS 32); and

(h) Hedge accounting (IAS 39).

Furthermore, there are certain differences between the old CMB rules and IFRS/IAS that could lead to reporting of different financial results and financial position. Major differences include:

(a) Measurement issues:

(i) According to CMB rules, foreign exchange losses that arise from acquisition of property, plant and equipment can be capitalized after related assets are put into use. IFRS and IAS, on the other hand, require recording of such foreign exchange losses as period expenses.

(ii) CMB rules require that construction contracts should be accounted for using the completed contract method, whereas IFRS and IAS require the use of percentage of completion or cost recovery methods.

(iii) Although IFRS and IAS treat organization and research costs as period expenses while permitting capitalization of development costs under special circumstances, CMB rules allow for capitalization of organization, research and development costs.

(iv) The amortization period of goodwill is different between the two sets of standards.

(v) While IFRS and IAS require discounting of the pension obligations to present value, CMB rules do not impose such a requirement.

(vi) All types of leases are accounted for as operating leases according to CMB rules.

(b) Disclosure issues:

(i) According to the CMB rules the applicability of related parties is limited to shareholders, subsidiary and equity investments whereas related parties are more broadly defined in IFRS/IAS.

(ii) There are no specific disclosure requirements relating to the fair value of financial assets and liabilities except for marketable securities under the CMB rules.

(iii) Statement of Changes in Shareholders' Equity is not required by the CMB rules.

(iv) CMB rules on format of the statement of cash flows do not require a breakdown of cash flows by type of activity.

In November 2003, CMB issued a communiqué to adapt the financial reporting standards of traded companies in ISE to IAS and IFRS (Series XI, No: 25). The standards were mandatory for all publicly-traded companies and intermediary institutions (brokerage firms) from the beginning of 2005. The new standards in the communiqué are essentially the same with IAS/IFRS except for the amendments by IASB after 2004. One of the differences between the new CMB rules and IFRS lies in the treatment of goodwill. According to CMB rules, goodwill is still amortized.

According to tax rules, on the other hand, in principle, accrual accounting is required, but the treatment of certain items is closer to cash accounting. At the same time, with CMB, the Ministry of Finance required a one-time application of inflation accounting to restate the balance sheet ending 31 December 2003 or at the end of the then current fiscal year.[98]

Through Law No: 4487 dated December 1999, an addendum was made to the Capital Markets Law for the establishment of the Turkish Accounting Standards Board (TASB) to issue Turkish Accounting Standards (TAS) that would facilitate fair disclosure of the financial position. The board has both administrative and financial autonomy. It held its first meeting in March 2002, and has nine representatives from the Ministry of Finance, Higher Education Council, CMB, the Under secretariat of Treasury, Ministry of Industry and Commerce, the Banking Regulation and Supervision Agency (BRSA), the Union of Chambers and Commodity Exchanges in Turkey (TOBB), a self-employed accountant and a certified financial consultant from Union of Certified Public Accountants and Sworn-in Certified Public Accountants in Turkey (TURMOB).[99]

TASB has an agreement with the IASB to officially translate and publish IFRS/IAS and the related interpretations. As of mid-2007, TASB had issued 31 TAS and seven Turkish Financial Reporting Standards (TFRS). All of these issued standards correspond to the respective IAS and IFRS.

---

98 Simga-Mugan and Akman N (2002). Turkey. Revised chapter in World Accounting, Release 24. Orsini LL, Gould JD, McAllister JP, Parikh RN and Schultzke K (eds). Lexis–Nexis/Matthew–Bender, November

99 www.turmob.org.tr

Currently, TASB has no enforcement authority to require any Turkish company to prepare financial statements in accordance with TAS or TFRS (hereafter referred to as TAS).

Consolidation rules are not required under the present Commercial Code and tax legislation. However, CMB issued a communiqué in 2003 (Serial XI, No:21) that stipulates consolidation of financial position of companies that meet the criteria which are the same as IFRS rules for publicly-owned companies whose shares are traded. Since adoption of new IFRS-based CMB rules, companies are required to comply with the new regulation. TASB also published TAS 27 – Consolidated and Separate Financial Statement, which is fully compatible with IAS 27.

Another major discrepancy between the tax rules and the accounting rules concerns fixed assets. According to the accounting rules, the cost of fixed assets includes – in addition to the acquisition cost – items such as interest expense on self-constructed assets (capitalized until the asset is ready for use), foreign exchange losses on the purchase price of the assets, the debts incurred for such assets, and long-term investments (capitalized until the debt for the asset or investment is paid in full). According to tax rules, however, companies may continue to capitalize the interest expense related to loans used to finance such assets after the asset is in use.

According to both the old CMB regulations and the Ministry of Finance requirements between 1983 and 2003, companies revalued their fixed assets (except land) and the related accumulated depreciation if they wished, provided that they have been using those fixed assets for more than one year. The revaluation rate was based on an index published by the Ministry of Finance every December that approximated the country's annual inflation rate. The difference between the net revalued fixed assets of the current period (revalued cost minus revalued accumulated depreciation) and the previous period was accumulated under the owners' equity section of the balance sheet under the name "revaluation fund". This revaluation surplus was non-taxable unless distributed, and may have been added to capital via issuance of bonus (free) shares. With the inception of inflation accounting in 2003, this practice was abandoned.

B.   Banks and financial institutions

Financial reporting of financial institutions is regulated by BRSA. Until recently, BRSA issued its own set of accounting standards that financial institutions had to comply with. However, since November 2006, these institutions have been required to apply TAS to prepare their financial statements, except for certain differences such as loan loss provisions.

In summary, financial reporting in Turkey has a multi-institutional structure. Turkish companies prepare their financial reports according to different sets of accounting standards, depending on the nature of their business and their shareholding structure. Table 1 summarizes the reporting requirements of different companies.

Table 1. Reporting requirements of different companies

Publicly owned but not traded in the stock exchange	Old CMB standards (Series XI, No. 1 and its amendments)
Publicly owned and traded in the stock exchange	New CMB standards (Series XI No. 25 and its amendments)
Brokerage companies	New CMB standards (Series XI No. 25 and its amendments)
Banks and financial institutions	TAS
Insurance companies	Communiqué of under secretariat of treasury

As illustrated in the table above, presently companies that are not publicly owned are not required to apply any accounting standards other than Ministry of Finance's communiqué of 1992 and the tax legislation.

C.   The accounting profession and auditing

The accounting profession was formally defined by Law No: 3968, enacted in 1989. The three categories of accountants according to the law are as follows:

(a) Independent Accountant (IA): The IA is a practicing accountant who may keep the accounting records of companies, and develop accounting systems within the companies.

(b) Certified Public Accountant (CPA): Apart from the responsibilities of IAs, CPAs may conduct audits and perform consulting services; and

(c) Sworn-in Certified Public Accountant (sworn-in CPA): Sworn-in CPAs may not keep accounting records for their clients. They have the responsibility of certifying the financial statements as defined by the law.

The law also defines the competencies that are required (education, certificates and diplomas) to become an IA, CPA and sworn-in CPA. The professionals are recognized by the Turkish Union of Chambers of CPAs and are sworn in as CPAs.

The chambers of CPAs and sworn-in CPA's are separate. Chambers are professional organizations regarded as legal entities carrying qualities of public institutions. They are established for the objectives of meeting the needs of members of the profession, facilitating their professional activities, providing the development of the profession in compliance with common requirements, maintaining professional discipline and ethics, and providing the prevalence of honesty and mutual confidence in the work of the members of the profession and in their relations with their clients.

Auditing activities and audit firms in capital markets are regulated by CMB (Communiqué Serial: X, No: 22). Existing CMB regulations have been revised following regulatory reforms that were passed in the United States and the European Union. These include:

(a) Separation of audit and consultancy;

(b) Establishment of audit committees for companies whose securities are publicly traded and for brokerage firms;

(c) Audit firm rotation; and

(d) Determination of responsibility for the preparation, presentation and accuracy of financial statements and annual reports.

The maximum number of years that an audit firm can audit a company whose securities are publicly traded is seven years. At the end of seven years of service, the audit of that company should be contracted to another audit firm. In order for the first auditing firm to resume the auditing services of the same company, at least two accounting periods should elapse.

Per CMB rules, in order to conduct auditing activities, an auditing firm should meet the following requirements:

(a) An audit firm should be incorporated as a corporation with shares written to the name.

(b) The major partner should own 51 per cent of the shares;

(c) Auditors should be university graduates in the fields of economics and business administration.

(d) The firm should only be engaged in auditing activities.

(e) The firm should be insured (new amendment in 2007).

As noted above, banks and financial institutions are regulated by BRSA, and thus this agency oversees independent audit processes of such institutions. BRSA authorizes and terminates the activities of the audit companies. It carries out these activities through two by-laws: the law on independent audit of banks and authorization of independent audit firms.

The information Technologies Auditing Project started in 2004 with a change in the by-laws of BRSA which resulted in a partial reorganization of the agency. A working group was established that studied the relevant standards and literature. In addition, a survey on the technical capacity of the banks was carried out around the same time. Finally, in May 2006, BRSA issued a communiqué on auditing of information technologies of banks (IT audit). It adopted the Control Objectives for Information and Related Technology (COBIT).[100]

III. Capacity-building

In code law countries, of which Turkey can be classified as one, standard setting and enforcement are primarily functions of governmental institutions. In such countries, there is a lower demand for high-quality financial reporting and disclosure, as the reporting model is oriented towards tax offices and financial institutions. In common law countries, on the other hand, the enforcement of high-quality financial reporting standards is needed for shareholder protection.

Therefore, in Turkey, issuing accounting standards is not enough for enforcement of those standards. Legally, companies should be required to use TAS for those IFRS-compatible standards to be fully enforced.

A new draft commercial code that will introduce new financial reporting requirements per TAS has been discussed in related commissions of the parliament since the beginning of 2007. However, it is not expected to be enacted before 2008. Article 64 of the draft code requires all companies excluding small and medium-sized enterprises (SMEs) to prepare financial statements in accordance with TAS. Developing accounting standards for SMEs is an ongoing project of TASB. These standards are expected to be a simplified version of TAS which would be in line with the IASB's SME project.

The dilemma of preparing financial statements per tax requirements or according to accounting standards was also apparent in the responses of the executives who participated in a survey that assessed the perceptions of the preparers regarding IFRS.[101] Eighteen per cent of the

---

100   http://www.bddk.org.tr/turkce/raporlar/sunumlar/332it_audit_bddk_yaklasimi_20_4_2006.

101   Akman N, Simga-Mugan C, Arikboga D (2005). Awaiting IFRS: Perceptions and Demands of Executives In An Emerging Market. AACF, 2nd Annual Accounting Conference. 10–12 November. Istanbul, Turkey.

respondents see the differences between the IFRS-based standards and tax regulations as a major obstacle in applying the standards.

Therefore, in Turkey, standards alone do not guarantee the quality of financial information disclosed, rather the institutional factors such as the incentive of preparers should be considered.

The accounting managers of publicly-owned companies are already familiar with IAS-based accounting standards. However, most of the accounting managers of family-owned businesses are not exposed to such standards and are not familiar with the content of TAS. Once the draft commercial code is enacted and companies start to apply TAS, these managers will be in significantly difficult positions with respect to preparing financial statements. Family-owned companies comprise more than 85 per cent of businesses in Turkey.

Training and education on IFRS are mostly provided by universities and academic organizations. Universities already incorporated IFRS courses in their graduate and undergraduate curriculums as elective courses. In some universities, principles of accounting courses are covered using IFRS. Accounting textbooks are revised to reflect the changes that are brought about by the implementation of IFRS.

One of the academic organizations, AACF (Accounting Academician's Collaboration Foundation), organizes international and national seminars and workshops open to practitioners and academicians on various issues of IFRS/TAS (such as implementation of IAS 39).[102] Similarly, the Turkish Expert Accountants' Association holds seminars on IFRS in general, and on some specific standards.[103]

In order to align auditing standards with international developments, CMB published revised auditing rules and regulations by Communiqué Serial X, No: 22 in 2006 and later amended it with No: 23 in 2007. This communiqué states that:

"Independent auditing firms, their auditors and other staff shall not provide any issuer or intermediary, contemporaneously with the audit, any non-audit service, with or without fee, including:

(a) Bookkeeping and other related services;

(b) Financial information systems design and implementation;

(c) Services on management, accounting and finance;

(d) Appraisal or valuation services and actuarial services;

(e) Internal audit outsourcing services;

(f) Legal services and expert services;

(g) Any other consultation services."

As mentioned in the Report on the Observance of Standards and Codes of the World Bank, TUDESK (Turkish Auditing Standards Board) was formed in 2003.[104] It issues national auditing standards which in essence are translations of IASs issued by the International Auditing and Assurance Standards Board of the International Federation of Accountants. However, before the new commercial code is enacted, there is no requirement for companies other than entities whose shares are publicly traded to have their financial statements audited.

---

102   http://www.modav.org.tr – 16 July 2007

103   http://www.tmud.org.tr/dokumanlar/2007_s.doc - 16 July 2007

104   www.imf.org/external/pubs/ft/scr/2006/cr06126.pdf - 16 July 2007

In addition to accounting and auditing standards, CMB initiated the Corporate Governance Code. This code is based on Organization for Economic Cooperation and Development (OECD) principles, and requires publicly-traded companies to publish their corporate governance ratings. Rating agencies can rate the level of compliance of companies with "Corporate Governance Practices" recommended by the Capital Markets Board of Turkey.

IV. Lessons learned

Turkey is one of the proactive countries that took steps to improve its financial reporting and auditing system to align the requirements with the commencement of IFRS in 2005 in Europe.

In essence, the adoption of IFRS-based standards turned out to be a three-step process where the first step was the early adoption of IFRS between 2003 and 2005 by companies whose shares are publicly traded. The second step was the compulsory adoption of IFRS starting in 2005, again by the traded companies. The third step was the mandatory adoption by all publicly-owned companies upon the enactment of the draft commercial code.

Encouraging the traded companies to adopt IFRS or IFRS-based CMB standards before 2005 led to two benefits:

(a) More transparent financial statements were introduced; and

(b) The experience of the early adopters during the transition period helped the other publicly-traded companies.

The adoption of IFRS-based rules by the traded companies before the other private companies will ease the way for the latter companies. Non-publicly-owned private companies will benefit from their publicly-traded counterparts' experience during the implementation.

TAS will affect many parties covering both the internal and external users of financial statements. For external users such as foreign and domestic stock investors, TAS will bring transparency and comparability. These users will find themselves at ease while making investment decisions with the help of comparable and consistent financial data.

A study[105] examining the market reaction to inflation accounting-based financial reports indicated that accounting earnings announcements have an effect on market prices at a 0.10 significance level. It also found that inflation-adjusted financial reports had an impact on abnormal returns during the event window surrounding the annual earnings announcements. The paired samples T-test performed included 36 pairs of cumulative standardized abnormal return data for 2002 and 2004. The test results showed that, at a 95 per cent confidence level, the hypothesis that these two samples have equal means was rejected. This implies that the market reacted to inflation-adjusted data.

One of the urgent issues in Turkey is to solve the multi-institutional structure of the accounting environment. There should be one accounting standard-setting body for all entities.

A related issue is the enforcement of TAS. Until the draft commercial code is enacted, TASB does not have any power to enforce the adoption of TAS by all companies. As stated above, BRSA is the only authority that requires the use of TAS. It could be beneficial for CMB

---

[105]   An ongoing study being carried by Professor F.N. Can Şimga-Muğan et al. – Middle East Technical University, Ankara.

and Under secretariat of Treasury to follow the BRSA example and entrust their standard-setting authority to TASB.

Significant amounts of training and education for financial statement preparers and small and local auditing companies are needed. A lesson learned from the initial implementation is the insufficient understanding of accounting standards by these groups.

Generally, accounting standards do not address the full details of application that requires judgment from the management of entities. TAS involve a great deal of management judgment. As significant judgment is exercised in applying the accounting standards, incomplete comprehension of standards would lead to lower-quality financial information.

The results obtained through the survey discussed above brought to light the inadequate level of understanding of the accounting standards by financial statement preparers. As the demand for independent auditors will increase upon the enactment of the draft commercial code, there should be enough training for the professional accountants and auditors with respect to both accounting and auditing standards.

Within this framework, the results of the Turkish survey with respect to the question of the sources of advisory services (or consulting services) for the implementation of the IFRS-based accounting standards points to a very important potential problem of infringement of independence of audit companies. It should be noted that a majority of the respondents indicated that they intend to ask for consultancy from their current auditors, although such a practice is forbidden by CMB regulations.

The proposed changes in disclosure and particularly in measurement issues stated above will bring additional responsibilities to auditing firms, which are expected to be knowledgeable on the new set of accounting rules. There are indications that finance executives and accounting department staff will need extensive training on the application of TAS.

CMB and TASB should jointly establish a technical inquiry service for companies and auditors to answer very specific questions coming from the users of the accounting standards, and based on the common questions and complaints develop recommendations to TASB.

There are currently private training programmes that are available to the public. Especially in cases when these programmes are offered by spin-offs of the auditing firms, conflict of interest might be a problem which could result in ethical dilemmas. Thus, TASB should oversee and regulate the content of these programmes and closely monitor the auditor–client relationship.

TASB already translated IASB interpretations. However, these interpretations might not adequately address the concerns within the Turkish context. Therefore, the board should establish an interpretations committee to resolve national and when necessary sector-specific issues that may come up during the implementation of TAS. This committee should also publish books on the application of various standards.

One of the basic objectives of IASB is "to bring about convergence of national accounting standards and International Accounting Standards and International Financial Reporting Standards to high quality solutions".[106] It might be beneficial if TASB communicates to IASB the concerns and questions of the Turkish practice, along with the solutions provided. Such an effort could assist Turkey as well as other developing countries in aligning their national standards with IFRS.

---

106   http://www.iasb.org/About+Us/About+the+Foundation/Constitution.htm-16 July 2007

Currently, there is no supervision of auditing companies as a whole. CMB carries out inspections to determine whether auditing companies are performing their audit engagements in accordance with auditing standards. There should be a public oversight board to supervise the implementation of auditing standards and make sure that auditing companies are acting with due care. While the establishment of a public oversight board has been discussed since 2004, no legal or regulatory action has yet been taken.

V. Conclusion

Over the years, the Turkish accounting system has undergone considerable change. Financial accounting and reporting started as a record keeping for tax purposes. Although Turkey could still be classified as a code law country, since the 1960s there is a trend toward Anglo-Saxon style reporting. This movement accelerated after the establishment of the Istanbul Stock Exchange. The growth of global trade and investment also accelerated the change in accounting and auditing standards. As a result, Turkey accepted to adopt the IFRS by translating them into Turkish. Similarly, International Auditing Standards have also been translated and put into effect.

In code law countries such as Turkey, laws need to be changed in order to enforce an accounting standard. The Turkish experience regarding the process of enacting the new commercial code is an excellent example. Well-known lawyers and accountants from the country have been working on the draft code for more than six years. Therefore, countries that intend to implement IFRS should have their transition plans ready well ahead of launching IFRS.

At present, Turkey faces two main obstacles. The first one relates to endowing TASB with enforcement authority; the second one to the training of the accountants and staff of the local auditing firms.

The Turkish experience on the way to converge with the international accounting and auditing standards could help other developing countries with respect to the following issues:

(a) It might be better to require the use of IFRS or IFRS-based national standards in the case of large companies that could already be familiar with the international accounting standards to some extent.

(b) It would be helpful to have a single authority that oversees the development and implementation of the standards.

(c) It would be advisable to train the trainers before launching the accounting and auditing standards.

Chapter V

Guidance on corporate responsibility indicators in annual reports

Summary of discussions

Under the agenda item "other business" during the 24th session of ISAR, the Chair introduced the subject of corporate responsibility indicators in annual reports and gave the floor to a resource person to present the topic in more detail. The resource person began with background information on ISAR's work in this area, providing a brief overview of developments from earlier sessions. It was noted that the Group of Experts had explored issues of users of corporate responsibility (CR) reporting and their information needs, developed selection criteria for a limited set of indicators, identified a limited set of indicators, and developed a draft methodology for reporting the selected indicators.

This background information was followed by a presentation of the main elements of the background documents "Guidance on Corporate Responsibility Reporting in Annual Reports" (TD/B/COM.2/ISAR/41) and "Guidance on Corporate Responsibility Reporting in Annual Reports: the information needs of stakeholders and the selection criteria for core indicators" (TD/B/COM.2/ISAR/42). These documents, it was explained, provided a draft guidance on CR reporting in annual reports, including background on users of the information, the selection criteria for the indicators, an explanation of the indicators and a methodology for compiling and reporting on the selected indicators. The two documents provided a revised and finalized version of ISAR's deliberations on this subject, including material developed for, and delegate feedback during, the 21st, 22nd, 23rd, and 24th sessions of ISAR.

The guidance included a detailed methodology for compiling and reporting each of the selected core indicators on corporate responsibility. This methodology includes four fundamental elements: 1) a background description of each indicator; 2) definitions of technical terms required for standardizing preparation and reporting of each indicator; 3) instructions on compiling each indicator; and 4) instruction on presentation and disclosure of the compiled information. The resource person observed that these four factors combine to create a practical and standardized step by step process for understanding, compiling and reporting each indicator. The resource person also stressed that effort was taken to be as consistent as possible with existing guidance and definitions developed by other organisations, including the Global Reporting Initiative, the ILO, the OECD, the WTO, the OECD as well as other UN bodies.

After these initial comments on the background document, the Chair introduced a panel of experts to discuss the background document and corporate responsibility reporting. The panellists provided a mix of professional and geographic perspectives. The work of ISAR on CR reporting was commended by the panellists for its usefulness and the robustness of its methodology. A number of panellists also highlighted economic development orientation of many of the selected indicators, and observed that ISAR's approach to CR reporting would fill gaps in existing reporting frameworks. The panellists from developing countries provided a unique perspective on the increasing need for CR reporting in developing countries, and the relevance and importance of ISAR's selected indicators. A panellist from industry observed that CR reporting in general was becoming increasingly important for enterprises, and the ISAR guidance provided a concise, comparable and easy to use set of indicators.

Following the presentations of the panel, the Chair opened the floor for questions or comments on the background papers. A number of issues were raised concerning broader issues of CR and the role reporting can play. For example, several delegates raised questions about the relationship between CR and philanthropy and how reporting on these issues should be treated. There were also questions on the relationship between CR reporting and corporate governance disclosure, with a number of panellists remarking that these two fields, while still distinct, were becoming increasingly interconnected. Many delegates engaged the panel in broader discussions on the current state of CR reporting in developing countries and the development dimension of corporate responsibility. These discussions highlighted the importance of economic development as an integral issue of corporate responsibility for many delegates. In addition to general discussions on CR reporting, a number of technical questions arose regarding the measurability of indicators and comparability over time, as well as reporting related to the tax treatment of philanthropic donations. Many delegates commended the work for its usefulness and quality and suggested that it should be published and widely disseminated.

I. Introduction

The São Paulo Consensus of UNCTAD XI stated that UNCTAD should "assist developing countries, in particular LDCs (least developed countries), to design and implement active policies for building productive capacity and international competitiveness based on an integrated treatment of investment, corporate responsibility, technology transfer and innovation, enterprise development and business facilitation [...], competitiveness, diversification and export capacity, to sustain a high level of growth and promote sustainable development" (TD/410, paragraph 49). The São Paulo Consensus also stated, "Corporate responsibility was recognized at the Johannesburg World Summit on Sustainable Development. In this regard, corporate actors have a positive role to play in stimulating the economic development of host countries and in supporting social and environmental development and the competitiveness of local enterprises." (TD/410, paragraph 45). Member states stated "UNCTAD should carry out analytical work with a view towards facilitating and enhancing positive corporate contributions to the economic and social development of host developing countries" (TD/410, paragraph 58).

Since its eighteenth session, ISAR has viewed reporting on corporate responsibility as a significant emerging issue in the area of corporate transparency. ISAR recognized at its twentieth session that enterprises continued to produce more information on corporate responsibility, and that the pressure for improving reporting on social issues was increasing. The twenty-first session of ISAR began examining existing indicators so that corporate reports could be made more relevant and comparable. For the twenty-second session, the group identified a set of selection criteria and guiding principles to use when selecting reporting indicators. More details on these selection criteria and guiding principles, as well as users of corporate responsibility reporting and their information needs, can be found in the document TD/B/COM.2/ISAR/42.

During both the twenty-second and twenty-third sessions of ISAR, the group of experts suggested that a measurement methodology for the selected indicators could be developed to ensure their consistent reporting. It was agreed at ISAR's twenty-third session that "UNCTAD should further refine and finalize the guidance on selected corporate responsibility indicators and their measurement methodology with a view to providing a voluntary technical tool for enterprises" (TD/B/COM.2/ISAR/35).

The objective of this report, which has been developed with reference to the Global Reporting Initiative (GRI) Guidelines and the International Financial Reporting Standards (IFRS), is to provide detailed work on measurement methodology with a view to providing voluntary guidance on the preparation of reports using the selected indicators. The present report is divided into two main sections and the conclusion. The first section provides a concise overview of the selected indicators in the form of a table. The second section provides detailed guidance on compiling each of the selected indicators and is organized around the following main points:

(a)   **Background:** On the selection and relevance of the indicator;

(b)   **Definitions:** Any specific terms that require clarification;

(c)   **Compilation:** How to calculate the indicator; and

(d)   **Presentation and disclosure:** Specific notes on reporting the indicator.

This work builds on earlier reports prepared by the secretariat for the twentieth, twenty-first, twenty-second and twenty-third sessions of ISAR.[107] In particular, the report further develops the measurement methodology which was first approached during the twenty-third session in the document TD/B/COM.2/ISAR/34. An ad hoc consultative group, consisting of experts from a range of countries and organizations, was formed in 2007 during the intersession period to provide inputs to the development of this chapter (see annex III).

I.   Overview of selected indicators

Table 1 provides an overview of the indicators that were selected during ISAR's deliberations on this subject, including further refinements.

---

[107] Previous papers prepared for ISAR on this subject include TD/B/COM.2/ISAR/20, TD/B/COM.2/ISAR/24, TD/B/COM.2/ISAR/29 and TD/B/COM.2/ISAR/34.

Table 1. Selected indicators

Group	Indicator
Trade, Investment and Linkages	1. Total revenues 2. Value of imports vs. exports 3. Total new investments 4. Local purchasing
Employment Creation and Labour Practices	5. Total workforce with breakdown by employment type, employment contract and gender 6. Employee wages and benefits with breakdown by employment type and gender 7. Total number and rate of employee turnover broken down by gender 8. Percentage of employees covered by collective agreements
Technology and Human Resource Development	9. Expenditure on research and development 10. Average hours of training per year per employee broken down by employee category 11. Expenditure on employee training per year per employee broken down by employee category
Health and Safety	12. Cost of employee health and safety 13. Work days lost due to occupational accidents, injuries and illness
Government and Community Contributions	14. Payments to Government 15. Voluntary contributions to civil society
Corruption	16. Number of convictions for violations of corruption related laws or regulations and amount of fines paid/payable

II. Review of measurement methodology for selected indicators

To ensure consistent reporting of the selected indicators presented in table 1, a measurement methodology is described for each of the indicators in the sections below. The methodology includes four parts: (a) *background* on the selected indicator; (b) *definitions* of terms used in compiling and presenting the indicator; (c) *compilation* guidance; and (d) *presentation* guidance.

To better reflect corporate contributions to social and economic development within host countries, the measurement methodology for each indicator is intended to be used to compile relevant data for the national reports of an enterprise, rather than consolidated global reports. The use of national data, rather than globally consolidated data, should also improve the usefulness and comparability of information: for example, it would allow for benchmarking against the operations of the same enterprise in different countries, or comparing, within the same country, the contributions of one enterprise with those of its peers.

As noted in previous papers (TD/B/COM.2/ISAR/29 and TD/B/COM.2/ISAR/34), the selected indicators are drawn from a range of existing reporting initiatives, including financial reporting practices, the practices of specific enterprises, government reporting guidelines and GRI. Wherever possible, due care has been taken to use the same methodology as other organizations where the same indicator has been used. Note that indicators drawn from GRI[108] (including related background, definitions, compilation and presentation) may have been modified to ensure consistency with ISAR's selection criteria and guiding principles.[109] For example, all GRI indicators have been modified to focus on nationally – rather than regionally or globally – consolidated reporting. Additional footnotes are provided which highlight areas of modification. Some indicators have also been modified to ensure consistency with IFRS.

This guidance recommends the use of accrual basis of reporting unless national law requires cash basis. The definitions have been based wherever possible on IFRS. The definitions of IFRS are recommended except where national law requires different definitions and accounting methodologies; in such situations, national accounting practices prevail. It is recommended to include a note explaining the definitions and accounting methodologies used in the annual report. Annex I of this document includes additional general definitions, which pertain to more than one indicator. Annex II contains additional notes relevant to specific indicators.

A.   Trade, investment and linkages

1. Total revenues

Background: The total revenues of an enterprise allows for an approximate calculation of the enterprise's overall economic relevance to the economy in which it operates.

Definitions[110]

(a) Revenue is the gross inflow of economic benefits during the period arising in the course of the ordinary activities of an enterprise when those inflows result in increases in equity, other than increases relating to contributions from equity participants.

(b) Fair value is the amount for which an asset could be exchanged, or a liability settled, between knowledgeable, willing parties in an arm's length transaction.

---

[108] All references to GRI indicators in this paper refer to version 3.0 of GRI's indicators, also known as the "G3" indicators, which were released in 2006.

[109] For further information on selection criteria and guiding principles, see document TD/B/COM.2/ISAR/42.

[110] These definitions are taken from IAS 18.

Compilation

(a) Revenues should be measured at the fair value of the consideration received or receivable.

(b) Revenues from the sale of goods should be recognized when all the following conditions have been satisfied:[111]

    (i) The enterprise has transferred to the buyer the significant risks and rewards of ownership of the goods;

    (ii) The enterprise retains neither continuing managerial involvement to the degree usually associated with ownership nor effective control over the goods sold;

    (iii) The amount of revenue can be measured reliably;

    (iv) It is probable that the economic benefit associated with the transaction will flow to the enterprise; and

    (v) The costs incurred or to be incurred respecting the transaction can be measured reliably.

(c) When the outcome of a transaction involving the rendering of services can be estimated reliably, revenue associated with the transaction should be recognized by reference to the stage of completion of the transaction at the balance sheet date. The outcome of a transaction can be estimated reliably when all the following conditions are satisfied:

    (i) The amount of revenue can be measured reliably;

    (ii) It is probable that the economic benefit associated with the transaction will flow to the enterprise;

    (iii) The stage of completion of the transaction at the balance sheet date can be measured reliably; and

    (iv) The costs incurred for the transaction and the costs to complete the transaction can be measured reliably.

Presentation and disclosure

(a) The figure for total revenues should correspond to the same data as reported elsewhere in the company's (audited) financial statements, or its internally (audited) management accounts. It is encouraged to disclose revenues on a segmental basis, with a reference to International Accounting Standard (IAS) 14.

(b) In addition, value added information may be provided. Value added in enterprises is measured by the difference between the revenue from the goods and services produced and the cost of goods and services bought in. The value added model can assist the user of information to form an opinion concerning the scale and composition of the production factors used by the enterprise to produce the goods and services it provides, the macroeconomic significance of the enterprise and the distribution of the value-added of the different stakeholders deriving income from the enterprise.

---

[111] These conditions are taken from IAS 18.

2. Value of imports vs. exports

Background: The value of an enterprise's exports in relation to its imports is an indicator of the contribution of an enterprise to the balance of payments of the country in which it operates. This issue is of particular relevance for developing countries which must manage their "hard currency" reserves.

Definitions

(a) Economic territory: This may not be identical with boundaries recognized for political purposes. A country's economic territory consists of a geographic territory administered by a Government. Within this geographic territory, persons, goods and capital circulate freely. For maritime countries, geographic territory includes any islands subject to the same fiscal and monetary authorities as the mainland.

(b) Residence of enterprises: An enterprise is said to have a centre of economic interest and to be a resident unit of a country (economic territory) when the enterprise is engaged in a significant amount of production of goods and/or services there or when the enterprise owns land or buildings located there, or otherwise meets the local entity requirements as defined by the country in which the enterprise is operating. The enterprise must maintain at least one production establishment (goods and/or services) in the country and must plan to operate the establishment indefinitely or over a long period of time.

(c) Export: Domestically produced good or service sold abroad.

(d) Import: A good or service purchased from foreign suppliers.

(e) FOB (free on board): The delivery of goods on board the vessel at the named port of origin (loading), at seller's expense. The buyer is responsible for the main carriage/freight, cargo insurance and other costs and risks.

(f) CIF (cost, insurance and freight): The cargo insurance and delivery of goods to the named port of destination (discharge) at the seller's expense. The buyer is responsible for the import customs clearance and other costs and risks.

Compilation: Data maintained for meeting generally accepted financial reporting requirements can be useful for calculating this indicator.

(a) Identify all cross-border transactions of the reporting company concerning its current, capital and financial account.

(b) Identify whether these transactions are exports or imports from the perspective of the reporting company.

(c) Calculate the contribution of the reporting company to the host country's balance of payments (CCBP) using the following formula:
$$CCBP = \sum Export - \sum Import.$$

(d) Transactions refer to:

   (i)   Current account: goods; services; income; current transfers;

   (ii) Capital and financial account:

      a. Capital transfers: acquisition or disposal of non-produced, non-financial assets; and

      b. Financial assets and liabilities.

Presentation and disclosure: In the disclosure, the data on import and export should be shown separately. The use of transfer pricing, where applicable, should be explained, especially how prices were derived. The reasons for any significant year-on-year changes in the contribution of the enterprise to the balance of payments of the country should also be explained. The enterprise may provide additional information on the type of goods and/or services making the most significant contributions to imports and or exports.

3. Total new investments

Background: New investments by enterprises can have a positive economic and social impact. This is especially the case when new investments go toward buildings, machinery, equipment and intangible assets, as these investments can lead to the development of productive capacity and the reduction of poverty in host developing countries.

Definitions

(a) Investments can be considered as both:

    (i) Direct investments made by the reporting enterprise into another entity in the same country; and

    (ii) Investments by the reporting enterprise to create, among others, new productive capacity or new technology (e.g. the purchase of new facilities, new production technology, etc.).

(b) Foreign direct investment made into the country of the reporting enterprise, and made by a related party of the reporting enterprise (e.g. a parent firm), should be reported as new investment by the reporting enterprise.

(c) Investments do not include ongoing operational costs of existing equipment or facilities. They do not include the costs of training or health and safety, which are already captured by other indicators in this guidance. They do not include financial instruments held for short-term cash management purposes.

(d) Financial instruments are any contract that gives rise to both a financial asset of one entity and a financial liability.

Compilation: Data on new investments the reporting entity made as detailed in the definition above identify new investments and calculate the total amount of new investments as described in the definitions based on invoices.

Presentation and disclosure: Figures on new investments should be presented with a breakdown by the different types of investment detailed in definitions (a) and (b) above. The reasons for any significant year-to-year changes should be explained. In addition, information may be provided on the expected amortization period of the most significant investments made.

4. Local purchasing

Background: Forging supplier linkages with domestic companies is an important channel for increasing local value added and creating employment. Costs of local purchasing are a general indicator of the extent of an enterprise's linkages with the local economy.

Definitions: Purchasing is defined as "local" when it:[112]

(a) Concerns "local products" which are those produced in the same country as the reporting enterprise, or otherwise meet the local content requirements as defined by the Government of that country; or

(b) Concerns "local services" which are those provided by an enterprise that is incorporated in the same country as the reporting enterprise, or otherwise meets the local entity requirements as defined by the Government of that country.

Compilation

(a) Identify the items of local purchasing included in the reporting period.

(b) Calculate the costs of local purchasing during the reporting period (i.e. accruals accounting).

Presentation and disclosure

(a) The total amount of local purchasing is presented as an absolute figure, and also as a percentage of total purchasing.

(b) Additional information may be included in the presentation, such as the number of local enterprises from which goods and services were purchased, the nature of the goods or services, or the identity of any major suppliers of goods or services. Further information may be provided on major commitments made during the reporting period.

B. Employment creation and labour practices

5. Total workforce with breakdown by employment type, employment contract and gender[113]

Background: One of the most significant positive economic and social contributions an enterprise can make to the country in which it operates comes through the creation of jobs. An enterprise's efforts towards eliminating discrimination are also a positive social contribution to the country in which it operates. The extent to which an enterprise reduces discrimination can be considered a measure of the management team's ability to recruit and retain people on the basis of merit, and will benefit the enterprise in recruiting and retaining the best talent. Given the guiding principles for selecting indicators, and in particular the universality principle, the selected indicator includes a breakdown by gender.

Definitions

(a) Employment types:

(i) Full-time employment: A "full-time employee" is defined according to national legislation, collective bargaining agreements and practice regarding working time. It is often defined in terms of months per year or hours per week employed.

---

[112] The reference to "local content requirements" and "local entity requirements" here refers to those terms as they are used under the rules of the World Trade Organization for determining local content and local entities.

[113] This indicator is based on GRI indicator LA1, with modifications including the additional breakdown by gender.

(ii) Part-time employment: A "part-time employee" is an employee whose working hours per week, or months per year are less than "full time" as defined above.

(iii)   Supervised contract worker: Person who directly supplies work and services to the reporting organization but whose formal contract of employment is with another organization.

(b) Employment Contract:

(i) A contract as recognized under national law or practice that may be written, verbal or implicit (i.e. when all the characteristics of employment are present but without a written or witnessed verbal contract).

(ii) Indefinite or permanent contract is a permanent contract of employment with an employee for full-time or part-time work for an indeterminate period.

(iii) Fixed term or temporary contract is a contract of employment as defined above that ends when a specific time period expires, or when a specific task that has a time estimate attached is completed. A temporary contract of employment is of limited duration and terminated by a specific event, including the end of a project or work phase, return of replaced personnel, etc.

Compilation

(a) Identify the total workforce (employees and supervised workers) working for the reporting entity at the end of the reporting period. Outsourced activities are not included in this compilation. Supply chain workers are not included in this indicator.

(b) Identify the contract type and full-time and part-time status of employees based on the definitions described above.

(c) Calculate the full-time equivalents of employees. This is the number of employees reflected in full time status, e.g. two employees working each 50 per cent equal one full-time equivalent.

Presentation and disclosure

(a) The following figures should be presented:

(i)   Total workforce broken down by employees and supervised workers;

(ii)   Total number of employees broken down by type of employment contract (permanent or temporary);

(iii)   Total number of employees broken down by employment type (full-time or part-time);

(iv)   Items i, ii and iii, above, broken down by gender; and

(v)   Full-time equivalents broken down by gender.

(b) Additional information that may be reported:

(i)   Companies may also want to provide additional information related to issues of discrimination, including information on minorities or historically disadvantaged groups, based on the circumstances of the country in which the reporting enterprise is located. Additionally, enterprises may choose to report information on the age of their workers, in which case it is recommended that the total number of employees be broken down by the following age groups: <30; 30-50; >50.

(ii)   If a substantial portion of the organization's work is performed by workers who are legally recognized as self-employed, or by individuals other than employees or supervised workers, it is recommended to include this information.

(iii)   Sometimes an average number of employees in the reporting period may provide more insight. In this case, it is recommended to include an overview of average number per quarter.

(iv)   Information on seasonal or temporary contract workers, agency workers and self-employed workers may be presented in the explanatory notes to the table. Agency workers are provided to companies by a temporary agency and usually are recognized as employees of the agency that provides them or as co-employees of the agency and the company using their labour. Self-employed workers are recognized as parties in a legitimate commercial relationship with the company. If applicable, any significant seasonal variations in employment numbers (e.g. in the tourism or agricultural industries) or of significant numbers of agency workers or of self-employed individuals should be explained.

(v)   Reasons for any significant variation between the indicators reported and those relating to previous periods may be explained.

6.   Employee wages and benefits with breakdown by employment type and gender

Background: Another significant positive economic contribution an enterprise can make to the community in which it operates comes through the payment of wages and other benefits to employees. The total payroll of an enterprise, through the multiplier effect, supports the economic activity and economic development of the community in which the employees live. This indicator should reflect the total costs of the employee workforce.

Definitions: Employee benefits:[114]

(a) Employee benefits are all forms of consideration given by an enterprise in exchange for services rendered by employees.

(b) Short-term employee benefits are those (other than termination benefits) which fall due wholly within 12 months after the end of the period in which the employees render the related service.

---

[114] The definitions and examples are taken from IAS 19.

(c) Post-employment benefits are those (other than termination benefits) which are payable after the completion of employment.

(d) Termination benefits are employee benefits payable as a result of either:

    (i) An enterprise's decision to terminate an employee's employment before the normal retirement date; or

    (ii) An employee's decision to accept voluntary redundancy in exchange for those benefits.

(e) Examples of employee benefits include:

    (i) Short-term employee benefits, such as wages, salaries and social security contributions, paid annual leave and paid sick leave, profit-sharing and bonuses (if payable within 12 months of the end of the period) and non-monetary benefits (such as medical care, housing, cars and free or subsidized goods or services) for current employees;

    (ii) Post-employment benefits such as pensions, other retirement benefits, post-employment life insurance and post-employment medical care; and

    (iii) Other long-term employee benefits, including long-service leave or sabbatical leave, or other long-service benefits, long-term disability benefits and, if they are not payable wholly within 12 months after the end of the period, profit-sharing, bonuses and deferred compensation.

Compilation

(a) Identify the types of benefits provided to employees.

(b) Identify the cost of benefits provided to employee as reported elsewhere in the company's (audited) financial statements, or its internally (audited) management accounts.

Presentation and disclosure

(a) The data on total benefits should be presented providing a breakdown by:

    (i) Payroll and other types of benefits;

    (ii) Major groups of employees as defined by the International Labour Organization's (ILO's) guidance International Standard Classification of Occupations;

    (iii) Type of employment contract (part-time/full-time/other); and

    (iv) Gender.

(b) Additional information may be provided on the type of benefits provided to full-time employees of the organization (e.g. insurance, housing, education, pensions, etc.).

(c) Reasons for any significant variation between the indicators reported and those relating to previous periods should be explained.

7. Total number and rate of employee turnover broken down by gender[115]

Background: Workforce turnover rates can reflect the job security of employees and the employment practices of an enterprise. Important issues should initially be reflected in an enterprise's turnover statistics, which should be compared to industry averages, best practice within the enterprise's industry, or even other industries.

Definition: Turnover: number of employees who leave the organization voluntarily (done or undertaken of one's own free will) or due to dismissal, retirement or death in service.

Compilation

(a) Identify total number of employees leaving employment during the reporting period.

(b) Identify the reason of departure (e.g. individual dismissal, retirement, death, restructuring, etc.).

(c) Calculate the absolute number and rate of employees leaving employment during the reporting period. Rates should be calculated using the total employee numbers at the end of the reporting period.

Presentation and disclosure

(a) The following figures should be presented:

(i) Total turnover of employees;

(ii) Total turnover of employees broken down by reason of departure; and

(iii) Total turnover of employees broken down by gender.

(b) Additional information may be provided on the reasons for retrenchments and dismissals or exceptional levels of employee turnover. Enterprises may also choose to report the total turnover of employees broken down by the following age groups: <30; 30-50; >50.

8. Percentage of employees covered by collective agreements[116]

Background: The right of workers to join or form their own organizations and to bargain collectively with their employer over the conditions of their work is internationally recognized. Whether or not employees exercise these rights in practice varies by location, industry and enterprise. Collective bargaining is recognized as an effective private means for increasing the

---

[115] This indicator is based on GRI indicator LA2, with modifications including a focus on breakdown by gender and reason for departure.

[116] This indicator is based on GRI indicator LA4.

positive social impact of business activity. Collective bargaining is an important form of governance that contributes to development. For those stakeholders who are trying to assess the relationship between management and workers, it is helpful to know how many employees are covered by collective bargaining agreements.

Definitions: This indicator refers to collective bargaining agreements signed by the reporting enterprise itself or by employer organizations of which it is a member. These agreements may be at the sectoral, national, regional, organizational or workplace level.

Compilation

(a) Use data from indicator number 1 above (total workforce) as the basis for calculating percentages for this indicator.

(b) Identify the number of employees covered by collective bargaining agreements.

(c) State the combined number of employees covered as a percentage of the total number of employees.

Presentation and disclosure: Reasons for any significant variation between the indicators reported and those relating to previous periods should be explained.

C. Technology and human resource development

9. Expenditure on research and development

Background: Process and product technologies are often the drivers behind an enterprise's competitive advantage, and such technologies are also acknowledged as a key ingredient in the economic development of host countries.

Definitions[117]

(a) Research:

(i) Basic research: Systematic study directed toward fuller knowledge or understanding of the fundamental aspects of phenomena and of observable facts without specific applications towards processes or products in mind;

(ii) Applied research: Systematic study to gain knowledge or understanding necessary to determine the means by which a recognized and specific need may be met;

---

[117] The definitions are taken from the United States National Science Foundation (www.nsf.gov).

(b) Development: Systematic application of knowledge or understanding, directed toward the production of useful materials, devices, and systems or methods, including design, development, and improvement of prototypes and new processes to meet specific requirements.

Compilation

(a) Research or development costs that:

    (i) Relate to an in-process research or development project acquired separately or in a business combination and recognized as an intangible asset; and

    (ii) Are incurred after the acquisition of that project shall be accounted for in accordance with IAS 38, pp. 54–62.

(b) To assess whether an internally intangible generated asset meets the criteria for recognition, an entity classifies the generation of the asset into a research phase and a development phase.

(c) No intangible asset arising from research (or from the research phase of an internal project) shall be recognized. Cost of research (or on the research phase of an internal project) shall be recognized as an expense when it is incurred.

(d) An intangible asset arising from development (or from the development phase of an internal project) shall be recognized if, and only if, an entity can demonstrate all of the following:

    (i) The technical feasibility of completing the intangible asset so that it will be available for use or sale;

    (ii) Its intention to complete the intangible asset and use or sell it;

    (iii) Its ability to use or sell the intangible asset;

    (iv) How the intangible asset will generate future economic benefits. Among other things, the entity can demonstrate the existence of a market for the output of the intangible asset itself or, if it is to be used internally, the usefulness of the intangible asset;

    (v) The availability of adequate technical, financial and other resources to complete the development and to use or sell the intangible asset; and

    (vi) Its ability to measure reliably the expenditure attributable to the intangible asset during its development.

Presentation and disclosure

(a) Total expenditure on research and development for the reporting entity should be presented as per the definitions and compilation formula above.

(b) Intangible assets arising from development should be disclosed.

(c) Additional information may be included in the presentation, such as an explanation of the reporting enterprise's principal research and development projects, expected results and the expected timeframe of the projects. Further details on significant differences in year-on-year expenditure could also be provided.

10. Average hours of training per year per employee broken down by employee category[118]

Background: One of the ways in which companies can best contribute to the capacity for innovation of local communities is by enabling employees to develop their skills. Training local employees enhances the quality of their employment position. In economic terms, training of employees represents the management's conscious effort to invest in its human resources. In addition, developing employee knowledge, or "know-how", is a key element of the broader development of technology and productivity which fuels enterprise development. Employee training can be measured in two ways: by average hours of training per employee and by expenditure on training per employee (see indicator number 11 below).

Definitions

(a)   Training: This includes all types of vocational training and instruction, paid educational leave provided by the reporting organization for its employees, training or education pursued externally and paid for in whole or in part by the reporting organization, and training on specific topics such as health and safety. It does not include on-site coaching by supervisors.

(b)   Employment category: Major groups of employees as defined by ILO's guidance International Standard Classification of Occupations.

Compilation

(a)   Identify the number of employees for each major group of employment category across the organization's operations at the end of the reporting year. The organization should use the definition of "major group" of employment category set out in ILO's guidance International Standard Classification of Occupations.

(b)   Identify total hours devoted to training personnel within each major group of employment category.

(c)   State the number of hours of training per year per employee by category of employee using the following formula:

$$\text{Average number of hours of training per employee per year per category} = \frac{\text{Total hours of training per year per category}}{\text{Total employees per category}}$$

Presentation and disclosure: The reasons for any significant variation between the indicators reported and those relating to previous periods should be explained. A distinction may be considered between general training focusing on personal development and specific training on knowledge development, e.g. leadership, information technology skills, communication skills, language, teamwork, knowledge, personal growth, etc. In addition, the disclosure of a reference to the employee's own time investment due to following training and preparing for training in their own time may also be considered. Also, information concerning on-the-job training can be disclosed when applicable.

---

[118] This indicator is based on GRI indicator LA10, with modifications including the use of the International Labour Organization International Standard Classification of Occupations to define employee categories.

11. Expenditure on employee training per year per employee broken down by employee category

Background: Expenditure on employee training is another indicator reflecting an enterprise's positive contribution towards the development of human resources.

Definitions

Costs of external and internal vocational training courses:

(a) Fees and payments (to vocational training providers and external trainers): This refers to the total amount paid in fees for external courses or for external trainers or instructors (including those providing internal courses). It also includes payments made to external consultants, assessors or examiners for course-related activities. Any payments made by employers for courses that have been undertaken in employees' own time are included. Fees for training courses undertaken by apprentices or trainees are excluded. Fees and payments for learning material for open and distance courses are, wherever possible, excluded.

(b) Travel and subsistence payments: This refers to actual payments made to cover the travel and subsistence costs of employees participating in vocational training courses. It also includes any additional payments made for time spent travelling to courses.

(c) Labour costs of internal trainers exclusively involved in managing and delivering vocational training courses.

(d) Labour cost of internal trainers, partly involved in managing and delivering vocational training courses. The staff engaged in designing, managing, conducting or supporting vocational training courses, comprising:

 (i) Internal trainers and staff of training centres;

 (ii) Directors and other top managers concerned with training policy;

 (iii) Instructors and training managers or officers; and

 (iv) Clerical/administrative and other personnel supporting these activities.

Anyone dealing solely with apprenticeship training and anyone who is not a member of the normal workforce of the enterprise were excluded. For staff engaged full time in course-related activities, the figures quoted should be the total annual labour costs of all those identified. For staff engaged part time in course-related activities, it should be a proportion of their labour costs, reflecting the proportion of time they spent on course-related activities.

(e) Costs of premises. These costs include:

 (i) The cost of running a training centre (excluding staff labour costs) or any other premises used for vocational training courses;

 (ii) Equipment or materials bought specifically for vocational training courses; and

 (iii) If the training centre or other premises or equipment are used only partly for vocational training courses, (e.g. if used also for training of apprentices), a proportion of the total cost should be included, representing the proportion of time they are used for vocational training courses.

89

(f) Contributions to collective funding arrangements.

(g) Receipts for vocational training courses. Receipts from collective funds, i.e. grants for vocational training courses, and from sources of revenue for vocational training courses like: Receipts from Regional/Sector funds; Receipts from National Funds; Government subsidies; Government rebates on expenditures; Tax concessions on the expenditures; External financial assistance from non-government sources, such as private foundations; Receipts for vocational training courses provided to external bodies and persons.

Compilation

(a) Identify the training costs from the sources, which are known in the enterprise (accounts, data files, minutes, etc.).

(b) Identify estimates of the training costs only if these data were not available.

(c) Calculate the cost using the following formula and provide the data broken down by each major group of employment category across the organization's operations at the end of the reporting year. The organization should use the definition of "major group" of employment category set out in ILO's guidance International Standard Classification of Occupations.

$$\text{Cost of employee training} = \text{Direct costs of training} + \text{Indirect costs of training}$$

(d) Direct costs:

$$\sum \text{Costs described under (52.a) to (52.f)} - \sum \text{Value of receipts, grants, rebates and other concessions and assistance described under (52.g)}$$

Presentation and disclosure: Reasons for any significant variation between the indicators reported and those relating to previous periods should be explained. It should be noted that this indicator can be distorted by the costs of expensive training courses that are provided for a few employees. Additional information may be provided on the type of training, such as general training focusing on personal development and specific training on knowledge development. Additional reference can also be made to employees' own time investment, as well as reference to training on the job.

D.   Health and safety

12.   Cost of employee health and safety

Background: Employee health and safety represent one of the most important corporate responsibility issues confronting organizations. This is particularly true for companies operating in an environment with weak regulatory infrastructure in an inherently hazardous industry. Occupational accidents lower employee productivity, undermine human capital development, divert management attention, and could be symptomatic of poor management quality and lack of adequate internal management systems.

Definitions: Employee safety: occupational safety, occupational health and working environment is related to the following fields (ILO R164, II, 3): (a) design, citing, structural features, installation, maintenance, repair and alteration of workplaces and means of access thereto and progress there from; (b) lighting, ventilation, order and cleanliness of workplaces; (c) temperature, humidity and movement of air in the workplace; (d) design, construction, use, maintenance, testing and inspection of machinery and equipment liable to present hazards and, as appropriate, their approval and transfer; (e) prevention of harmful physical or mental stress due to conditions of work; (f) handling, stacking and storage of loads and materials, manually or mechanically; (g) use of electricity; (h) manufacture, packing, labelling, transport, storage and use of dangerous substances and agents, disposal of their wastes and residues, and, as appropriate, their replacement by other substances or agents which are not dangerous or which are less dangerous; (i) radiation protection; (j) prevention and control of, and protection against, occupational hazards due to noise and vibration; (k) control of the atmosphere and other ambient factors of workplaces; (l) prevention and control of hazards due to high and low barometric pressures; (m) prevention of fires and explosions and measures to be taken in case of fire or explosion; (n) design, manufacture, supply, use, maintenance and testing of personal protective equipment and protective clothing; (o) sanitary installations, washing facilities, facilities for changing and storing clothes, supply of drinking water, and any other welfare facilities connected with occupational safety and health; (p) first-aid treatment; (q) establishment of emergency plans; and (r) supervision of the health of workers.

Compilation

(a)   Identify the company's cost of occupational safety and health-related insurance programmes (when such programmes exist). Do not include in this figure expenditures on employee health insurance programmes, as this should be included in employee benefits (indicator 6). Include a distinction between operating costs and investments.

(b)   Identify the company's cost of health care activities financed directly by the company as such, either through self-insurance or in operating the company's own health care facilities.

(c)   Identify the company's cost incurred on working environment issues related to occupational safety and health (see "employee safety" under definitions below).

(d)   Calculate the company's total cost of employee health and safety by adding up the figures obtained in identification steps (a) through (c) in paragraph 53. (Note: Costs of training should not be included in this figure.)

Presentation and disclosure: The disclosure should include the details of compilation items (a), (b), and (c) in paragraph 53 above, as well as the total (item d).

13. Work days lost due to occupational accidents, injuries and illness[119]

Background: Work days lost due to occupational accidents, injuries and illness can reflect the degree to which the enterprise contributes to creating a healthy, safe and productive work environment.

Definitions

(a) Occupational injury: A non-fatal or fatal injury arising out of or in the course of work.

(b) Occupational disease: A disease arising from the work situation or activity (e.g. stress or regular exposure to harmful chemicals), or from a work-related injury.

(c) Fatality: The death of a worker occurring in the current reporting period, arising from an occupational injury or disease sustained or contracted while in the reporting organization's employ.

(d) Lost day: Time ("days") that could not be worked (and is thus "lost") as a consequence of a worker or workers being unable to perform their usual work because of an occupational accident or disease.

(e) Lost day rate: Refers to the impact of occupational accidents and diseases, as reflected in time off work by the affected workers. It is expressed by comparing the total lost days against the total number of hours scheduled to be worked by the workforce in the reporting period.

Compilation

(a) This indicator should provide a breakdown according to:

   (i) The total workforce (i.e. total employees, plus supervised contract workers); and

   (ii) Independent contractors working on site towards whom the reporting organization owes liability for the general safety of the working environment.

(b) Data on "lost days" should be based on the definitions under the national law of the country in which the lost days took place. In calculation of lost days, it should be noted: (i) whether "days" means "calendar days" or "scheduled work days"; and (ii) at what point the "lost days" count begins (e.g. the day after the accident or three days after the accident).

(c) State lost day rate (LDR) by calculating as follows:

$$\text{LDR per 100 employees} = \frac{\text{No. of lost days}}{\text{Hours worked}} \times 200{,}000$$

   Note: The factor 200,000 is derived from 50 working weeks at 40 hours per 100 employees. By using this factor, the resulting rate is related to the number of employees and not the number of hours.

---

[119] This indicator is based on GRI indicator LA7, with modifications including a focus on LDR and fatality statistics.

Presentation and disclosure

(a) Present the data used in compiling the lost day rate. The breakdown of data on total workforce and independent contractors may be presented in a table.

(b) Reasons for any significant variation between the indicators reported and those relating to previous periods should be explained.

(c) Report fatalities in the reporting period using an absolute number, not a rate.

E.   Government and community contributions

14.   Payments to Government

Background: Enterprises make a significant economic contribution to government finances in the form of taxes, royalties and other fees paid to Governments. This is particularly important for some industries which do not have large payrolls or strong business linkages, and whose principal contribution to economic development is in the form of taxes and other payments to Governments.

Definitions

(a) Current tax is the amount of income taxes payable (recoverable) in respect of the taxable profit (tax loss) for a period.[120]

(b) Payments to the Government exclude acquisition of government assets (e.g. purchase of formerly state-owned enterprises).

Compilation

(a) All company taxes and related tax penalties cost at the national and local levels. This should include corporate tax, income tax, property tax, excise duties, value added tax, local rates and other levies and taxes, but exclude deferred taxes.

(b) All royalties, license fees, and other payments to Government.

(c) All fees paid included should be on a cash-paid basis.

(d) Excluded from this figure should be penalties and fines for non-compliance issues unrelated to tax payment (e.g. environmental pollution).

---

[120] The definition of current taxes is not restricted to income taxes, but also refers to excise duties, value added taxes, local rates, and other levies and taxes.

(e) Excluded from this figure should be any payments for government assets, e.g. the acquisition of a state-owned enterprise, government land, etc.

Presentation and disclosure

(a) Present the total amount related to reporting year with a distinction between amounts *paid* to the Government and amounts *payable* to the Government.

(b) Present the information, in conjunction with a breakdown of the major categories of payments (e.g. income taxes, customs duties, royalties, etc.).

15. Voluntary contributions to civil society

Many enterprises support the communities in which they operate through the voluntary donation of cash, goods and services. These direct contributions can result in significant positive contributions, for example, to the development of local infrastructure such as schools and hospitals, as well as the provision of emergency relief in times of natural disaster. This indicator reflects an enterprise's voluntary contributions to the community.

Definition: Voluntary contributions are charitable donations and investments of funds in the broader community where the target beneficiaries are external to the company. These include contributions to charities, non-governmental organizations and research institutes (not related to the company's commercial research and development), funds to support community infrastructure (e.g. education, medical and or recreation facilities) and direct costs of social programmes (including arts and educational events). The amount included should account for actual expenditures in the reporting period, not commitments.

Compilation

(a) Voluntary contributions are recognized as an expense when they are paid and are not deductible for tax purposes.

(b) For infrastructure investments, the calculation of the total investment should include costs for ancillary, related or incidental goods and labour, in addition to capital costs. For support of ongoing facilities or programmes (e.g. an organization funds the daily operations of a public facility), the reported investment should include operating costs.

(c) The infrastructure investment excludes legal and commercial activities. Any infrastructure investment which is primarily driven by core business needs (e.g. building a road to a mine or factory) or to facilitate the business operations of the organization, should not be included. The calculation of investment may include infrastructure built outside the main business activities of the reporting organization, such as a school or hospital for employees and their families.

Presentation and disclosure: The total amount should be presented for the reporting period, together with an itemization of major contributions or categories of contributions (e.g. education, health and arts).

F.   Corruption

16.   Number of convictions for violations of corruption-related laws or regulations and amount of fines paid/payable

Background: Corruption is internationally recognized as an obstacle to economic development and a hindrance to international trade and investment. Corporations can make a positive contribution to respect for anti-corruption laws and international norms by ensuring that they are not involved in corruption. A basic measurable performance indicator in this regard is the number of legal infractions a company incurs as a result of corrupt practices. This indicator can provide useful information to stakeholders about legal liabilities and areas of the enterprise's internal control that require attention.

Definitions

(a) Corruption: The Organization for Economic Cooperation and Development (OECD) defines corruption as the "active or passive misuse of the powers of public officials (appointed or elected) for private financial or other benefits".

(b) Bribery: The offering, promising, giving or accepting of any undue pecuniary or other advantage to or by (a) a public official, at the national, local or international level; (b) a political party, party official or candidate; and (c) a director, officer, employee or agent of a private enterprise; in order to obtain or retain a business or other improper advantage, e.g. in connection with regulatory permits, taxation, customs, judicial and legislative proceedings.

(c) Extortion or solicitation: The demanding of a bribe, whether or not coupled with a threat if the demand is refused. "Bribery" as used in these rules shall include extortion.

Compilation

(a) Identify all convictions for violations of corruption related laws or regulations.

(b) Identify the amount of fines paid/payable.

Presentation and disclosure

(a) The total number of convictions should be presented together with the total amount of fines paid and or payable.

(b) Additional information would be an itemization of individual fines or penalties, along with an indication of the particular regulation or law violated.

(c) The enterprise may also provide information about any actions taken in response to incidents of corruption, for example new or revised enterprise policies to prevent such incidents.

III. Conclusion

In accordance with the agreed conclusions of the twenty-third session of the group of experts, the UNCTAD secretariat is presenting for consideration by the twenty-fourth session of ISAR this detailed work on measurement methodology with a view towards finalizing ISAR's guidance on voluntary disclosures in this subject area. The group of experts may choose to recommend dissemination of this document, combined with the contents of TD/B/COM.2/ISAR/42, as a voluntary technical tool aimed towards improving the comparability and relevance of corporate responsibility reporting in annual reports. A technical tool such as this could be used by enterprises to improve their corporate reporting, by other organizations working on corporate responsibility reporting to further inform their work, and as a benchmark for research on corporate disclosures in this area.

Annex I

Additional definitions

Except where noted, the following definitions are taken from the IFRS glossary of terms produced by the International Accounting Standards Board.

Accrual basis: The effects of transactions and other events are recognized when they occur (and not as cash or its equivalent is received or paid) and they are recorded in the accounting records and reported in the financial statements of the periods to which they relate.

Cost: The amount of cash or cash equivalents paid or the fair value of the other consideration given to acquire an asset at the time of its acquisition or construction or, when applicable, the amount attributed to that asset when initially recognized in accordance with the specific requirements of other IFRSs.

Expenditures:[121] A decrease in an asset (usually cash) or an increase in a liability (often accounts payable) associated with the incurrence of a cost. The expenditures in an accounting period equal the cost of all the goods and services acquired in that period.

Expenses: Decreases in economic benefits during the accounting period in the form of outflows or depletions of assets or incurrences of liabilities that result in decreases in equity, other than those relating to distributions to equity participants.

Revenue: The gross inflow of economic benefits during the period arising in the course of the ordinary activities of an entity when those inflows result in increases in equity, other than increases relating to contributions from equity participants.

---

[121] The term "expenditures" is not defined by the IASB. This definition is taken from Anthony, Reece and Hertenstein (1995) *Accounting Text and Cases*, ninth edition.

Annex II

Additional references

References by indicator

1. Total revenues: Applicable accounting standards, such as International Financial Reporting Standards (IFRS) 18 and IFRS 7 on revenues and fair value, respectively, could be consulted.

2. Value of imports vs. exports: Balance of payments manual of the International Monetary Fund; European Balance of Payments/International Investment Position Statistical Methods.

5. Total workforce: ILO International Classification of Status in Employment; ILO Key Indicators of the Labour Market; ILO Laborstat Internet Indicators. Number of female employees: The OECD Guidelines for Multinational Enterprises, Chapter IV Employment and Industrial Relations, Article d); ILO C111 Discrimination (Employment and Occupation) Convention (1958), Article 1.

6. Employee wages and benefits: Applicable accounting standards, such as IAS 19 on Employee Benefits, could be consulted. Ratio of male to female wages and benefits: The OECD Guidelines for Multinational Enterprises, Chapter IV Employment and Industrial Relations, Article d); ILO C111 Discrimination (Employment and Occupation) Convention (1958), Article 1.

7. Percentage of employees represented by independent trade union organizations or covered by collective bargaining agreements: ILO Convention 87, "Freedom of Association and Protection of the Right to Organize", 1948; ILO Convention 98, "Right to Organize and Collective Bargaining", 1949; ILO Convention 135, "Workers' Representatives Convention", 1971; ILO Convention 154, "Collective Bargaining Convention", 1981; and Recommendations 91, "Collective Agreements Recommendation' 1951, and 163, "Collective Bargaining Recommendation", 1981; ILO Declaration on Fundamental Principles and Rights at Work, 86th Session, 1998, Article 2 (a); OECD Guidelines for Multinational Enterprises, Section IV, Paragraph 2 (a).

8. Research or development expenditure and tangible assets: IAS 38.

9. Average hours of training per year per employee broken down by employee category: ILO International Standard Classification of Occupations (ISCO-88); ILO Convention 142, "Human Resources Development Convention", 1975; ILO Convention 140, "Paid Educational Leave Convention", 1974; ILO Convention 155, "Occupational Safety and Health Convention", 1981; OECD Guidelines for Multinational Enterprises, Revision 2000, Articles II, 4 & IV, 2 (c), 3 and 5; ILO R117, "Vocational Training Recommendation", 1962.

10. Expenditure on employee training per year per employee broken down by employee category: ILO International Standard Classification of Occupations (ISCO-88); ILO Convention 142, "Human Resources Development Convention", 1975; ILO Convention 140, "Paid Educational Leave Convention", 1974; ILO Convention 155, "Occupational Safety and Health

Convention", 1981; OECD Guidelines for Multinational Enterprises, Revision 2000, Articles II, 4 & IV, 2 (c), 3 and 5; ILO R117, "Vocational Training Recommendation", 1962; European Commission, European social statistics Continuing vocational training survey (CVTS2).

11. Cost of employee health and safety: OECD publication "A system of health accounts"; ILO C155 Occupational Safety and Health Convention, 1981; ILO P155 Protocol of 2002 to the Occupational Safety and Health Convention, 1981; ILO R164 Occupational Safety and Health Recommendation, 1981; International classification for health accounts (ICHA); World Health Organisation "Guide to producing national health accounts", Annex B.

12. Work days lost due to occupational accidents, injuries and illness: ILO Convention 155, "Occupational Health and Safety Convention" and Protocol 155, 1981; ILO Code of Practice on Recording and Notification of Occupational Accidents and Diseases, 1995.

13. Payments to Government: Applicable accounting standards, such as IAS 12 on Income Taxes; IAS 7 on Cash Flow statements; and IAS 19 on Employee Benefits, could be consulted.

14. Number of convictions for violations of corruption-related laws or regulations and amount of fines paid/payable: OECD Convention of Combating Bribery of Foreign Public Officials; OECD Recommendation on Combating Bribery in International Business Transactions; OECD Recommendation on the Tax Deductibility of Bribes to Foreign Public Officials; International Criminal Court (ICC) Report on Extortion and Bribery in Business Transactions; ICC Commission on Anti-Corruption "Fighting Corruption: A Corporate Practices Manual"; United Nations Convention against Corruption.

Annex III

Members of the 2007 ad hoc consultative group[122]
Chairperson of the 2007 ad hoc consultative group:

Ms. Nancy Kamp–Roelands - Ernst & Young, Netherlands

Members of the 2007 ad hoc consultative group:

Mr. Sean Ansett – Independent Consultant, Spain
Ms. Geneviève Besse – European Commission, Belgium
Ms. Jesse Dillard – Portland State University, Oregon, United States
Mr. Damir Dragičević – Global Reporting Initiative, Netherlands
Mr. Burkhard Feldman – Ciba Specialty Chemicals, Switzerland
Mr. Stephen Gardner – Baylor University, Texas, United States
Mr. Stephen Hine – Ethical Investment Research Services, United Kingdom
Mr. Dwight Justice – International Trade Union Confederation, Belgium
Mr. Douglas Kativu – African Institute of Corporate Citizenship, South Africa
Mr. Michael Kelly – KPMG, United Kingdom
Mr. Robert Langford – Independent Consultant, United Kingdom
Ms. Barbara Leon – International Organization of Employers, Switzerland
Ms. Marcelle Colares Oliveira – University of Fortaleza, Brazil
Mr. David Pritchett – PricewaterhouseCoopers, United Kingdom
Ms. Emily Sims – International Labour Organization, Switzerland
Ms. Aracéli Cristina de Sousa Ferreira – Universidade Federal do Rio de Janeiro, Brazil
Mr. Peter Utting – United Nations Research Institute for Social Development, Switzerland
Mr. Mark Vesser – Ernst & Young, Switzerland

---

[122] The views contained in this document do not necessarily reflect those of the organizations with which the members of the ad hoc consultative group are affiliated.

The information needs of stakeholders and the selection criteria for core indicators

I. Introduction

It was agreed at the twenty-third session of ISAR that "UNCTAD should further refine and finalize the guidance on selected corporate responsibility indicators and their measurement methodology with a view to providing a voluntary technical tool for enterprises" (TD/B/COM.2/ISAR/35). This document presents an overview of an enterprise's stakeholders and their information needs, and provides useful background on the selection criteria and guiding principles employed by ISAR in the development of corporate responsibility indicators. The material presented in this report is based on material previously presented to the twenty-second session of ISAR in the report TD/B/COM.2/ISAR/29. It forms an integral part of the report "Guidance on corporate responsibility indicators in annual reports" (TD/B/COM.2/ISAR/38), and should be considered in conjunction with that report.

Among the guiding principles discussed in this document are three key dimensions which evolved during the deliberations of the group of experts:

(a) The development dimension;

(b) The performance orientation; and

(c) The focus on national reporting.

At its twenty-first session, the group noted that UNCTAD XI had provided a broader context in which the issue of corporate responsibility could be addressed. In particular it was agreed that "such information could also reflect corporate contributions to the economic and social development of host countries, as well as the need for capacity building" (TD/B/COM.2/ISAR/26). The development dimension of corporate responsibility reporting was again emphasized at ISAR's twenty-second session, where it was agreed that this work "should continue to reflect corporate contributions to the economic and social development of host countries" (TD/B/COM.2/ISAR/31). This emphasis on the development dimension of corporate responsibility has also been complemented by an emphasis on performance-oriented indicators. At ISAR's twenty-third session, the group of experts recognized "the increased interest among corporate responsibility reporters in creating more concise, more useful and more performance-oriented reports" (TD/B/COM.2/ISAR/35). A third key dimension of ISAR's work on corporate responsibility reporting arose during deliberations at the twenty-second session of ISAR, where it was emphasized that the indictors should focus on national reporting. It was noted that national reports were more useful for stakeholders interested in specific countries; it was also noted that users could, if they chose, aggregate national reports to a regional or global level.

While environmental issues are also recognized as an important feature of corporate responsibility, this project does not focus on environmental issues, as ISAR has previously conducted extensive work in this area. In 1989, ISAR took up the topic of corporate environmental accounting. In the following years, several recommendations were published in this area: (a) the 1999 report *Accounting and Financial Reporting for Environmental Costs and Liabilities* (UNCTAD/ITE/EDS/4); (b) the 2000 report *Integrating Environmental and Financial*

Performance at the Enterprise Level (UNCTAD/ITE/TED/1); and (c) the 2004 manual *Eco-Efficiency Indicators* (UNCTAD/ITE/IPC/2003/7). The five eco-efficiency indicators identified in the 2004 manual are listed in the annex.

II.   Stakeholders and their information needs

The concept of corporate responsibility draws upon the strategic management theory that says managers can add value to an enterprise by taking into account the social and economic effects of an enterprise's operations when making decisions.[1] This theory claims that managers can best promote the long-term viability of an enterprise by balancing the needs of its stakeholders with the financial requirements of sustaining and growing a business. Reporting on an enterprise's performance in this area is therefore a means to provide shareholders and other stakeholders (as well as managers themselves) an account of an enterprise's impact on society. This added transparency can lead to greater accountability of the enterprise to its principal stakeholders.

Enterprises should demonstrate how and to what extent they fulfil their responsibilities toward their stakeholders. These responsibilities are often, though not exhaustively, described and defined in existing regulations, codes, laws and international agreements. As organs of society, enterprises are increasingly being called upon to demonstrate support for both international law as well as internationally-agreed normative statements; this is most clearly reflected in the United Nations Global Compact. Failure to meet society's expectations in these areas may undermine an enterprise's license to operate or public acceptability.

Stakeholders are understood as groups of persons that are affected by and/or can influence an enterprise, without necessarily holding an equity share of the enterprise. Their actions can affect an enterprise's brand and reputation, its financial performance, and even its license to operate.

Communicating with stakeholders and ascertaining their views, therefore, is very important for enabling enterprises to provide relevant information. In doing so, enterprises ought to consider that the perception of usefulness and the use of such reporting are highly specific to the target group. To identify key issues, enterprises may engage in stakeholder dialogue. This can be done in several ways, for example by community panels, staff surveys, industrial relations, consumer surveys, opinion polls, workshops with combined stakeholder dialogues on specific issues, and meetings with external experts. Another method is providing stakeholders with contact details and/or comment or feedback forms in published reports or by employing company websites to encourage stakeholders to give input about the information they are interested in and about their opinions on the company's behaviour.[2]

Presented below are key stakeholder groups and their information needs:

(a)   Investors and financial institutions;

(b)   Business partners;

(c)   Consumers;

---

[1]   Freeman RE (1984). *Strategic Management: A Stakeholder Approach*. New York, Pitman.
[2]   For example, the "Tell Shell" portion of the Shell Group's website www.shell.com.

(d)   Employees;

(e)   Surrounding community;

(f)   Civil society organizations; and

(g)   Governments and their institutions.

This list mainly comprises groups already identified as users of financial reports, for example by the International Accounting Standards Board.[3] It is expected that the inclusion of corporate responsibility information into annual reports would not only provide existing users with additional useful information, but would also broaden the scope of users to include additional stakeholder groups with a particular interest in the impact of the enterprise on society.

Investors and financial institutions: The financial markets consist of various stakeholders, including shareholders, lenders, banks, rating agencies and analysts. While there are differences with regard to the information requirements of these entities, there is nevertheless a growing recognition within this stakeholder category of the importance of non-financial information, including corporate responsibility information, in the evaluation of long-term enterprise performance. The differences that do exist are largely dependent upon the time-frame of the various investor groups: whereas short-term investors may not take much interest in corporate responsibility reporting, long-term investors, such as pension funds, are increasingly interested in such reporting in order to better judge future opportunities, risks, legal liabilities, and the general quality of management. Additionally, there are factors beyond time-frame driving demand for more reporting on these issues. For example, there are non-financial pressures on pension fund trustees to align the social values of pension fund beneficiaries with the social performance of the companies in which the fund invests.[4] Another example would be the growth of "socially responsible investment" funds that base their investments on social and environmental information, as well as financial information.[5]

Non-financial performance indicators are taken into account by financial institutions when valuing companies, in particular from the perspective of risk assessment. In general, financial institutions seek information enabling them to assess both the current and future performance of an enterprise. Typically, they are not primarily concerned with improving corporate responsibility issues; rather, their concern is about the material impact these issues can have on the valuation of a company.

Corporate responsibility information required by the financial sector includes the financial consequences of such issues, the overall strategy of an enterprise, its risk and reputation management, compliance with laws and regulations, the consequences of plant additions or closures and similar decisions. In benchmarking exercises (for example, when financial

---

[3]   The International Accounting Standards Board identifies users of general purpose financial statements in its framework. It includes present and potential investors, employees, lenders, suppliers and other trade creditors, customers, Governments and their agencies and the public. IASB (2005). *Framework for the Preparation and Presentation of Financial Statements.* www.iasb.org.

[4]   The United Nations Environment Programme Finance Initiative project, the "The principles for responsible investment" is a reflection of non-financial pressures driving demand for social reporting (www.unpri.org).

[5]   Further information on socially responsible investment (SRI) funds in the United States, for example, can be obtained from the Social Investment Forum, an SRI industry association (www.socialinvest.org).

institutions select enterprises for inclusion in social–ethical investment funds or indices) information needs to be presented in a way that allows comparisons.

Business partners: Business partners include potential or existing joint venture partners, suppliers and customers. They are particularly interested in the enterprise from the point of view of business relationships. Enterprises that use corporate responsibility reporting as part of the due diligence on a future business partner, or a target of future merger or acquisition, need information that enables them to assess risks that might impact the enterprise's operations. They would like to know how the enterprise addresses corporate responsibility issues, including labour practices, human rights, legal compliance and fair business practices (e.g. anti-corruption, anti-trust, respect for contracts, technology transfer, fair pricing and timely payment of invoices). This information should relate to both the enterprise as well as the key business partners making up the extended value chain of that enterprise. An important element of this information would be disclosure on governance and management systems in place to address corporate responsibility issues.

Consumers: Consumers are interested in information on product safety measures, the effect of products on health, product quality, product liability and warranty, new product development, and the manufacturing process of products. Interest in the manufacturing process includes information about the circumstances in which products are produced, for example, information on working conditions. Consumers would not be limited to "present and future", but would also include former consumers who have a stake in product liability and product warranty issues arising from past purchases.

Employees: An enterprise's present and future employees are interested in remuneration, plans and intentions of the business, job prospects, working conditions, health and safety, industrial relations, the management of risks, and personnel development opportunities. An enterprise's former employees, to the extent that they receive pension and other retirement benefits from the enterprise, also have an interest in the enterprise's present and future financial condition. Trade unions, as representatives of employees, already have access to employee-related information, at least for those enterprises with which they are affiliated. However, they may still find disclosure on employee issues useful to benchmark against other enterprises, industries or countries.

Surrounding community: Issues related to economic development are often the primary area of interest for an enterprise's surrounding community. This includes questions about jobs, contributions to the tax base, and the secondary impact of an enterprise (through local business linkages and the multiplier effect of the local payroll). Equally among a community's primary interests are issues related to the management of local health, safety and security risks and information on community complaints about corporate activities and how these are dealt with. In regard to security risks, communities have a natural interest in positive corporate contributions to the avoidance of human rights abuses, especially in the assurance that armed enterprise security is the subject of proper training and supervision. In some contexts, the local community may also have concerns about the impact of an enterprise's operations on local culture. Such impacts can result from the introduction of new products or services, or from the generation of internal migration.

Civil society organizations: Civil society organizations, especially activist and relief-oriented non-governmental organizations, use the information in corporate responsibility reports, among other things, as a basis for dialogue with the reporting enterprise. The interest of civil society organizations covers a wide range of corporate responsibility issues, including labour practice, human rights, anti-corruption, economic development and environmental protection. Civil society organizations are particularly interested in information that allows for benchmarking, or relative comparison, of an enterprise's performance in this area. They also seek information on corporate responsibility policy and implementation.

Governments and their institutions: Governments are interested in the way in which enterprises assume responsibilities toward society, in the voluntary initiatives of enterprises in this field and in the impact of enterprise's social engagement. Governments need such information to help them formulate social and economic policies, as well as to help identify gaps in regulation and enforcement. Some government offices also use such information to influence their choice of suppliers.

III. Criteria for the selection of core indicators

A. Quality characteristics

Drawing a parallel to the existing financial reporting framework that provides principles underlying the usefulness of companies' reported information, the following quality criteria should be taken into account in selecting indicators that meet the common needs of a wide range of users of corporate responsibility reporting:

(a) Comparability;

(b) Relevance and materiality;

(c) Understandability; and

(d) Reliability and verifiability.

Comparability: Users should be able to compare the indicators over time and between enterprises to enable them to identify and analyse the outcome of changes in policy and management. For purposes of comparison over time, it is important to disclose corresponding information for the preceding periods. If changes are made in the measurement, presentation or classification of information, comparative figures should be adjusted, unless it is not practical to do so. The reason for a change should be explained by means of notes, and where it is not practical to adjust comparatives, the reason for that should also be explained, as should the nature of the changes that would be required.

Relevance and materiality: To be useful, information should be relevant in meeting the needs of users in forming an opinion or decision. Information has the quality of relevance when it influences the opinion or decision of users by helping them to evaluate past, present or future events, or confirming or correcting their past evaluations.

The relevance of information is affected by its nature and materiality. In some cases, the nature of the information alone is sufficient to determine its relevance. In other cases, both the nature and materiality, as expressed in the relative quantitative variables, is important. Relevance, moreover, often depends on the circumstances relating to topics and recent events. Therefore, it could be relevant to provide more details such as a breakdown by a specific category or other details in relation to some of the indicators.

Information is material if its omission or misstatement could influence users' decisions. Materiality depends on the size of the item or error judged in the particular circumstances of its omission or misstatement. Thus, it provides a threshold or cut-off point rather than being a primary qualitative characteristic which information must have if it is to be useful. If enterprises choose not to include an indicator due to materiality considerations, the enterprise is encouraged to state the reasons why.

There is presently still much discussion as how to develop further guidance on a consistent application of the concept of materiality as it relates to non-financial reporting.[6] The management of the enterprise is responsible for making adequate decisions with respect to the application of the materiality principle and its effects on the content of its corporate responsibility reporting. The decision-making process of the enterprise's management in relation to materiality should preferably have a structured and substantiated process that is consistently applied to determine what information it considers to be of material importance and therefore for inclusion in its reporting. This could include (a) internal consultations with responsible officers, supervisory boards and/or audit committees; (b) identification of and consultations with important stakeholder groups; (c) considerations of particular issues that play a role in politics and public debate associated with an enterprise's activities, products and locations; and (d) specific industry reporting guidelines. This decision-making process about reporting materiality should be sufficiently transparent and understandable for third parties, and preferably be disclosed in the reporting of an enterprise.

Understandability: The information on corporate responsibility must be understandable to the reader. This means that the manner of presentation has to be in keeping with the knowledge and experience of users, and should include the following: (a) a good design; (b) systematic classification of topics and indicators; (c) concise use of language; and (d) an explanation of unknown terms in the text, or the inclusion of a glossary to enhance understandability. Relevance takes priority over understandability, but the two concepts should not be seen as mutually exclusive. Information about complex matters that is relevant to users is not to be omitted merely on the grounds that it may be too difficult for some users to understand. For a proper interpretation, these indicators would have to be reported in the appropriate context, such as information on related policies, management systems and past performance. It would also be helpful to make use of targets, both for measuring past performance relative to past targets and for providing forecasts of future performance.

Reliability and verifiability: Information has the quality of reliability when it is free from material error and bias, and when it gives a true, complete and balanced view of the actual situation. The information should be faithful and representative of the actual situation in the business, complete within the boundaries of what is relevant, well-balanced on both positive and negative events, presented in the right context, and free of material misstatement. It should be neutral (free from bias). Corporate responsibility reporting is not neutral if, by the selection or presentation of information, it influences the making of a decision or judgment in order to achieve a predetermined result or outcome.

---

[6]   See, for example, the deliberations of the United Kingdom Department of Trade and Industry in the publication, *The Operating and Financial Review Working Group on Materiality: A Consultation Document* (www.dti.gov.uk).

The indicator selected should allow for internal or external verification. The indicator should enable comparison with underlying evidence.

B. Guiding principles

ISAR (during its twenty-first and twenty-second sessions) identified the following five principles that could be used in selecting core indicators on corporate responsibility reporting:

(a) Universality to maximize comparability: The indicators would in principle apply to all enterprises, regardless of sector, size or location, the intention being to maximize the comparability of reported information.

(b) Incremental approach: This means that selected indicators should first address issues that an enterprise has control over and for which it already gathers, or has access to, relevant information.

(c) Capability of consistent measurement: The selected indicators should be able to be recognized, measured and presented in a consistent way. This enables comparison over time and across entities.

(d) Performance orientation rather than process orientation: The selected indicators should assist users of corporate reports to identify areas of corporate responsibility that require attention, and to measure the performance of the organization in addressing these areas. The social impact of business operations cannot be assessed solely on the basis of the management processes and policies adopted by enterprises in the context of corporate responsibility.

(e) National reporting and positive corporate contributions to development: Indicators should help to analyse positive corporate contributions to the economic and social development of the country in which it operates. For this reason, indicators should be reported on a nationally consolidated basis, so that they are useful to stakeholders within a specific country, and so that the indicators can be understood within the context of a specific country. In the selection of the indicators, consideration was given to UNCTAD's work on corporate contributions to development (TD/B/COM.2/EM.17/2).

C. Constraints

ISAR recognized (during its twenty-first session) the following constraints in selecting core topics and indicators on corporate responsibility reporting:

(a) Costs and benefits: The measurement of indicators and the provision of additional information in relation to indicators should not impose an unreasonable burden on enterprises, particularly those in developing countries and in the small and medium-sized enterprise sector. The incremental approach helps to address this issue through a focus on indicators that can be derived from data that enterprises already gather or have access to in their regular course of business, without incurring significant additional costs.

(b) Confidentiality: The confidentiality of commercial information is often a crucial practical consideration for the success of an enterprise. Therefore, the selection of indicators should respect the confidentiality of commercial data, as well as the confidentiality of any enterprise data that relates to the right to privacy of natural persons (e.g. employee data). However, if a particular indicator is deemed to be material to the needs of stakeholders, then materiality could take precedence over commercial confidentiality, where this does not conflict with legal requirements to keep the information confidential.

(c) Timeliness: If there is undue delay in the reporting of information, it may lose its relevance. Conversely, if the reporting is delayed until all aspects are known, the information may be highly reliable but of little use to users who have had to make decisions in the interim. For the timeliness (and hence frequency) of reporting, the enterprise has to find a balance between relevance and reliability. The overriding consideration in this respect is how the information needs of users can best be met.

IV. Conclusion

In accordance with the agreed conclusions of the twenty-third session of the group of experts, the UNCTAD secretariat is presenting for consideration by the twenty-fourth session of ISAR this report on corporate responsibility reporting with a view towards finalizing ISAR's guidance on voluntary disclosures in this subject area. ISAR may choose to integrate this document with the detailed reporting methodology presented in the document TD/B/COM.2/ISAR/38 and disseminate the combined work as a voluntary technical tool on corporate responsibility reporting in annual reports. A technical tool such as this could be used by enterprises in improving their corporate reporting, by other organizations working on corporate responsibility reporting to further inform their work, and as a benchmark for research on corporate disclosures in this area.

Annex

Eco-efficiency indicators

(a)   Water consumption per net value added;

(b)   Global warming contribution per unit of net value added;

(c)   Energy requirement per unit of net value added;

(d)   Dependency on ozone-depleting substances per unit of net value added; and

(e)   Waste generated per unit of net value added.

For more information on eco-efficiency indicators, please see the UNCTAD publication *A Manual for the Preparers and Users of Eco-Efficiency Indicators* (UNCTAD/ITE/IPC/2003/7).

Chapter VI

2007 Review of the implementation status of corporate governance disclosures

Summary of discussions

Under the agenda item "other business" during the 24th session of ISAR, the Chair introduced the subject of corporate governance disclosure and gave the floor to a member of the Secretariat who presented the findings of the "2007 Review of the Implementation Status of Corporate Governance Disclosures: an inventory of disclosure requirements in 25 emerging markets" (TD/B/COM.2/ISAR/CRP.6). The Secretariat highlighted a number of important trends influencing corporate governance (CG) disclosure, including: increased pressure on investment funds and other institutional investors to disclose their voting on proxy statements; the impact of electronic technologies on shareholder voting and CG disclosure; increasing convergence among national CG standards around the world; and a global wave of stock exchange mergers that is adding pressure for convergence in CG practices. The Secretariat also presented the findings of the 2007 review, which showed that nearly all of the 25 markets in the study required the disclosure of more than half of the 53 items in the ISAR benchmark on good practices in CG disclosure.

Following this presentation the Chair introduced one professor from China and one professor from Egypt who had each conducted a country level case study using the ISAR benchmark on good practices in CG disclosure. These country case studies highlighted the reporting practices of enterprises in both countries, providing an indication of what information is being disclosed. In addition to these presentations the Chair introduced a panel of experts to discuss corporate governance disclosure around the world. The panellists commended the Secretariat's 2007 survey and the case studies of Egypt and China. The panellists also highlighted a number of key issues in CG disclosure, including: the role of CG disclosure requirements in the development of stock exchanges and capital markets; the challenge and need for measuring the quality of CG disclosure; the need for guidance for SMEs on this subject; and the increasing integration of environmental and social issues into the broader corporate governance framework.

After the panellists had made their presentations, the Chair opened the floor and a broad discussion on the subject of corporate governance disclosure ensued. Several delegates commented on the Secretariat's 2007 inventory of disclosure requirements, recognizing its usefulness and making suggestions for future research in this area. Some delegates considered the possibility of whether or not an international corporate governance disclosure standard might be developed in the future to harmonize disclosure practices around the world. Some topical issues also arose in the discussion, such as the current sub-prime mortgage problems which are causing problems for financial institutions around the world; in this context, questions arose about the ability of disclosure to keep abreast of rapidly evolving and complex financial instruments. The Group also heard discussions of the role of regulators in requiring disclosure and how this might be balanced with market based voluntary initiatives. The Group concluded their discussion with calls for the Secretariat to continue its work in this area.

I. Introduction

Corporate governance has been a key area of work for the Intergovernmental Working Group of Experts on International Standards of Accounting and Reporting (ISAR) since 1989 (E/C.10/AC.3/1989/6). Since the twenty-first session of ISAR, the Group of Experts has request an annual review of the implementation status of corporate governance disclosure. Annual reviews were presented at the twenty-first, twenty-second and twenty-third sessions of ISAR. At the twenty-third session, ISAR considered the document 2006 Review of the Implementation Status of Corporate Governance Disclosures (TD/B/COM.2/ISAR/CRP.3, hereafter the "2006 Review").

This 2007 Review, the fourth annual Review conducted on this subject, uses as a benchmark ISAR's conclusions on corporate governance disclosure found in the 2006 UNCTAD publication *Guidance on Good Practices in Corporate Governance Disclosure*. This 2007 Review broadens the scope of research presented in 2005 and 2006. While those earlier Reviews examined the actual reporting practices of enterprises, based on their public reports, the present Review examines the disclosure related requirements of Government and stock exchange regulations. Thus, while the 2005 and 2006 Reviews were studies of what enterprises were actually reporting, the present study is an examination of what publicly listed enterprises are required to report. This new line of enquiry is expected to complement the earlier studies and present a broader picture of the implementation status of corporate governance disclosure.

The objectives of this Review are to: (a) provide a brief overview of recent developments in corporate governance since the twenty-third session of ISAR; and (b) present and analyze the results of the 2007 review of corporate governance disclosure practices. The overview of recent developments is provided in chapter I, which examines significant developments in the area of corporate governance disclosure. Chapter II presents the findings of the 2007 Review, along with detailed analysis.

The findings of the 2007 Review show that nearly all of the economies in the sample studied have mandatory disclosure rules for a majority of the items in the ISAR benchmark of good practices in corporate governance disclosure. Detailed analysis of the data presented in chapter II below shows that some categories of disclosure are subject to more disclosure rules than others. The analysis in chapter II also provides some insights into differences between the markets in the sample group, both in regards to the particular disclosure items required, as well as the degree of specificity of the rules regarding disclosure. The findings show a high degree of consensus among the markets studied, not only regarding the subjects of disclosure, but also regarding the use of mandatory disclosure rules. This is noteworthy given that non-financial disclosure is often considered to be regulated largely by non-binding voluntary codes of best practice. This research, however, suggests that government regulators and stock exchanges are playing a large role in corporate governance disclosure through the use of binding disclosure rules.

II. Overview of recent developments in the area of corporate governance disclosure

Over the 2006/07 ISAR intersession period, there has been increased international focus on how to encourage institutional investors to exercise their fiduciary duty towards beneficiaries by voting proxies responsibly. This represents an intensification of a trend that was identified in the 2006 Review. Most of the pressure takes the form of legislative and other initiatives to require funds to disclose their voting records to beneficiaries. Efforts to improve the governance of mutual and pension funds, described in the 2006 Review, continue as a strategy to promote fund accountability to beneficiaries. A number of initiatives encourage investors to go further than merely exercising voting rights: promoting voting, engagement and activism on environmental, social and governance (ESG) issues are also described below.

International consolidation of the proxy advisory and proxy voting industry continued in the present period with acquisitions involving two of the largest players in the global industry as well as a number of cooperative ventures. These acquisitions increasingly allow firms to provide bundled offerings addressing a broad range of investor services. Consolidation in the industry prompted renewed calls in the United States for an investigation into the potential conflicts of interest that come with providing both voting advice and consulting services, and into the competitiveness of the market. A United States Governmental Accountability Office (GAO) report, released at the end of July 2007, found no apparent conflicts, either in the nature of services provided or in the power of individual proxy advisory firms to influence vote outcomes.

With the recognized cost, efficiency and access advantages of electronic proxy voting, usually called e-proxy voting, international regulatory and industry developments are promoting its uptake in jurisdictions outside the United States. This therefore may be a trend to watch for developing countries and economies in transition. Within the United States, the Securities and Exchange Commission (SEC) has taken steps towards allowing electronic distribution of proxy materials and electronic proxy communications as the default method of communication between management and shareholders and amongst shareholders. Cross-border voting has emerged as a key area of regulatory attention in the European Union and across Asia, and regulatory proposals in both regions recognize the benefits of electronic proxy voting and proxy material distribution in increasing cross-border access for investors.

Two governance issues continue to draw much media and shareholder attention internationally: executive compensation and director elections. Initiatives designed to reign in compensation and tie compensation to performance have focused on promoting a shareholder advisory vote on executive compensation policies. The way directors are elected to boards in the United States is being scrutinized from a number of angles. Having achieved widespread support for the principle of requiring a majority affirmative vote in the election and re-election of director nominees to the board during the 2005/06 intersession review period, shareholder activist efforts in the 2006/07 period have focused on "proxy access", or allowing shareholders to place their own nominees on the proxy ballot. Efforts have also been focused on the practice of casting "broker non-votes"; these are votes cast by brokers on routine matters, including director elections, where beneficial owners fail to vote within ten days of an annual general meeting (AGM). In such cases, the brokers almost always vote with management.

Convergence in standards of governance and corporate governance disclosure has been driven by efforts to enhance the cross-border participation of investors in the governance of companies and by the activism of groups of large institutional investors with international holdings. A number of developments indicate that foreign institutional investor activism will promote convergence with international governance practices. A merger wave in the global stock exchange industry is also likely to have the effect of promoting further convergence in governance reporting standards.

A.   Corporate governance developments in Asia

The Asian Corporate Governance Association's (ACGA) Asian Proxy Voting Survey, a survey of large international institutional investor concerns regarding proxy voting in the region, which was released in September 2006, highlighted 10 areas of concern regarding proxy voting across Asia.[1] Of these, five concerns stood out as particularly urgent: (a) lack of independent audit of vote results; (b) lack of publication of vote results; (c) insufficient information on which to vote; (d) no confirmation that a vote has been received; and (e) the prevalence of voting by show of hands rather than by ballot/poll. Recommendations made by the report focus on identified areas of concern, but the overarching recommendation is that national electronic voting platforms be put in place as a matter of priority. This would provide a voting audit trail, increasing shareholder participation given the difficulties of cross-border voting, and address the problems inherent in voting by show of hands and clustering of AGM dates. In addition, electronic technologies could be used to make proxy materials more accessible and available on a timely basis and to publish the vote results. According to the ACGA survey, the markets with the weakest voting systems were identified as Japan, the Republic of Korea and Taiwan Province of China. Hong Kong, China had the strongest voting system, although still not up to the standard of the voting systems in Australia, the United Kingdom and the United States, which were used as benchmarks of best practice. Implicit in the ACGA recommendations is the importance of international convergence in proxy voting standards, in particular to facilitate cross-boarder voting, but more generally to emulate the standards already in place in the "best practice" benchmark countries identified in the study.

The annual Asian Corporate Governance Roundtable, sponsored by the Organization for Economic Cooperation and Development, met in Singapore in June 2007. Singapore itself put out a critical self-assessment of the state of its corporate governance practices in an independent report commissioned by the Monetary Authority of Singapore and Singapore Exchange. The Singapore Code of Corporate Governance relies on the "comply or explain" approach described in the 2006 Review, and contrasted with the "rules-based" approach. However, the report finds that most companies do not routinely adhere to this principle. The report sees lack of institutional investor activism in Singapore, particularly by international institutions, as partly responsible for lack of compliance with the "comply or explain" principle. An important barrier to institutional investor involvement was identified as relating to proxy voting, in particular the inability to attend general meetings because of lack of time for informed voting, lack of control over the counting of votes, clustering of meeting dates, and the common practice of voting by a show of hands.[2] These findings echo those of the ACGA Asian Proxy Voting Survey, which ranked Singapore second among 11 Asian markets studied, just behind Hong Kong, China.

---

[1] ACGA (2006). Report on Proxy Voting Across Asia. Asian Corporate Governance Association , September. www.acga-asia.org.
[2] Mak Yuen Teen (2007). Improving the Implementation of Corporate Governance Practices in Singapore. Monetary Authority of Singapore and Singapore Exchange, June.
http://www.mas.gov.sg/resource/news_room/press_releases/2007/CG_Study_Complete_Report_260607.pdf

At the bottom of the ACGA ranking is Japan, due to concerns over clustering of AGMs (for example, more than half of Japan's traded companies held their AGMs in 2007 on the same day, 28 June), bundling of resolutions and inadequate time to receive and vote proxies. This set the stage for a big year in international institutional investor activism in Japan, with foreign funds estimated to have put forward a record 40 of the 85 shareholder resolutions at around 21 Japanese companies during the short period in June in which over 2,000 AGMs took place.[3] Japan did, however rank first in the ACGA's survey in providing for electronic proxy voting, being the only Asian market to do so since the introduction of an electronic proxy voting platform in 2006 as a joint venture between the Tokyo Stock Exchange, the Japan Securities Dealers Association and ADP Investor Communications Services. This, along with increased foreign shareholdings in Japanese companies (up to 28 per cent in March 2007[4] from 19 per cent in 2000[5]) encouraged international shareholder involvement in the 2007 proxy season.[6] Much of the 2007 shareholder activism took aim at takeover defences, a particularly important issue for foreign investors in other markets. This suggests that increased foreign institutional investor activism will promote convergence with international governance practices. The issue of takeover defenses was drawn into the spotlight following a change in Japanese corporate legislation in May 2007 making hostile takeovers easier; this legislative change was followed by management efforts in Japan to set up barriers to hostile takeovers (i.e. takeover defences). While the results of the proxy season demonstrate continued loyalty to management by most domestic investors, some activist investors report that management is becoming more responsive to investor concerns.[7]

Japan has made moves to strengthen and formalize its corporate governance rules with its new internal control and financial reporting mandates, dubbed "J-SOX" in reference to their primary inspiration, the United States Sarbanes–Oxley Act of 2002 (SOX). These rules, released in November 2006 by Japan's Financial Services Agency and due to take effect in April 2008, grew out of accounting fraud scandals at large Japanese companies (e.g. Seibu Railway, Kanebo and Livedoor). The new rules draw heavily on SOX, so companies that trade on the NYSE and already file SOX-compliant reports will be considered compliant with the new J-SOX rules. A key difference between SOX and the new internal control and financial reporting rules is that the latter do not stipulate a particular governance model, whether the United States independent audit committee structure or the Japanese statutory audit system. Another key difference is that, whereas under SOX auditors are required to assess the actual internal controls in place in companies, under J-SOX auditors are only required to assess management's evaluation of the effectiveness of internal controls. A further difference is the threshold of "materiality" against which governance-related problems are to be reported, set at 5 per cent under J-SOX, which is considered much looser than SOX. As with SOX, there are concerns that J-SOX rules will place a disproportionate burden on small companies.[8]

---

[3] Takahiko Hyuga and Eijiro Ueno (2007). Steel Partners Loses in Bid to Stop Bull-Dog Defense. <u>Bloomberg</u>, 28 June:
http://www.bloomberg.com/apps/news?pid=20601080&sid=akcNXDDiTf2w&refer=asia.

[4] Turner D (2007). Foreigners surge into Japanese shares. Financial Times, 18 June:
http://www.ft.com/cms/s/4687d812-1dc4-11dc-89f7-000b5df10621.html.

[5] Santin L (2006). Proxy-Voting Systems Improve, But Investors Still Face Hurdles. Wall Street Journal, 18 September:
http://online.wsj.com/article/SB115823596061663013-search.html?KEYWORDS=Laura+Santini&COLLECTION=wsjie/6month.

[6] ADP Brings Electronic Proxy Voting to Japan, and more. FinanceTech, 9 February 2006:
http://www.financetech.com/showArticle.jhtml?articleID=179102659.

[7] Activist Shareholders in Japan Rebuffed, Associated Press, 28 June 2007:
http://www.forbes.com/feeds/ap/2007/06/28/ap3867593.html.

[8] Aritake T (2006). Why J-Sox is Not Sarbanes–Oxley. Directorship Magazine, December:
http://www.directorship.com/publications/1206_news_jsox.aspx.
Armin J (2007). Tokyo calling. Corporate Secretary Magazine, The Cross Border Group, June:
http://www.thecrossbordergroup.com/pages/1006/June+2007.stm?article id=11851.

B.   Proxy voting reform in Europe

As with Asia, a key corporate governance theme in Europe is strengthening shareholder rights, particularly the cross-border exercise of shareholder rights by institutional investors. Over the 2006/07 ISAR intersession period, the focus has been on corporate governance disclosure and proxy voting reform, with the formal adoption in June 2007 of the Shareholder Rights Directive, initially proposed on 5 January 2006. The directive has to be transposed into member States' laws by summer 2009. It requires "that shareholders have timely access to the complete information relevant to general meetings and facilitates the exercise of voting rights by proxy. Furthermore, the directive provides for the replacement of share blocking and related practices through a record date system."[9] Already, France and Germany use record dates in place of share blocking, with only Austria, Belgium, Greece, Hungary, Italy, Poland, Portugal and Spain still practicing share blocking.[10] Most of the proposed measures are to be achieved through the use of available technologies: proxy material distribution, voting and publication of voting results can all be done by electronic means and the directive encourages member States to take advantage of this capability in achieving increased participation by, and improved and timelier disclosures to, shareholders. The directive also requires that member States ensure that shareholders holding a specified threshold level of shares (member States are not to set this threshold at more than 5 per cent) are able to table items on the agenda of general shareholder meetings and submit draft resolutions in this regard.

Reports indicate that European Union Commissioner Charles McCreevy initially intended that this directive was to require the one-share-one-vote model across the European Union, but widespread use of unequal voting rights and other control-enhancing mechanisms, such as voting caps and ownership ceilings (up to 44 per cent of listed companies across Europe, according to a study published in June 2007[11]), raised strong opposition to this provision. According to subsequent remarks by Commissioner McCreevy, there appears at this point to be no clear economic advantage to requiring that one-share-one-vote prevail as an ownership principle across Europe.[12] Survey evidence suggests that institutional investors view control-enhancing mechanisms negatively, particularly multiple voting rights shares, and expect discounts on share prices where multiple voting rights apply. Yet few appear to call for legislated abolition of multiple voting rights, preferring to deal with this issue on a case-by-case basis with improved transparency.[13]

While question of "proportionality" has been a particularly contentious issue in Europe over the 2006/07 ISAR intersession period, observers recognize that even where companies do have a one-share-one vote shareholding structure in place, there are other ways to slant the relationship between ownership and control (or "economic power" and "voting power"). Practices such as "vote lending" by brokerages or institutional fund managers allow for the "decoupling" of economic and voting power, since, under Delaware law,[14] whoever holds the

---

[9] http://ec.europa.eu/internal_market/company/shareholders/indexa_en.htm.

[10] EUROSIF (2006). Active Share Ownership in Europe: 2006 European Handbook, European Social Investment Forum: http://www.eurosif.com.

[11] Institutional Shareholder Services (ISS). Report on the Proportionality Principle in the European Union. Proportionality Between Ownership and Control in EU Listed Companies External Study Commissioned by the European Commission.
http://ec.europa.eu/internal_market/company/docs/shareholders/study/final_report_en.pdf.

[12] McCreevy C (2007). Regulators: help or hindrance? Speech by European Commissioner for Internal Market and Financial Services to the 12th Annual Conference of the International Corporate Governance Network (ICGN), 6 July:
http://www.icgn.org/conferences/2007/documents/mcreevy_speech.pdf.

[13] Institutional Shareholder Services (ISS). Report on the Proportionality Principle in the European Union. Proportionality Between Ownership and Control in EU Listed Companies External Study Commissioned by the European Commission.
http://ec.europa.eu/internal_market/company/docs/shareholders/study/final_report_en.pdf.

[14] Note that most large companies in the United States are incorporated in the State of Delaware, thus the relevance of Delaware law for corporate practices.

shares on the record date that a company sets for a shareholder vote gets to vote those shares, regardless of whether they actually own the shares. In May 2006, an academic paper was published showing the use of these strategies in specific cases.[15] The practices described by the authors – Henry Hu and Bernard Black of the University of Texas – collectively called "vote borrowing", are often used by hedge funds for the purpose of exercising voting power disproportionate to economic interest (which they call "empty voting") to influence the outcome of key shareholder elections. Most strikingly, they describe instances where the interests of the borrower ran counter to those of the rest of shareholders by reducing the share price of the company. Much of the vote borrowing behaviour that leads to empty voting goes undisclosed, and is therefore difficult to detect. The extent of this practice, therefore, is not clear, but regulators are taking seriously the threat to market integrity that this practice represents, especially as shareholders gain greater voting power with respect to board elections in the United States.[16] The United States SEC, the United Kingdom Financial Services Authority and Hong Kong, China's Securities and Futures Commission are considering additional disclosures to address the problem. One approach would be to require greater disclosure of agreements that hedge funds reach with brokerages to secure greater voting rights. Another approach would require improved tracking of economic and voting power in order to reveal decoupling of economic from voting interests, as recommended by the authors of the 2006 study.[17] The SEC's chairman has requested a study and recommendations from SEC staff by the end of 2007.[18]

C.   Proxy advisory and governance ratings industry

Consolidation in the proxy advisory and governance ratings industry, identified as a trend in the 2006 Review, continued through the present review period. This industry consists of firms that provide proxy voting advice and/or ratings of individual company corporate governance structures and processes. These services are provided primarily to institutional investors and can influence the investment decisions of these investors.

On 11 January 2007, United States-based RiskMetrics purchased Institutional Shareholder Services (ISS), headquartered in Rockville, Maryland, for $553 million. On the same day, Glass Lewis, based in San Francisco, which had previously received investment from China-based Xinhua Finance, and which had purchased Corporate Governance International (CGI), a Sydney-based proxy advisory firm, in September 2006, was purchased by Xinhua Finance for $45 million.

Three key strategic drivers of consolidation in the industry are: (a) expanded global coverage, which drove many of the developments that were reported on in the 2006 Review; (b) the emerging strategy of providing technical services – electronic communication, proxy delivery and voting services – along with proxy voting advice and analytic content that make for informed voting decisions; and (c) access to new market segments with complementary analytical services.

---

[15] Hu HTC and Black B (2006). Hedge Funds, Insiders, and the Decoupling of Economic and Voting Ownership: Empty Voting and Hidden (Morphable) Ownership. European Corporate Governance Institute (ECGI) Finance Working Paper No. 56/2006. http://papers.ssrn.com/sol3/papers.cfm?abstract_id=874098.
[16] Scannell K (2007). How borrowed shares swing company votes, Wall Street Journal, 26 January: http://www.wsj.com.
[17] Judd E (2007). The new vote buying, Corporate Secretary Magazine, The Cross Border Group, June. http://www.thecrossbordergroup.com/pages/1006/June+2007.stm?article_id=11845.
[18] Scannell K (2007). Hedge Funds Vote (Often). In Proxies Borrowed Shares fill Ballot Box; SEC May Act. Wall Street Journal, 22 March.

Consistent with the second objective, in September 2006 ISS and Swingvote entered into a strategic partnership to bundle voting services to retail investors with proxy voting advice, which until then could only be afforded by larger institutions. Automatic Data Processing (ADP) has dominated the United States proxy delivery industry up to the present. However the additional services provided through the ISS–Swingvote partnership could win over some business from ADP.[19]

Likewise in Europe, Proxinvest, offering e-proxy voting for French companies, joined the European Corporate Governance Services (ECGS) partnership of organizations to provide e-proxy voting services bundled with voting recommendations provided through ECGS partners, including: Avanzi, Corporate Governance Services Spain, DSW, Dutch Sustainability Research, PIRC and Sustainable Governance. Similar European developments involve a partnership between IVOX proxy voting service with Centre Français d'Information sur les Entreprises-Conseil, which provides proxy voting advice, and Manifest's partnership with Exchange Data International to offer clients expanded agenda coverage and analysis, starting in January 2007.

In line with the third strategy outlined above, RiskMetrics recently announced that it intends to buy the forensic accounting firm Center for Financial Research and Analysis (CFRA). Together with the analysis provided by ISS, the acquisition was described as strengthening RiskMetrics' corporate governance services and risk assessment capacity for institutional clients.[20]

A number of criticisms over potential conflicts of interest continue to be levelled at the proxy advisory industry. Noted in the 2006 Review is the potential conflict of providing proxy voting advice and corporate governance ratings on public corporations while also marketing services to corporate clients, as ISS does. Criticisms to this effect are behind the call, in September 2006, for a report from the GAO on conflicts of interest and the state of competition in the proxy advisory industry, which was published on 30 July 2007. As noted above, the report found no major conflicts and found that advisory firms' ability to influence votes is limited due to the way in which large institutional investors use the proxy voting advice provided by proxy advisory firms.[21]

Another important criticism to emerge is the state of governance at firms that provide governance ratings and proxy advice, with Xinhua Finance falling into the spotlight as allegations of bad governance practices were made against it. RiskMetrics has suggested plans for an IPO of ISS, leading to concerns about ISS falling into the same category of entity as those it rates, namely, public company. Competitors such as Egan-Jones, Proxy Governance International and PIRC have been using their "conflict free" credentials as a marketing tool.

D.   Investment fund accountability: proxy voting disclosure

There has been much international focus on disclosure of voting records by investment institutions. Disclosure of full proxy voting records by investment companies registered with the SEC, including mutual funds and investment advisors, is mandatory in the United States (since

---

[19] Sale Tactics (2006). Global Proxy Watch, Vol. 10 (34): http://www.davisglobal.com.
[20] http://www.riskmetrics.com/release/cfra.html.
[21] Tomoeh Murakami Tse (2007). Proxy Advisers Are Not Found To Have Conflicts by the GAO. Washington Post, 31 July, p. D02: http://www.washingtonpost.com/wp-dyn/content/article/2007/07/30/AR2007073001603.html.

2004) and Canada (since 2006). Although there has been a gradual increase in the number of United Kingdom funds voluntarily disclosing their proxy voting records over the period 2003–2007, pressure is mounting in the United Kingdom for more compliance. For example, the Treasury Minister in early 2007 called for voluntary disclosure of proxy voting records by investment funds, including pension funds, and suggested the possibility of a legislated requirement for disclosure should the voluntary approach fail. Pressure in the United Kingdom also comes from the trade union movement, with the Trades Union (TUC) being particularly vocal on this issue. In response to this pressure, the United Kingdom Institutional Shareholders' Committee (ISC), which is comprised of the Association of British Insurers (ABI), the Association of Investment Companies (AIC), the Investment Management Association (IMA) and the National Association of Pension Funds (NAPF), published the "Industry framework on voting disclosure" on 27 June 2007. This follows, and provides substance to, the ISC's "Principles on the Responsibilities of Institutional Shareholders and Agents", revised and issued in September 2005.[22] The framework sets out in very general terms what is to be disclosed and how it is to be disclosed. However, it goes nowhere near as far as the United States SEC in providing for a standard set of fields or providing for a centralized repository of the disclosures.[23] A survey of all NAPF members' engagement practices was published in October 2006: 41 responses were received and these showed that pension funds in the United Kingdom are slowly starting to provide voluntary disclosures as to how they vote shares in their plans, with only two plans voluntarily publishing their voting records on their website for general public access.[24]

While many large national public pension funds – such as California's CaLPERS, South Africa's Public Investment Corporation (PIC) (managing funds for the Government Employees Pension Fund), the Ontario Teachers Pension Plan and Britain's Universities Superannuation Scheme – voluntarily provide some information on their voting behaviour, pension plans in the United States and Canada are not yet required to publicly report their proxy voting records as is now the case with mutual funds in both those jurisdictions. However, there is some pressure in both jurisdictions for this to become a regulated duty of plan management. A survey of proxy voting by Canadian pension fund investment managers and proxy voting services provided on behalf of Canadian pension funds, conducted by The Shareholder Association for Research and Education (SHARE), shows that most private plans delegate complete discretion for proxy voting to fund managers. This suggests that most Canadian private pension plans do not have proxy voting policies.[25] An August 2004 report by the United States GAO showed that many of the same conflicts that apply to the mutual fund industry in exercising fiduciary duty towards beneficiaries also apply to United States private pension funds. In the report, the GAO recommends to Congress that the Employee Retirement Income Security Act of 1974 (ERISA) be amended to require private pensions funds to develop proxy voting guidelines and disclose both the guidelines and their votes annually.[26] Ten years before, in what has become known as the "Avon Letter", Alan D. Lebowitz, Deputy Assistant Secretary for the United Statues Pension and Welfare Benefits Administration (PWBA), had established the voting of proxies as part of the fiduciary duty of pension plan asset management. He further identified plan trustees as

---

[22] Institutional Shareholders' Committee. Review of the Institutional Shareholders' Committee Statement of Principles on the Responsibilities of Institutional Shareholders and Agents. September 2005:
http://www.ivis.co.uk/pages/gdsc6_5_1.pdf.
[23] Institutional Shareholders' Committee framework on voting disclosure, June 2007:
http://institutionalshareholderscommittee.org.uk/sitebuildercontent/sitebuilderfiles/ISCframeworkvotingdisclosureJun07.pdf.
[24] National Association of Pension Funds (NAPF). Pension Funds' Engagement with Companies – 2006. October 2006:
http://www.napf.co.uk/engagement%20survey%20final.pdf.
[25] Shareholder Association for Research and Education (2006). 2006 Key Proxy Vote Survey. SHARE, Vancouver, Canada. http://www.share.ca.
[26] United States Government Accountability Office. Pension Plans: Additional Transparency and Other Actions Needed in Connection with Proxy Voting. Report to the Ranking Minority Member, Committee on Health, Education, Labor, and Pensions, U.S. Senate. August 2004:
http://www.gao.gov/new.items/d04749.pdf.

responsible for the execution of the proxy vote, either directly or by designating this responsibility to an investment manager under condition of periodic monitoring.[27] As the importance of the fiduciary duty of investment institutions towards their beneficiaries becomes more generally acknowledged against existing evidence of conflicts in exercising this duty, pressure on pension funds and investment institutions in other jurisdictions to disclose their voting results is likely to increase.

While disclosure is a first step, accessibility of proxy voting disclosures is also a concern for users of this information. The SEC's EDGAR database provides a central repository for all proxy voting reports by registered investment companies. However, the Canadian framework does not provide for a central repository of proxy voting disclosures by funds, which are obligated only to make these disclosures available to members, although some go further and make them publicly available on their websites. The same is the case in the United Kingdom regarding the voluntary disclosure of proxy voting records. Centralized access to proxy voting records would vastly increase the value of these disclosures. Some initiatives are underway to provide access to compiled voting records, including the website "fundvotes.com", which covers the disclosures of large United States and Canadian mutual funds, and the TUC's database of pension fund voting based on survey data.

E.   Investment fund accountability: fund governance

The two-pronged approach to making investment institutions more accountable to their members was elaborated on in the 2006 ISAR corporate governance review. Proxy voting disclosure is one approach and the other entails improvements in fund governance. The International Corporate Governance Network's (ICGN) Statement of Principles on Institutional Shareholder Responsibilities[28] was endorsed by the ICGN board in March 2007 and received final approval by ICGN membership at the 6 July AGM in Cape Town, South Africa. Described more fully in the 2006 Review, the code sets out principles for both internal governance as well as engagement with companies.

The theme of aligning a long-term approach to investing and engagement with good internal governance is the foundation of the newly established "Marathon Club" in London, as revealed in their investment mandate Guidance Note for Long-Term Investing, produced in April 2007. The Marathon Club consists of 20 members, including British fund trustees, executives and investment specialists, and aims to "stimulate pension funds, endowments and other institutional investors and their agents to be more long-term in their thinking and actions, place a greater emphasis on being responsible and active owners and increasing knowledge about how their investment strategy and process can improve the long term financial and qualitative buying power of fund beneficiaries."[29]

Strengthening institutional investor oversight is also the theme underlying the Clapman Report, which was published in May 2007 by a committee of the Stanford Institutional Investors' Forum at Stanford Law School. The committee is comprised of representatives of large United

---

[27] See Department of Labor's Letter on ERISA Fiduciary Standards: http://www.lens-library.com/info/dolavon.html.
[28] International Corporate Governance Network: Statement of Principles on Institutional Shareholder Responsibilities. International Corporate Governance Network (ICGN):
http://www.icgn.org/organisation/documents/src/Revised%20Statement%20on%20Shareholder%20Responsibilities%20130407.pdf.
[29] The Marathon Club. Guidance Note for Long-Term Investing. Spring 2007:
http://www.marathonclub.co.uk/Docs/MarathonClubFINALDOC.pdf.

States institutional investors, academics and corporate governance practitioners and is chaired by Peter Clapman, CEO of the advocacy group Governance for Owners, USA. The report outlines best practice principles for investment fund governance in the United States applicable to pension, endowment and charitable funds. A key recommendation of the report is that funds should "clearly define and make publicly available their governance rules".[30]

In 2007, PIC (South Africa's largest public pension fund) successfully engaged the Barloworld Company over board diversity and the independence of the CEO from the chairman of the board. This action marked a milestone in shareholder activism in South Africa. The PIC, which represents civil service retirement savings, models itself on CalPERS.[31]

Shareholder engagement takes a longer-term view of investment in corporations. Short-termism in investment is seen by many as undermining efforts to achieve well-governed companies, since it leads to over-concern with quarterly profits and, therefore, unsustainable business practices. This sentiment is behind the efforts of the Aspen Institute, through the Corporate Values Strategy Group (CVSG), to achieve consensus around a set of investment and business principles, called the "Aspen Principles". These principles were endorsed by a range of stakeholders including a group of large corporations, shareholder groups, the Business Roundtable and the Council of Institutional Investors. The principles were published on 18 June 2007 in a document entitled Long-term Value Creation: Guiding Principles for Corporations and Investors. The principles are intended to provide guidance for voluntary corporate action as well as public policy on how to achieve a longer-term business strategy.[32]

F.   Transparency and communication using electronic technologies

The spread of e-proxy voting as a proxy voting tool has been dealt with above and has been recognized as a way of reducing cross-border barriers to voting and providing a mechanism for vote auditing and reporting. Other ways in which electronic technologies are being leveraged to improve transparency, timeliness and accessibility of corporate information and reduce the cost of preparing and disseminating reports is through the promotion of so-called "interactive data" or tagged data, more specifically, eXtensible Business Reporting Language (XBRL), and through the use of electronic distribution channels for proxy materials and communications. Both of these developments are taking place in the United States due to recent SEC rule adoptions.

In July 2007, the SEC published a rule, to come into effect on 20 August 2007, allowing mutual funds to voluntarily submit tagged information contained in the risk/return summary section of their prospectuses as a supplement to the full prospectus. The tagged reports are to be prepared according to a specially designed XBRL taxonomy for mutual fund reporting developed by the Investment Company Institute, a trade association for the mutual fund industry.[33] This new rule expands the XBRL voluntary reporting programme introduced by the SEC in 2005 and discussed in the 2006 ISAR corporate governance review. Through the United States jurisdictional arm of the XBRL International Consortium, the SEC is promoting the finalization

---

[30] The Stanford Institutional Investors' Forum, Committee on Fund Governance. Best Practice Principles. 31 May 2007. http://www.law.stanford.edu/program/executive/programs/Clapman_Report-070316v6-Color.pdf.
[31] Rumney R (2007). Buzzword bingo. Mail & Guardian Online, 19 March: http://www.mg.co.za.
[32] See: http://www.aspeninstitute.org/site/c.huLWJeMRKpH/b.2286629/k.5EAB/Corporate_Values_and_Strategy_Group.htm.
[33] United States Securities and Exchange Commission (SEC). Extension Of Interactive Data Voluntary Reporting Program On The Edgar System To Include Mutual Fund Risk/Return Summary Information. Final Rule. File Number S7-05-07. http://www.sec.gov/rules/final/2007/33-8823.pdf.

of XBRL taxonomies for financial reporting in all industries. At present, XBRL taxonomies are limited to information contained in financial reports and do not cover governance-related information that is typically reported in the form of narrative text. However, the potential exists for such data to be standardized according to a tagging system. The SEC's Interactive Financial Report Viewer is an open-source online tool that enables users to interact with XBRL filings submitted as part of the SEC's Voluntary XBRL Filing Program.[34] It allows for viewing of individual company reports, including graphing of fields of interest to the user, export to Microsoft Excel and printing of sections of the financial report, as well as cross-company comparisons. This tool demonstrates the power of analysis facilitated by tagged financial reporting. Besides the SEC's public interface for searching and analyzing XBRL reports, there are a number of private vendors with more powerful products in various stages of development that are geared towards the analyst industry. There are also a number of products targeted at reporting entities that create the XBRL documents. The SEC hopes to encourage the further development of these tools through its open-source project.[35]

Using electronic technologies to facilitate shareholder communications has been one of main themes behind reforms promoted by SEC Chairman Christopher Cox. In July 2007, the SEC finalized the Internet Availability of Proxy Materials Rule, S7-10-05, also known as the "Notice and Access Rule", requiring large companies to send only a Notice of Internet Availability of Proxy Materials to shareholders and then make proxy materials available on their company websites. Large corporate filers will be required to comply with this rule from 1 January 2008 onwards. Under this rule, shareholders are still able to specifically request a paper copy of a particular company's proxy materials, and the company is obligated to send this out upon such a request; however, the default will be electronic availability. The estimated cost and paper savings of this rule change are substantial. Already some proxy service firms are offering to provide services tailored to allowing companies to take advantage of this new rule.[36] This process of proxy solicitation includes all subsequent communications from the company to its shareholders that would usually fall under SEC-regulated communications, and also applies to others soliciting proxies in the case of proxy contests[37] which, it has been argued, would reduce the cost of mounting proxy contests, where cost is considered to be the greatest barrier faced by shareholder groups.

G.   Stock exchange mergers and convergence in governance standards

While the two models of corporate governance reporting identified in the 2006 Review continue to prevail, namely the principles-based "comply or explain" model characteristic of European corporate governance reporting and the rules-based reporting format of the United States, there are some important developments that promote convergence of the governance measures representing both reporting traditions. One of the key drivers is likely to be cross-border stock exchange listings and cross-border mergers within the stock exchange industry.

In December 2006, the merger between the New York Stock Exchange and Euronext was approved and trading began on the combined exchanges in April 2007. This merger was triggered

---

[34] See SEC Interactive Financial Report Viewer: http://216.241.101.197/viewer.
[35] Thomas C (2007). Opening up XBRL, <u>IR Magazine</u>, The Cross Border Group, June:
 http://www.thecrossbordergroup.com/pages/1506/June+2007.stm?article_id=11865.
[36] Computershare Launches ProxyAccess Solution. Press Release:
http://www.earthtimes.org/articles/show/news_press_release,128953.shtml-
[37] SEC Rule 14a-16 – Internet Availability of Proxy Materials, see: httn://www.law.uc.edu/CCL/34ActRls/rule14a-16.html.

by earlier attempts by NASDAQ to acquire the London Stock Exchange (LSE)[38] and trumped an alternate bid by Deutsche Börse for Euronext.[39] The NYSE, which demutualized earlier in 2006, was already the world's largest stock exchange. Euronext, with exchanges in Paris, Amsterdam, Brussels and Lisbon, and with LIFFE in London, was Europe's second-largest stock exchange group after the LSE.

The merged exchange company, known as NYSE Euronext, continues to actively seek new acquisitions in Europe and maintains a number of special arrangements with other exchanges, including with the Luxembourg Exchange for the development of corporate bonds business, and with the Warsaw Exchange for information and communications technology (ICT) cooperation. Meanwhile in Asia, the NYSE Euronext has indicated intentions to expand operations, including a strategic alliance in Japan with the Tokyo Stock Exchange, a sizeable stake in the National Stock Exchange of India, as well as intentions to become more involved in China when authorities allow foreign minority ownership stakes in Chinese stock exchanges.[40]

With stiff global competition amongst exchanges (contributing to decreasing trading, settlement and clearing costs) for cross-border reach and a broader product range, the NYSE Euronext merger triggered further consolidation in the global stock exchange industry.[41] Germany's Deutsche Börse plans to acquire the United States options exchange ISE, and the LSE intends to acquire Borsa Italiana SpA after rejecting an acquisition bid by NASDAQ earlier in 2007. Also in 2007, NASDAQ beat out a rival bid from the Dubai Exchange and completed the acquisition of OMX AB, the Nordic stock exchange group, to form NASDAQ OMX Group. The OMX exchange group not only provides a common offering spanning Helsinki, Copenhagen, Stockholm, Iceland, Tallinn, Riga and Vilnius, but also provides exchange technology, clearing services and central securities depositories in a number of countries.

A probable outcome of this global stock exchange merger wave over the longer term is some degree of regulatory convergence around corporate governance practices. Companies wishing to access capital in one of the larger capital markets of Europe or the United States are already required to comply with at least some of the governance standards for these jurisdictions. Local jurisdictions themselves may push for changes with respect to local regulation in an effort to compete globally, and many of the changes may resemble European or United States style governance practices. An example, already noted above, is Japan's new J-SOX rules modelled on the United States SOX. Furthermore, larger exchange groups, such as the NYSE Euronext, may push for governance improvements through exchange listing rule changes at smaller exchanges in which they hold substantial stakes, such as the India National Stock Exchange.[42] At the moment, developments in this area are moving slowly. For example, to allay fears of European listed companies having to comply with SOX-driven NYSE listing rules, the NYSE Euronext Group has continued to operate on separate listing processes and separate order books for trading, which continues to fall under the jurisdiction of local regulators.

---

[38] MacDonald A and Manuel G (2006). NASDAQ Gets Tough in LSE Bid, Wall Street Journal, 13 December 13:
http://online.wsj.com/article/SB116591445456147486.html.
[39] Taylor E, Lucchetti A and MacDonald A (2006). Deutsche Börse Exiting Euronext Chase. Wall Street Journal, 15 November 15:
http://online.wsj.com/article/SB116355794762023471.html.
[40] Kanter J (2007). Newly merged NYSE Euronext has Asian Ambitions. International Herald Tribune, 4 April:
http://www.iht.com/articles/2007/04/04/business/exchange.php.
[41] Tran M (2006). New York stock exchange and Euronext merge. Guardian Unlimited, 2 June:
http://business.guardian.co.uk/story/0,,1789127,00.html.
[42] Armin J (2007). Cultural Club, Corporate Secretary Magazine, The Cross Border Group, June:
http://www.thecrossbordergroup.com/pages/1006/May+2007.stm?article id=11796.

H.   Executive compensation

Internationally, the prerogative of shareholders to have a say on executive compensation policies is gaining acceptance from shareholders and regulators, and is even causing some executives to engage in dialogue over the issue. Already annual, non-binding votes on compensation policies are required in the United Kingdom (the first adopter of this measure, in 2002) and Australia, while public companies in Sweden, Norway and the Netherlands are to hold annual binding votes on compensation policies. A non-binding shareholder vote on the board's remuneration committee report is now included in the provisions of South Africa's new Companies Bill, 2007, (to replace the Companies Act of 1973) as one of the four standard issues that are to be transacted at shareholder meetings and as part of the Government's effort to "[enhance] corporate governance, transparency and accountability of large and widely-held firms".[43]

The movement promoting shareholder advisory votes on compensation policies, or compensation committee reports, is now also gaining acceptance in the United States. A number of ad hoc groups that span not only national boundaries ("International Roundtable on Executive Remuneration", consisting of 13 funds from five different countries), but also institutional investors and corporate executives ("Working Group on the Advisory Vote on Executive Compensation Disclosure", led by the Business Roundtable and consisting of representatives of large United States corporations such as Pfizer and American International Group as well as shareholder activists such as AFSCME[44] and Walden Asset Management), have engaged in dialogue over the issue of an advisory vote on executive compensation at United States public corporations.[45] In April 2007, the "Shareholder Vote on Executive Compensation Act," was passed in the United States House of Representatives and was pending a vote in the Senate as of the date of writing this report. Additionally in the United States, a large number of shareholder resolutions, around 60, calling for the implementation of an advisory vote on executive compensation policies, have been voted on at shareholder meetings held during the 2007 United States proxy season, and have achieved high levels of support, with some achieving majority support (for example, those voted on at Blockbuster and Verizon Communications, Ingersoll-Rand Co. and Motorola Inc.). The retirement plan provider TIAA-CREF, a major institutional investor, is one of the main promoters of such resolutions in the United States, and has adopted this measure with respect to its own executive pay policies.[46] As with the issue of majority voting in director elections discussed in the 2006 Review, these developments indicate, at the very least, a widespread voluntary adoption of the so-called "say-on-pay" measure by large corporations. It is expected that Canada will be the next jurisdiction to face pressure to adopt this measure, and this could come as soon as the 2008 proxy season.[47]

---

[43] See Companies Bill, 2007: http://www.thedti.gov.za/ccrdlawreview/COMPANIESBILL07.htm.

[44] The American Federation of State, County and Municipal Employees, is the largest union for workers in the public service in the United States with 1.4 million members.

[45] Davis S and Lukomnik J (2007). Activists Have Sudden Outbreak Of Dialogue. Compliance Week, 13 February: http://www.complianceweek.com.

[46] http://www.tiaa-cref.org/about/governance/corporate/topics/exec_comp_qa.html.

[47] McFarland J (2007). Say on Pay Fight Heads North. Globe and Mail, 11 June. http://www.theglobeandmail.com/servlet/ArticleNews/TPStory/LAC/20070611/RSAYONPAY11/Columnists/Columnist?author=Janet+McFarland.

I.   Board elections

More action on reforming board elections in the United States took place during the 2006/07 ISAR intersession period. Having established the majority affirmative vote as the standard for director elections through a successful shareholder resolution campaign, labour groups (who are also significant institutional investors) turned their attention to the issue of proxy access and shareholder nomination of candidates for the board. This issue came into focus following the 5 September 2006 ruling by a United States Court against the AIG Company to allow a shareholder resolution calling for a bylaw change to permit shareholder access to the proxy ballot. Similar resolutions came to a vote at a number of companies during the 2007 proxy season and achieved as much as 40 per cent support in the case of Hewlett-Packard. Two company boards, those of Apria Healthcare and Comverse, voluntarily adopted proxy access provisions into their bylaws. The United States SEC is considering comments from the public on two alternate proposals, one of which would allow shareholders to nominate candidates to the board, with restrictions; the other would prevent shareholder nominations.

A further development served to bring into question the level of support that management nominees have traditionally enjoyed in United States board elections. In October 2006, a working group of the NYSE proposed reassigning director elections from a routine to non-routine voting matter, thereby abolishing "broker voting" with respect to director elections. Broker voting (also referred to as "broker non-votes") is the practice of allowing brokers to vote shares held in their accounts for which they have not received voting instructions from beneficial shareholders within 10 days before a company's AGM. As noted above, brokers almost always vote with management, thereby boosting observed support for such matters voted on. Strong opposition from management groups lead to a delay in ratifying the stock exchange listing rule changes that this would entail. The opposition called for a review of the system by which corporations are able to communicate with shareholders before considering abolishing broker voting in director elections. Such a review was launched through a series of three round tables hosted by the United States SEC to address stockholder rights and the federal proxy rules held during May 2007.[48] The status of broker voting in director elections, at the time of writing, continues to be the subject of debate.

Both of these developments have the potential to turn director elections into a more accurate barometer of shareholder satisfaction with board members, and possibly even shape the structure of the board based on the performance of individual directors.

J.   Climate risk and corporate governance

Institutional investors continue to increase their attention on the issue of global climate change, and this is drawing corporate environmental performance toward the centre of mainstream corporate governance considerations around the world. A number of investor-led initiatives both signal and drive this trend. Perhaps the most significant development is the widespread endorsement of the United Nations Principles for Responsible Investment (PRI). Just one year after their formal launch in 2006, more than 200 institutional investors from around the

---

[48] Roundtable Discussions Regarding the Proxy Process. Securities and Exchange Commission (SEC): http://www.sec.gov/spotlight/proxyprocess.htm.

world, representing over $9 trillion, have signed onto the PRI. The principles provide guidance on how to integrate environmental, social and governance issues into investment decision-making and ownership practices. They also express the intent of signatories to promote ESG reporting at corporations and to promote the uptake of the principles by other institutional investors.[49]

In October 2006, the Investor Statement on Climate Change, sponsored by the Institutional Investors Group on Climate Change (IIGCC), was signed by a number of Europe's largest pension funds and asset managers, collectively managing more than GBP 850 billion. The statement affirms the significant risk that climate change poses to individual savers whose assets are managed by institutional investors, the centrality of investment decisions to this risk, and therefore the responsibility of institutional investors to consider climate change in making investment decisions and appointing advisors and asset managers.[50]

In order for institutional investors to make decisions that incorporate climate change risk considerations, they need information on corporate environmental performance. In October 2006, CERES, a United States-based coalition of investors and environmental organizations working toward environmentally sustainable business practices, published the "New Global Framework for Climate Risk Disclosure", which provides guidance for companies on how to report on "business risks and opportunities resulting from climate change, as well as how to report on the company's efforts to address those risks and opportunities" through existing reporting channels, namely, financial reports, the Carbon Disclosure Project, the Global Reporting Initiative and forward-looking disclosures.[51]

K.   Chapter conclusion

The main regulatory and market developments shaping corporate governance internationally during the 2006/07 intersession period have served to promote shareholder participation in voting and engagement. In particular, a number of developments have focused on facilitating cross-border shareholder voting, increasing the use of electronic technologies for reporting to and communicating with shareholders. A number of other issues were also the subject of significant developments in the 2006/07 period, including new activities to address management compensation and director elections. This period also saw major developments in the mainstream inclusion of environmental and social issues in the broader governance framework, creating a new integrated focus on ESG issues. One final trend that may continue to shape global corporate governance practices into the future is the ongoing wave of mergers and acquisitions among stock exchanges. As the globalization of the stock exchange industry continues, it is likely that further convergence will take place among existing corporate governance practices around the world.

---

[49] PRI Progress Report 2007: Implementation, Assessment and Guidance. UNEP Finance Initiative (UNEP FI) and The United Nations Global Compact: http://www.unpri.org/report07/index.php.
[50] http://www.iigcc.org.
[51] http://www.ceres.org/pub/docs/Framework.pdf.

III. Status of implementation of good practices in corporate governance disclosure at the regulatory level

A. Background and methodology

The purpose of this study is to evaluate the level of implementation of good practices in corporate governance disclosure highlighted in the 2006 UNCTAD publication *Guidance on Good Practices in Corporate Governance Disclosure* (based on the ISAR document TD/B/COM.2/ISAR/30). This 2006 UNCTAD guidance forms a benchmark (hereafter the "ISAR benchmark") of 53 disclosure items on corporate governance. This benchmark was used in earlier ISAR studies on this subject, namely the 2005 Review and the 2006 Review. The complete set of 53 disclosure items are grouped into five broad categories, or subject areas, of corporate governance disclosure, and are presented and analysed by category in section B below. These categories are:

(a) Board and management structure and process;

(b) Financial transparency and information disclosure;

(c) Ownership structure and exercise of control rights;

(d) Auditing; and

(e) Corporate responsibility and compliance.

In an effort to continually improve the research methodology of ISAR's annual review of corporate governance disclosure, and to expand understanding of disclosure practices around the world, the present study is substantially different in its approach when compared to the earlier Reviews. While the 2005 and 2006 Reviews evaluated the disclosure practices of a sample of 105 enterprises from around the world, the present study evaluates the corporate governance disclosure requirements of regulators and stock exchanges in 25 emerging markets. While the previous Reviews provided a useful picture of what enterprises were actually disclosing, there was insufficient understanding of the requirements placed on companies by regulators and stock exchanges, and how these requirements might vary from country to country. In order to gain a better understanding of the regulatory environment in which publicly listed enterprises operate, this study compares the corporate governance disclosure requirements of regulators and stock exchanges with the ISAR benchmark on good practices.

The sample of 25 markets examined in this study was drawn from the Emerging Markets Index produced by Morgan Stanley Capital International (hereafter the "MSCI EM Index"). MSCI is a leading commercial provider of financial information, including equity indices tracking publicly listed enterprises around the world. The MSCI EM Index is considered by institutional investors to be the industry standard to gauge emerging markets performance, and is an important tool for facilitating foreign portfolio investment to developing countries and countries with economies in transition. The current MSCI EM Index tracks approximately 850 publicly listed enterprises, which account for roughly 85 per cent of the market capitalization of 25 emerging markets. Table 1 below provides a list of the economies included in the MSCI EM Index.

Table 1. The 25 economies included in the MSCI EM Index

1. Argentina	14. Republic of Korea
2. Brazil	15. Malaysia
3. Chile	16. Mexico
4. China	17. Morocco
5. China, Taiwan Province of	18. Pakistan
6. Colombia	19. Peru
7. Czech Republic	20. Philippines
8. Egypt	21. Poland
9. Hungary	22. Russia
10. India	23. South Africa
11. Indonesia	24. Thailand
12. Israel	25. Turkey
13. Jordan	

The research question applied to this sample was: which of the ISAR benchmark disclosure items are required to be reported by enterprises listed on the major stock exchanges of each of the 25 markets studied? The study examined government laws and regulatory instruments as well as the listing requirements of major stock exchanges. The origin of disclosure requirements varied from market to market, with some markets primarily relying on regulatory instruments and others relying on stock exchange rules. The research was performed primarily using publicly available documents from the Internet, but in some cases relied on direct communication with regulators and or stock exchange officials. A preliminary copy of the findings for each market was submitted to regulators or stock exchange authorities in that market for comment; a number of replies were received and their comments and suggestions were incorporated into the findings below. While every effort was made to be thorough in this research, this report cannot claim to have covered all applicable laws and regulations; the reader can gauge the thoroughness of the research by examining the complete list of sources by market contained in annex I. Note also that this survey does not take into account voluntary codes; it is an inventory of mandatory requirements. This should not be interpreted as discounting the value of voluntary codes; it is merely an attempt to gauge the role of regulators and stock exchanges in setting disclosure requirements. In some markets, for example the United Kingdom, when voluntary codes are taken into account, all of the items in the ISAR benchmark are covered. Given the high compliance rate of companies in some markets with voluntary codes, additional mandatory requirements may not be necessary. Therefore, the data presented below should not be interpreted as a measure of the overall rate of disclosure by enterprises in the selected markets: some markets may have mandatory requirements that are not complied with by enterprises, while other markets may have voluntary codes that are the subject of a high rate of compliance. Readers should also note that, as was the case with ISAR's previous annual reviews on this subject, this report is not intended as a measure of the quality of disclosure within individual markets; it is a measure of the existence of regulations requiring the selected disclosure items.

B. Disclosure requirements of 25 emerging markets

Table 2 below displays the results of the survey within each of the five broad categories discussed in section A above. This grouping of the disclosure items allows readers to draw their own conclusions based on the importance they assign to a particular category or subject area and, within that category, a particular disclosure item. It also facilitates the analysis that follows on the relative level of disclosure within each category.

Table 2. Main findings of survey of disclosure requirements in 25 emerging markets
(Number of markets requiring this item)

Disclosure item	No. of markets (max. = 25)
Ownership structure and exercise of control rights	
Ownership structure	25
Process for holding annual general meetings	25
Changes in shareholdings	25
Availability and accessibility of meeting agenda	25
Control structure	24
Control rights	24
Control and corresponding equity stake	23
Rules and procedures governing the acquisition of corporate control in capital markets	23
Anti-takeover measures	20
Financial transparency and information disclosure	
Financial and operating results	25
Nature, type and elements of related-party transactions	22
Company objectives	22
Disclosure practices on related party transactions where control exists	22
Rules and procedures governing extraordinary transactions	22
The decision-making process for approving transactions with related parties	21
Board's responsibilities regarding financial communications	21
Critical accounting estimates	14
Impact of alternative accounting decisions	12
Board and management structure and process	

Disclosure item	No. of markets (max. = 25)
Governance structures, such as committees and other mechanisms, to prevent conflict of interest	24
Composition of board of directors (executives and non-executives)	24
Role and functions of the board of directors	24
Composition and function of governance committee structures	23
Qualifications and biographical information on board members	23
Determination and composition of directors` remuneration	23
Material interests of members of the board and management	22
Independence of the board of directors	22
Existence of procedure(s) for addressing conflicts of interest among board members	21
"Checks and balances" mechanisms	18
Risk management objectives, system and activities	18
Duration of directors' contracts	18
Types and duties of outside board and management positions	15
Existence of plan of succession	14
Professional development and training activities	14
Number of outside board and management position directorships held by the directors	13
Performance evaluation process	9
Availability and use of advisorship facility during reporting period	8
Compensation policy for senior executives departing the firm as a result of a merger or acquisition	7
Auditing	
Process for interaction with external auditors	22
Process for appointment of external auditors	22
Internal control systems	21
Process for interaction with internal auditors	19
Process for appointment of internal auditors/scope of work and responsibilities	18
Rotation of audit partners	18
Auditors` involvement in non-audit work and the fees paid to the auditors	14
Board confidence in independence and integrity of external auditors	13
Duration of current auditors	12
Corporate responsibility and compliance	
Policy and performance in connection with environmental and social responsibility	13
Mechanisms protecting the rights of other stakeholders in business	12

Disclosure item	No. of markets (max. = 25)
A code of ethics for the board and waivers to the ethics code	10
A code of ethics for all company employees	10
Impact of environmental and social responsibility policies on the firm's sustainability	7
The role of employees in corporate governance	5
Policy on "whistle blower" protection for all employees	3

General Overview

As shown in table 2, most of the disclosure items recommended in the ISAR benchmark are already the subject of mandatory disclosure requirements for listed companies in most of the markets studied. Twenty-eight of the 53 items in the ISAR benchmark, or just slightly more than half, are required by 20 or more of the 25 emerging markets included in the study. This suggests a growing consensus among emerging market regulators. In contrast, the findings also show that some of the disclosure items in the ISAR benchmark are only required by a minority of the markets studied: 11 of the 53 items in the ISAR benchmark are required by less than half of the markets in the study. This may reflect the relative novelty of some disclosure items (e.g. those in the corporate responsibility category, or a preference for voluntary disclosure for certain topics.

Considering the disclosure items by category, table 2 shows that the first three categories of disclosure items are strongly supported by disclosure requirements in the sample markets. All nine of the disclosure items in the ownership structure category were required of listed enterprises by 20 or more of the 25 markets studied. Seven of the nine disclosure items in the financial transparency category were required by 20 or more markets. And nine of the 19 disclosure items in the board and management structure category were required by 20 or more markets. In contrast, the disclosure items in the last two categories in table 2 are the subject of less mandatory disclosure requirements. The auditing category has three of nine disclosure items required by 20 or more markets, though eight of the nine items in this category are supported by at least half the 25 markets studied. The disclosure items in the category of corporate responsibility were required by the lowest number of markets, with most of the items required in less than half the markets studied. Figure 1 provides an overview of the maximum and minimum number of markets supporting individual disclosure items in each category, along with the median number of markets supporting all disclosure items within each category.

Figure 1. Overview of disclosure requirements by category
(Maximum and minimum number of markets requiring disclosure items in this category –
vertical line indicates the median number)

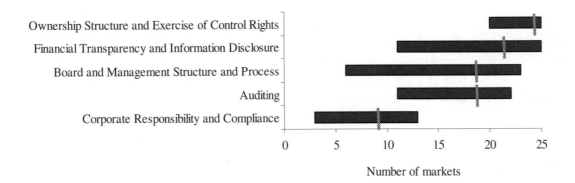

Figure 1 provides an illustration of the extent of mandatory disclosure requirements in each of the five categories. This analysis shows a different picture of reporting than that provided in the previous ISAR studies of corporate governance disclosure. In the 2005 and 2006 Reviews, which examined the actual disclosure practices of enterprises, it was the auditing category that was consistently the subject of the lowest level of disclosure among emerging markets. This contrasts with the present review of requirements, which shows that for the 25 emerging markets under review, requirements for disclosure of auditing-related information is more common than disclosure requirements related to corporate responsibility. Indeed, the latter category is subject to the least number of required disclosures. As noted above, this may be a result of the relative novelty of this category of disclosure. As seen in table 3 below, six of the bottom 10 least prevalent disclosure items are from the corporate responsibility category, while only one is from the auditing category.

Table 3. Most prevalent and least prevalent disclosure items
(Number of markets requiring this item)

Top 10 most prevalent disclosure items required among 25 emerging markets	No. of markets	Bottom 10 least prevalent disclosure items required among 25 emerging markets	No. of markets
Ownership structure*	25	Duration of current auditors*	12
Process for holding annual general meetings*	25	Mechanisms protecting the rights of other stakeholders in business	12
Changes in shareholdings	25	A code of ethics for the board and waivers to the ethics code	10
Availability and accessibility of meeting agenda	25	A code of ethics for all company employees	10
Financial and operating results*	25	Performance evaluation process	9
Control structure*	24	Availability and use of advisorship facility during reporting period*	8
Control rights	24	Compensation policy for senior executives departing the firm as a result of a merger or acquisition*	7
Governance structures, such as committees and other mechanisms to prevent conflict of interest	23	Impact of environmental and social responsibility policies on the firm's sustainability	7
Composition of board of directors (executives and non-executives)*	23	The role of employees in corporate governance*	5
Role and functions of the board of directors	23	Policy on "whistle blower" protection for all employees*	3

* Disclosure item also appears among the top/bottom 10 of most/least prevalent disclosure items among enterprises from low- and middle-income countries in the 2006 Review.

Of the 10 most prevalent disclosure items, six are from the ownership structure category. This contrasts somewhat with the findings of the 2005 and 2006 Reviews, which found that while disclosure items in this category were relatively widespread, the highest category of disclosure items was that of financial transparency. It is also noteworthy that five of the top 10 most prevalent disclosure items are required in all 25 of the markets studied. This provides an indication that for at least a few disclosure items, there is an international consensus among leading emerging markets.

Some limited comparisons can be made between the data in table 3 and the findings of the 2006 Review on most and least prevalent disclosure items. Half of the disclosure items (5 of 10) listed in the top and bottom 10 were also found among the top and bottom 10 most/least prevalent disclosure items reported by enterprises from developing countries and economies in transition. These are marked by an asterisk. The correlation between the two sets of data could be related to a number of factors. In the case of the five items found among the 2006 Review's top 10 most prevalent disclosure items among enterprises, the reason these disclosure items are so widely reported may result from the fact that they are required by many emerging markets. Likewise, the situation with the least prevalent disclosure items from the 2006 Review is that many of these are also not subject to requirements.

The data, however, would suggest caution before assigning a direct causality between regulation and disclosure. While it is true that correlation exists in many cases, it does not exist in all. Some items are the subject of mandatory requirements in few markets, yet appear relatively widespread in the 2006 Review's study of actual company reports. This relationship between the requirements and actual practice suggests a more complex situation, wherein a number of factors, including investor expectations, are influencing the disclosure practices of enterprises beyond what is mandatory. In other cases, some items that are mandatory in the 25 emerging markets studied are not prevalent among the enterprises examined in the 2006 Review. In part, this is caused by differences in the samples being studied, which do not allow for precise comparison, but in part this may also reflect poor compliance among enterprises regarding mandatory corporate disclosure.

C.   Gap analysis of disclosure requirements

Table 4 below provides another view of the main findings of the study, illustrating where gaps exist in corporate governance disclosure requirements. The top line of the table lists the numbers of the 53 disclosure items found in the ISAR benchmark, grouped according to general category. The blank or white spaces in the table indicate an absence of a mandatory requirement for disclosure of that item. The markets in the table are listed from top to bottom in order of the total number of disclosure items required. The three large developed markets are included at the bottom of the table for comparison purposes.

This presentation of the data provides an overview of the categories of disclosure where consensus exists. As noted above, in nearly all of the markets reviewed, most of the disclosure items in the ownership structure category are the subject of disclosure requirements. Seventeen of the 25 emerging markets studied require all of the items in this category.

The financial transparency category is also the subject of mandatory disclosure in most of the markets studied. However, one of the consistent gaps in this category highlighted in table 4 below is the disclosure of the impact of alternative accounting decisions (disclosure item 14 in table 4). Fourteen of the 25 emerging markets do not make disclosure of this information mandatory. The one item from this category required by all markets is the disclosure of financial and operating results (item 10 in table 4).

The auditing category demonstrates the rapid adoption of rules which were largely inspired by the corporate scandals and collapses of the early 2000s. Many of the disclosure items in this category relate to issues of the reporting enterprise's relationship to its auditors. For example, the disclosure of the duration of the current auditors (item 25 in table 4) and the rotation of audit partners (item 26), and the disclosure of auditors' involvement in non-audit work and the fees paid to the auditors (item 27), are the type of disclosure items that were popularized by the 2001 Enron scandal and the resulting 2002 Sarbanes-Oxley Act of the United States. While some of these disclosure requirements were seen as controversial at the time of introduction, they now appear as requirements in many of the markets studied.

Table 4 also highlights the gap in requirements for the corporate responsibility category. Given the relative novelty of many of the items in this category, it is perhaps unsurprising that it is not the subject of more disclosure requirements. It is noteworthy, however, that in the United Kingdom and the United States, the two largest securities markets in the world, every item in this category is the subject of mandatory disclosure.

As noted in figure 1 above, the broad category board and management structure shows the largest variation in requirements between items. For some items, such as disclosure of governance structures to prevent conflict of interest (item 35 in table 4) or disclosure of the role and functions of the board of directors (item 39), most markets require disclosure. Other items, however, are among the least required of all the items in the ISAR benchmark, for example the disclosure of the enterprise's compensation policy for senior executives departing the firm as a result of a merger or acquisition (item 46). Note, however, that while this item is rarely required in emerging markets, it is a requirement in the two largest securities markets, the United Kingdom and the United States.

Table 4. Gap analysis of disclosure requirements in 25 emerging markets and three large developed markets*

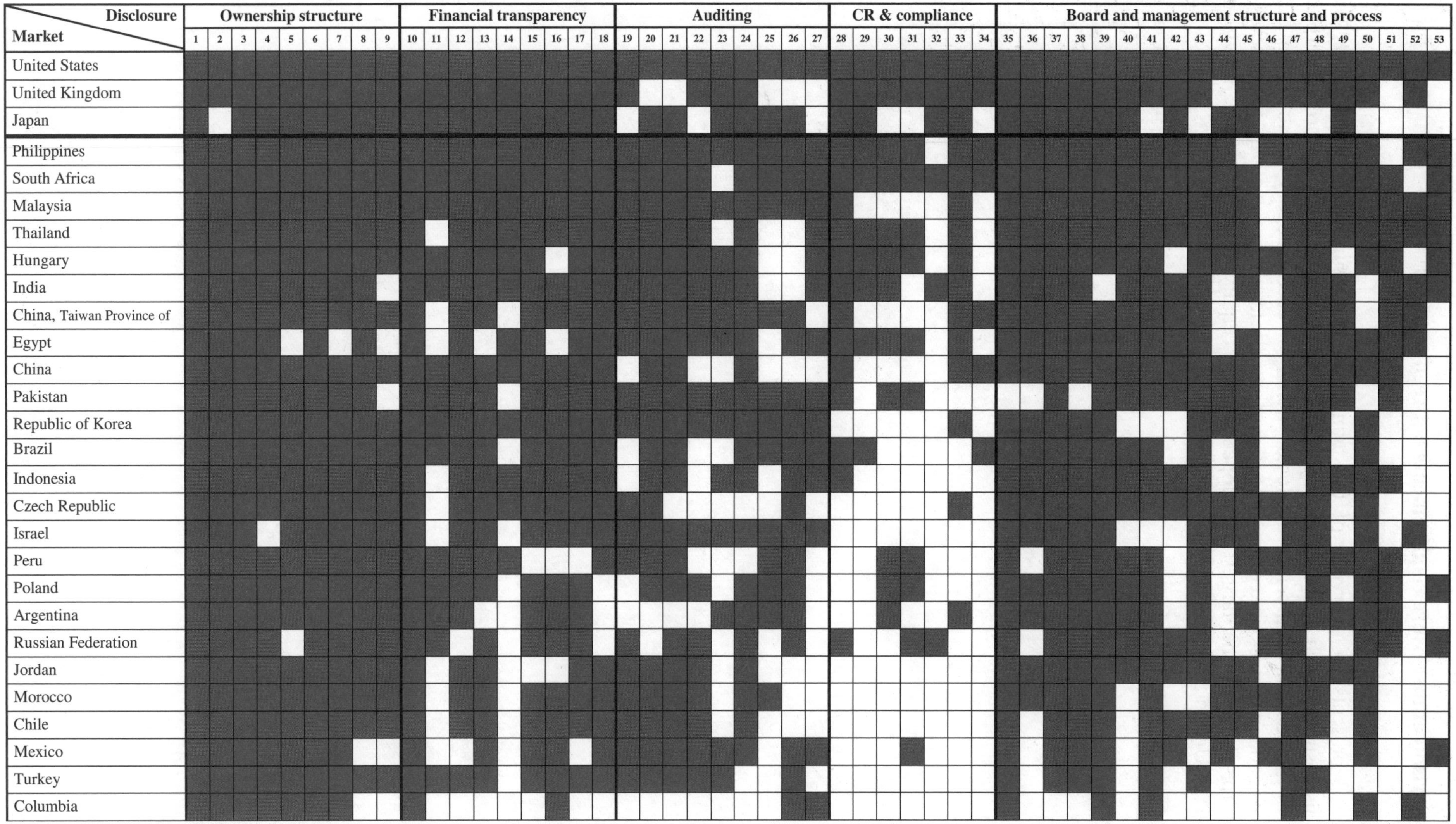
Disclosure
Market
Ownership structure
Financial transparency
Auditing
CR & compliance
Board and management structure and process
1 2 3 4 5 6 7 8 9 10 11 12 13 14 15 16 17 18 19 20 21 22 23 24 25 26 27 28 29 30 31 32 33 34 35 36 37 38 39 40 41 42 43 44 45 46 47 48 49 50 51 52 53
United States
United Kingdom
Japan
Philippines
South Africa
Malaysia
Thailand
Hungary
India
China, Taiwan Province of
Egypt
China
Pakistan
Republic of Korea
Brazil
Indonesia
Czech Republic
Israel
Peru
Poland
Argentina
Russian Federation
Jordan
Morocco
Chile
Mexico
Turkey
Columbia

Empty white squares indicate that the disclosure item is not required. The name of individual disclosure items can be found in the list in Annex II.

D.   Comparison of disclosure requirements between markets

Figure 2 presents an overview of the number of disclosure items required for each category of disclosure in each of the 25 emerging markets reviewed. For comparison purposes, the figure also includes the number of disclosure items for each category found in the ISAR benchmark of good practices in corporate governance disclosure, as well as the disclosure requirements for three of the largest developed country equity markets: Japan, the United Kingdom and the United States.

Figure 2. Disclosure requirements by market and category

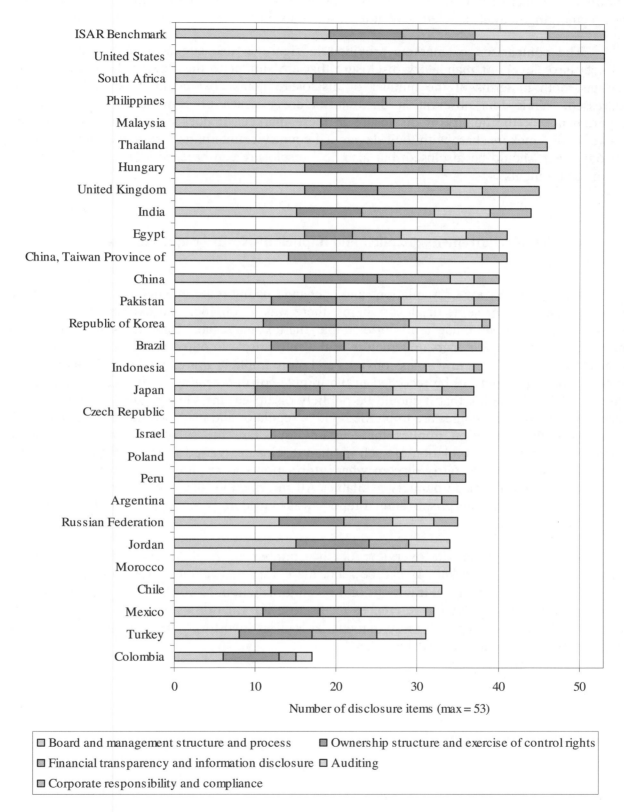

Number of disclosure items (max = 53)

☐ Board and management structure and process ☐ Ownership structure and exercise of control rights
☐ Financial transparency and information disclosure ☐ Auditing
☐ Corporate responsibility and compliance

This overview of disclosure items makes clear the relatively strong support for mandatory disclosure in many emerging markets. Nearly all of the markets studied required the disclosure of more than half the items in the ISAR benchmark. And despite the relatively low number of requirements overall for the category of corporate responsibility, figure 2 indicates that a significant number of markets have many mandatory disclosure requirements in this area: 18 of the 25 emerging markets studied have at least some disclosure requirements in this area.

The comparison of markets provided in figure 2 also suggests that many emerging markets have levels of mandatory disclosure that are similar to the leading developed country markets, both in terms of the number of disclosure items covered and the range of topics addressed. While this observation does not address issues of compliance with disclosure requirements, or the quality of disclosure in these markets, it does make clear that emerging market policy makers share with their developed country counterparts a similar understanding of not only *what* should be disclosed, but also *how* disclosure can be encouraged, i.e. through the use of requirements.

E. Clarity of requirements: explicit and implicit disclosure requirements

During the review of regulations and exchange listing requirements, it was observed that in some instances, for some disclosure items, there was an obvious and explicit requirement to disclose or report a particular item. For example, the text may state "enterprises must disclose in their annual reports the ownership structure of the enterprise". In other instances, the requirement to disclose a particular item was less obvious and more implicit. For example, a regulation might require a particular item to be recorded in the minutes of the meeting of the board of directors; without explicitly stating that it should be publicly disclosed, the same regulation may go on to state that the Board's minutes are to be filed with a regulator and made available to the public. In such cases, the regulation implies that certain issues are the subject of mandatory public disclosure. The exact formulation of such implied disclosures varied from market to market, but every effort was made to fairly discern what information was required, and whether or not that information would be made publicly available. All information that is made publicly available, even if it is not in the enterprise's annual report, was considered "disclosure" for the purposes of this study.

Figure 3 presents an overview of the number of explicit and implicit disclosure requirements for each market. As can be seen, these vary considerably from market to market, and may be related to the legal traditions of a given jurisdiction. Nevertheless, it may be useful to increase the number of explicit references to disclose information as an aid to both enterprises wishing to list on exchanges in these markets, as well as investors wishing to better understand the disclosure requirements of such markets.

Figure 3. Explicit and implicit disclosure requirements

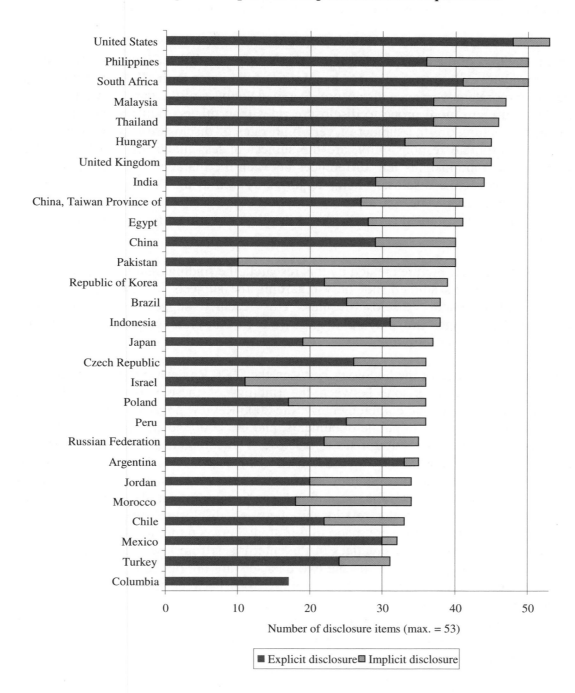

IV. Conclusions

This report is the fourth annual study of corporate governance disclosure prepared by the UNCTAD secretariat for ISAR. This study differs from earlier studies by focusing on the disclosure requirements applied to publicly listed firms by regulators and stock exchanges in the

25 economies that make up the MSCI Emerging Markets Index. The economies of the MSCI EM index were chosen as the sample for the study due to the influential role this index plays in facilitating foreign portfolio investment towards developing economies and economies in transition.

The main findings of the 2007 Review show that nearly all of the economies in the MSCI EM index have mandatory disclosure rules for a majority of the items in the ISAR benchmark of good practices in corporate governance disclosure. Detailed analysis of the data shows that some categories of disclosure are more prone to disclosure rules than others. While some categories, such as ownership structure, are the subject of very high rates of disclosure requirements, other categories, such as corporate responsibility, are the subject of less mandatory rules. The data analysis also provided some insights into differences between the markets in the sample group, both in regards to the particular disclosure items required, as well as the degree of specificity of the rules regarding disclosure. The existence of "implicit" disclosure rules, for instance, was noted to exist in every market studied (even the larger developed markets) for at least some of the items under review.

Looking at the broader picture created by this research, the findings show a high degree of consensus among the markets studied, not only regarding the subjects of disclosure, but also regarding the use of mandatory disclosure rules. This research suggests that government regulators and stock exchanges are playing a large role in corporate governance disclosure through the use of binding disclosure rules.

Although the difference in methodology between the 2006 Review and the 2007 Review does not allow for direct comparisons between the findings of these two studies, the data produced by each study is somewhat complementary: the 2006 Review provides a picture of what enterprises are actually disclosing in public documents, and the 2007 Review provides a picture of what regulators are requiring the enterprises to disclose. The complementary role of this data was designed to address the question of whether or not the low rates of disclosure of some enterprises, particularly in developing countries and economies in transition, was influenced by local regulations within these markets. Likewise, this type of research can also begin to address some of the questions surrounding the relationship between disclosure rates and disclosure requirements. Tentative comparisons were made in this study between the disclosure rules of the 25 markets studied, and the disclosure practices of the enterprises from low- and middle-income countries studied in the 2006 Review. While the two data sets are not directly aligned (the 2006 data includes more markets than the 2007 data), comparisons between the data suggest some tentative conclusions. For example, while some disclosure items are widely disclosed by enterprises, the same items are not the subject of mandatory disclosure rules. This suggests that other forces, such as investor pressure, are driving disclosure practices. In contrast to this example, some items that are required by most of the markets in the 2007 Review are the subject of very low rates of disclosure among the enterprises in the 2006 Review. This may indicate that compliance with disclosure rules is weak in some markets. Future research can seek to clarify some of these points by further aligning the data and more precisely comparing the actual disclosure practices of enterprises with the disclosure requirements of the markets in which those same enterprises are based.

Annex I: List of sources by market

Argentina
- o   Reglamento de Cotización BCBA;
- o   Normas de la Comisión Nacional de Valores;
- o   Decree Nro. 677/01;
- o   Ley de Sociedades Comerciales Nro. 19.500.

Brazil
- o   Listing Regulations of the Novo Mercado and Levels 1 and 2 of Differentiated Corporate Governance Practices;
- o   Law No. 10.303, of October 31, 2001 (Corporate Law);
- o   Law No. 6.404 of December 15, 1976;
- o   Law No. 6385 of December 7, 1976 (Securities Law).

Chile
- o   Characteristics of the Chilean Stock Market, Bolsa de Comercio de Santiago, 2003;
- o   Questionnaire of the Santiago Stock Exchange, Serie Institucional N° 3, Bolsa de Comercio de Santiago, 1999;
- o   Law No. 18,045 (Securities Market Law);
- o   Law No. 18,046 (Corporations Law).

China
- o   Interpretation of Listing Rules of the Shanghai Stock Exchange (2005–01–21) (summary), 新股票上市规则解读（汇总稿）；
- o   Shanghai Stock Exchange Listing Rules (amended in 2004), 上海证券交易所股票上市规则(2004年修订);
- o   Securities Law of the People's Republic of China (revised in 2005);
- o   Company Law of the People's Republic of China (revised in 2005).

China, Taiwan Province of
- o   Corporate Governance Best-Practice Principles for TSEC/GTSM Listed Companies, 上市上櫃公司治理實務守則;
- o   Taiwan Stock Exchange Corporation Rules Governing Information Reporting by Listed Companies;
- o   Taiwan Stock Exchange Corporation Procedures for Verification and Disclosure of Material Information of Listed Companies;
- o   Securities and Exchange Act;
- o   Company Act.

Colombia
- o   Código de Comercio;
- o   Código de mejores prácticas corporativas: Código País.

Czech Republic
- o   Section III of the Exchange Rules of the Prague Stock Exchange;
- o   Act No. 591/1992 Sb. on Securities;
- o   Commercial Code No. 513/1991 ("Obchodní zákoník").

Egypt
- o   Egyptian Code of Corporate Governance (2005);
- o   Listing Rules of the Cairo Alexandria Stock Exchange.

Hungary
- o   Corporate Governance Recommendations, Budapest Stock Exchange, 2004;
- o   Regulations of the Budapest Stock Exchange for listing, continued trading and disclosure;

- o   Act CXLIV of 1997 on Business Associations (Companies Act);
- o   C Act of 2000 on Accounting.

India

- o   Listing Agreement for Equity, Bombay Stock Exchange.

Indonesia

- o   Regulation Number I-A Listing Requirements, Jakarta Stock Exchange;
- o   Regulation Number I-E Concerning the Obligation of Information Submission, Jakarta Stock Exchange;
- o   Bapepam Rules Number VIII.G.11;
- o   Bapepam Rules Number VIII.G.2.

Israel

- o   Company Law 5759-1999;
- o   The Securities Law.

Japan

- o   Security Listing Regulations, Tokyo Stock Exchange (TSE);
- o   Principles of Corporate Governance for Listed Companies, TSE;
- o   Criteria of Listing, TSE;
- o   Listing Guides for Foreign Companies, TSE;
- o   Securities Listing Regulations, TSE;
- o   Rules on Timely Disclosure of Corporate Information by Issuer of Listed Security and the Like, TSE;
- o   New Legislative Framework for Investor Protection, Financial Services Agency;
- o   Law Concerning the Promotion of Business Activities with Environmental Consideration by Specified Corporations, Ministry of the Environment;
- o   The Whistle Blower Protection Act.

Jordan

- o   Directives for Listing Securities on the Amman Stock Exchange, 2004;
- o   The Securities Law, 2002;
- o   The Companies Law No. 22 of 1997.

Republic of Korea

- o   Stock Market Disclosure Regulation, 2006, Korea Exchange (KRX);
- o   Stock Market Operational Guidelines on Fair Disclosure, 2005, KRX;
- o   Stock Market Listing Regulation, 2005, KRX;
- o   Enforcement Rule of Stock Market Listing Regulation, 2006, KRX;
- o   Commercial Act, Republic of Korea.

Malaysia

- o   Best Practices in Corporate Disclosure, Kuala Lumpur Stock Exchange (KLSE);
- o   Statement on Internal Control – Guidance for Directors of Public Listed Companies, KLSE;
- o   Listing Requirements for Main Board and Second Board, KLSE;
- o   Malaysian Code on Corporate Governance, Securities Commission Malaysia.

Mexico

- o   Ley General de Sociedades Mercantiles;
- o   Ley del Mercado de valores;
- o   Code of Best Corporate Practices, 2006, Bolsa Mexicana de Valores (BMV);
- o   Corporate Governance Code for Mexico, 2002, BMV;
- o   Code of Professional Ethics of the Mexican Stock Exchange Community, BMV.

Morocco

- o   General Rules of the Stock Exchange (Casablanca-Bourse);
- o   Loi N° 17-95 Relative aux Societes Anonymes.

Pakistan

- o   General Rules of the Karachi Stock Exchange;

- o Listing Regulations of the Karachi Stock Exchange:
- o Code of Corporate Governance, Securities and Exchange Commission of Pakistan.

Peru
- o Reglamento de inscripción y exclusión de valores mobiliarios en la Bolsa de Valores de Lima;
- o Ley General de las Sociedades;
- o Reglamento de Hechos de Importancia, Información Reservada y Otras Comunicaciones;
- o Reglamento de Propiedad Indirecta, Vinculación y Grupos Económicos;
- o Reglamento de Oferta Pública de Adquisión y de Compra de Valores por Exclusión;
- o Reglamento de Información Financiera y Manual para la Preparación de Información Financiera;
- o Manual para la Preparación de Memorias Anuales y Normas Comunes para la determinación del contenido de Documentos Informativos.

Philippines
- o Listing rules for the Philippines Stock Exchange (PSE);
- o Financial Disclosure Checklist (Philippines Securities and Exchange Commission);
- o Philippines Code of Corporate Governance.

Poland
- o The Warsaw Stock Exchange Rules, 2006;
- o Detailed Exchange Trading Rules, 2007 (Warsaw Stock Exchange);
- o Best Practices for Warsaw Stock Exchange Listed Companies;
- o The Law on the Public Trading of Securities, 2004, as amended;
- o ACT on Public Offering, Conditions Governing the Introduction of Financial Instruments to Organized Trading, and Public Companies, 2005.

Russian Federation
- o Кодекс корпоративного поведения (Corporate Behaviour Code);
- o Listing rules for the Moscow Interbank Currency Exchange (MICEX).

South Africa
- o Stock exchange listing rules for the Johannesburg Stock Exchange;
- o The King Code of Corporate Practices and Conduct 2002.

Thailand
- o Disclosure Manual, 2007, Stock Exchange of Thailand (SET);
- o Principles of Good Corporate Governance for Listed Companies, 2006, SET;
- o SET Code of Best Practice for Directors of Listed Companies.

Turkey
- o Disclosure Requirements Regarding Financial Statements (Istanbul Stock Exchange);
- o Communiqué on Principles Regarding Public Disclosure of Material Events (Capital Markets Board of Turkey);
- o Istanbul Stock Exchange Listing Regulation;
- o The Capital Markets Law (Capital Markets Board of Turkey).

United Kingdom
- o Disclosure Rules and Transparency Rules, Finance Service Association (FSA);
- o FSA Handbook;
- o The City Code on Takeovers and Mergers, The Panel on Takeovers and Mergers.

United States
- o Final NYSE Corporate Governance Rules (303A), New York Stock Exchange (NYSE);
- o Listed Companies Manual, NYSE;
- o Sarbanes-Oxley Act;
- o Ownership Reports and Trading by Officers, Directors and Principal Security Holders, Securities and Exchange Commission (SEC);

o   Universal Internet Availability of Proxy Materials, SEC;
o   Regulation S-K, SEC.

Annex II: List of disclosure items in the ISAR benchmark

No.	Disclosure item
Ownership structure and exercise of control rights	
1	Ownership structure
2	Process for holding annual general meetings
3	Changes in shareholdings
4	Control structure
5	Control and corresponding equity stake
6	Availability and accessibility of meeting agenda
7	Control rights
8	Rules and procedures governing the acquisition of corporate control in capital markets.
9	Anti-takeover measures
Financial transparency and information disclosure	
10	Financial and operating results
11	Critical accounting estimates
12	Nature, type and elements of related-party transactions
13	Company objectives
14	Impact of alternative accounting decisions
15	Disclosure practices on related party transactions where control exists
16	The decision-making process for approving transactions with related parties
17	Rules and procedures governing extraordinary transactions
18	Board's responsibilities regarding financial communications
Auditing	
19	Process for interaction with internal auditors
20	Process for interaction with external auditors
21	Process for appointment of external auditors
22	Process for appointment of internal auditors/scope of work and responsibilities
23	Board confidence in independence and integrity of external auditors
24	Internal control systems
25	Duration of current auditors
26	Rotation of audit partners

No.	Disclosure item
27	Auditors` involvement in non-audit work and the fees paid to the auditors
Corporate responsibility and compliance	
28	Policy and performance in connection with environmental and social responsibility
29	Impact of environmental and social responsibility policies on the firm's sustainability
30	A code of ethics for the board and waivers to the ethics code
31	A code of ethics for all company employees
32	Policy on "whistle blower" protection for all employees
33	Mechanisms protecting the rights of other stakeholders in business
34	The role of employees in corporate governance
Board and management structure and process	
35	Governance structures, such as committees and other mechanisms to prevent conflict of interest
36	"Checks and balances" mechanisms
37	Composition of board of directors (executives and non-executives)
38	Composition and function of governance committee structures
39	Role and functions of the board of directors
40	Risk management objectives, system and activities
41	Qualifications and biographical information on board members
42	Types and duties of outside board and management positions
43	Material interests of members of the board and management
44	Existence of plan of succession
45	Duration of director's contracts
46	Compensation policy for senior executives departing the firm as a result of a merger or acquisition
47	Determination and composition of directors` remuneration
48	Independence of the board of directors
49	Number of outside board and management position directorships held by the directors
50	Existence of procedure(s) for addressing conflicts of interest among board members
51	Professional development and training activities
52	Availability and use of advisorship facility during reporting period
53	Performance evaluation process

2007 review of the implementation status of corporate governance disclosures: Case study of Egypt[*]

I. Introduction

The Intergovernmental Working Group of Experts on International Standards of Accounting and Reporting (ISAR) has been working in the area of corporate governance since 1989 (E/C.10/AC.3/1989/6). During the twenty-first session of ISAR in 2004, the group of experts requested the development of an annual study to assess the state of reporting on corporate governance. This resulted in a series of annual reviews presented at each of the subsequent ISAR sessions, including the twenty-second and twenty-third sessions. These annual reviews examined corporate governance disclosure practices around the world, including a number of enterprises from different regions. They were facilitated by the development of ISAR's benchmark of good practices in corporate governance disclosure. This benchmark consists of 53 disclosure items and is explained in detail in the UNCTAD publication *Guidance on Good Practices in Corporate Governance Disclosure*. This publication was the outcome of ISAR deliberations, particularly those of the twenty-second session.

This report is a case study of corporate governance disclosure in Egypt. It was conducted in cooperation with the American University in Cairo[1] and with support from the Cairo Alexandria Stock Exchange (CASE). The study utilizes the ISAR benchmark and the general methodology employed in the 2005 and 2006 reviews conducted by the UNCTAD secretariat.[2]

The objectives of this study are to: (a) provide a brief overview of key recent developments in Egypt related to corporate governance disclosure; and (b) present and analyse the results of the review of corporate disclosure practices among leading enterprises in Egypt. The overview of recent developments is provided in chapter I, which also examines the statutory framework in Egypt related to corporate governance and recent reforms to Egypt's capital markets, and rules and regulations related to corporate practices. Chapter II presents and analyses the results of the review, looking in detail at disclosure rates for each individual item in the ISAR benchmark.

II. Overview of recent developments in corporate governance disclosure in Egypt

This chapter provides a brief overview of the regulatory framework in Egypt as it relates to corporate governance disclosure, along with an overview of recent reforms directed at

---

[1] This document was prepared and edited by the UNCTAD secretariat based on research conducted by Dr. Khaled M. Dahawy, Associate Professor of Accounting, Head of the Accounting Unit, Department of Management, the American University in Cairo.

[2] For example, see the 2006 review of the implementation status of corporate governance disclosures (TD/B/COM.2/ISAR/CRP.3).

improving the state of corporate governance in the country. Since the high-profile collapses of a number of large United States firms such as Enron and WorldCom, there has been considerable interest among developed and developing nations alike in the corporate governance practices of modern corporations. As in many developing nations, corporate governance remains a relatively new subject for Egyptian businesses and regulatory bodies.

In the late 1990s, even before the Enron-type scandals broke, Egypt had already begun engaging in a number of activities aimed at improving its corporate governance practices. Government and business leaders in Egypt recognized that if applied properly, corporate governance helps countries to realize high and sustainable rates of growth. When practiced widely, good practices in corporate governance disclosure can boost investor confidence in a country's economy, help deepen capital markets, and increase the ability of a country to mobilize savings and increase investment flows. Corporate governance disclosure facilitates access to a wider pool of investors by helping to protect the rights of minority shareholders and small investors. It also encourages the growth of the private sector by supporting its competitive capabilities, helping to secure financing for projects, generating profits and creating job opportunities.

The importance of corporate governance for developing countries was shown by a study that was performed in 2002 by McKinsey Consulting that surveyed over 200 institutional investors.[3] The results of the survey showed that 80 per cent of the respondents were ready to pay a premium for well-governed companies. The study further indicated that this premium amounted to 40 per cent in the case of Egypt. Improving corporate governance in Egypt, therefore, is a means of creating value for the country's enterprises and economy as a whole.

A. Overview of the statutory framework in Egypt

Generally, the French civil law is the primary source of Egypt's corporate legal framework (companies' law 159/1981). However, Anglo-American common law concepts prevail in the Capital Market Law and the Central Depository Law. The main laws governing the legal framework that impacts the concepts of corporate governance in Egypt can be divided into two main groups:

Laws governing incorporation of companies:

1. *Companies' Law* (CL 159/1981), which regulates joint stock companies, limited liability companies and partnerships limited by shares;

2. *Investment Law* (IL 8/1997), which endorses investment in specific industrial locations or economic sectors by offering specific income tax exemptions or tax free zones;[4] and

3. *Public Business Sector Law* (PBLS 203/1991), the law that governs the incorporation of public business sector companies; and

Laws governing public and private sector companies listed on the Cairo Alexandria Stock Exchange (CASE):

---

[3] McKinsey (2002). Emerging Market Policy Maker Opinion Survey on Corporate Governance.
[4] Many of the tax exemptions offered in this law have been cancelled by the new tax law 91/2005.

4. *Capital Market Law (CML 95/1992),* the main law regulating the Egyptian financial market in terms of monitoring the market status in general and maintaining steadiness and growth; and

5. *Central Depository Law (CDL 93/2000),* which aims at reducing risks associated with trading physical securities, enhancing market liquidity, in addition to assuring fast securities exchange. In other words, the law maintains all registration, clearance and settlement procedures associated with trading transactions.

Efforts are currently under way to draft and discuss a unified law that would replace many laws and dispersed provisions. This unified law would ensure that all businesses in Egypt adhere to the same law following a modernized regulatory system that facilitates investor's dealings with administrative authorities and promotes transparency. The unified companies' law is expected to replace the current laws to remove conflicts and obstacles to local and foreign investments in Egypt. The first draft of the law was initially prepared in 1998 and several amendments have since been made by the ministry of investment and the General Authority for Investment and Free Zones (GAFI). However, as of the fourth quarter of 2007, this draft law is still being discussed in the people's assembly and has not yet been formally issued.

B.   Corporate governance reforms in Egypt since the late 1990s

In the late 1990s, a well-tailored economic reform programme, fully supported by the World Bank and the International Monetary Fund (IMF), was cumulatively implemented to cover the whole economic spectrum. As part of its privatization program, the Government of Egypt decided to revitalize its capital market by improving its reputation and building confidence among investors. The aim was to raise new foreign capital and to encourage more Egyptians to invest in the domestic markets rather than continuing to invest abroad. This development programme aimed at sound financial principles, availability of reliable corporate information, and adoption of international accounting and auditing standards. Thus, Egyptian authorities understood the need for good corporate governance practices to reach these goals.

In 2001, an assessment of Egypt's corporate governance was conducted jointly by the World Bank and the IMF, as the first Arab country to undergo a ROSC analysis.[5] This assessment evaluated corporate governance practices in Egypt against the recommendations of the Organization for Economic Cooperation and Development (OECD) Principles of Corporate Governance. The results indicated that Egypt applied 62 per cent of the principles. Following on from the ROSC assessment, Egypt started issuing new rules to guarantee companies' implementation of corporate governance practices. The most important among these rules were the new CASE listing rules issued in 2002.

The new listing rules included comprehensive corporate governance disclosure requirements (Article 12-19), as well as detailed requirements for financial statements preparation and presentation (Article 20-33). In addition, the new rules required the presentation of complete information about a company's board members, signed contracts with other companies, auditors, and the audit committee (Article 4). Finally, CASE issued strict delisting rules (Article 34-35) which forced the publicly listed companies of Egypt to make a commitment to corporate

---

[5] World Bank (2001). Report on the Observance of Standards and Codes (ROSC). Corporate Governance Country Assessment: Arab Republic of Egypt.

governance requirements, or risk losing their listing on the stock exchange. In 2007, CASE was working on producing new listing rules that incorporate a number of changes to further strengthen the corporate governance practices of the companies that are listed on the CASE.

In another effort to strengthen corporate governance, the Government of Egypt established the Egyptian Institute of Directors in 2003. The Institute works jointly with a range of international organizations, including the World Bank, International Finance Corporation, UNCTAD and the Centre for International Private Enterprise. One of the main goals of the Institute is to spread awareness and improve corporate governance practices in Egypt. The Institute seeks to fulfil its mission through a range of training and advocacy activities, including the provision of information on corporate governance principles, codes and best practices.

As one of the first institutes in the Arab region dealing with corporate governance issues, the Egyptian Institute of Directors not only serves Egypt, but also Middle Eastern and North African (MENA) countries. It serves senior company officials and other stakeholders at listed enterprises, State-owned enterprises and financial services companies. Accordingly, the Institute organizes conferences, seminars and training sessions on corporate governance, targeting different categories including directors, auditors and accountants, businessmen, and anyone interested in knowing more about corporate governance.

From its inception, the Institute was supervised by the Ministry of Investment according to Presidential decree No. 231/2004. The Institute is expected, however, to become a non-governmental, not-for-profit organization, by the end of 2007. The institute will be established on the principles of membership, which will be available to various categories including both corporate and individual members. Membership will also be available to foreigners who are interested in the Egyptian market and/or would like to make use of Egypt's role as an emerging leader on corporate governance issues in the MENA region.

The Egyptian Institute of Directors has taken several steps in its continuing efforts towards improving good corporate governance practices and strengthening the boards of directors in regional companies. For example, in April 2007, Institute hosted on its premises the first meeting of the ''Certified Director Forum of Egypt''. The founding members of the forum are the graduates of the first and second intakes of the Board Development Series, a certificate programme offered by the Institute jointly with the International Finance Corporation, aimed at promoting awareness of corporate governance issues to senior company officials. In 2007, the Institute has also conducted competitions for the best annual report and best website, with corporate governance disclosure as one of the main criteria. The intent of these competitions is to promote world-class standards in corporate reporting and to underscore the vital role of annual reports and websites in propagating full disclosure and transparency, and effective corporate governance. In May 2007, the Institute issued a manual for audit committees to ensure that corporate governance principles will be applied properly. In addition, it has launched a national campaign to update the corporate governance code issued in October 2005 for listed companies.

In 2004, the World Bank conducted a re-assessment of corporate governance implementation in Egypt, concluding that Egypt applied 82 per cent of the OECD principles (ROSC 2004). This indicates that Egypt is continuously improving in the area of corporate governance. The report observed that the major areas of improvement included basic shareholders rights, cost/benefit to voting, and disclosure standards. However, all items of the third principle – "Role of stakeholders in corporate governance" – remained the same in both assessments, thus signalling an area for improvement.

In 2005, the Capital Market Authority (CMA) further contributed to the corporate governance reforms by restructuring its organization and initiating a separate sector focused on corporate finance and corporate governance. The new CMA organization structure (shown in figure 1 below) includes three major sectors: (a) the Corporate Finance and Corporate Governance sector; (b) The Market Regulation sector; and (c) the Market Surveillance and Enforcement sector, in addition to other central departments and units.

Figure 1. New CMA organization

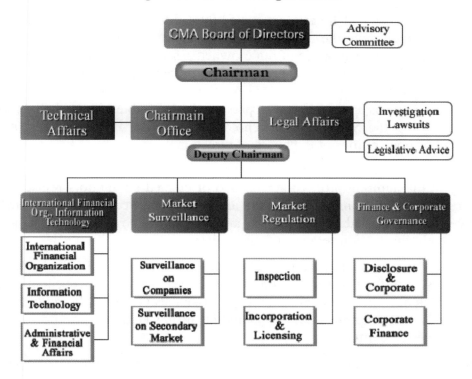

Source: Capital Market Authority, Government of Egypt.

Also in 2005, the Ministry of Investment and GAFI took the initiative to introduce the first Egyptian Code of Corporate Governance (ECCG) written in Arabic. These guidelines are to be primarily implemented in joint-stock companies listed on the stock exchange, especially those undergoing active trading operations, and financial institutions in the form of joint stock companies. These are the enterprises with ownership disbursed over numerous shareholders and necessitate a definition of the relation between ownership and management, and are also the enterprises that directly affect a vast number of stakeholders. The ECCG is also applicable to companies that use the banking system as a major source of financing; in this case, compliance with corporate governance standards assists in strengthening the rights of creditors. The code indicates that its rules should be considered in addition to the corporate related provisions stated under various laws (especially CL 159/1981 and CML 95/1992) and the executive regulations and decrees regarding their implementation. The ECCG is divided into nine related chapters that introduce the rules and procedures related to the following subjects:

(a) Scope;

(b) General Assembly;

(c) Board of directors;

(d) Internal audit department;

(e) External auditor;

(f) Audit committee;

(g)   Disclosure of social policies;

(h)   Avoiding conflict of interest; and

(i)   Corporate governance rules for other corporations.

In 2006, the Ministry of Investment issued the Code of Corporate Governance for State-Owned Companies based on the ECCG and the report of the OECD working group on privatization and corporate governance of State-owned assets.[6] The code introduces the principles of governing State-owned companies by presenting an organizational and legal framework within which such companies should operate. In addition, the code focuses on the actions of the State as a regulator versus its role as an owner. It also presents the principles for equitable treatment of all shareholders, including the State as a shareholder, conflict of interest issues, disclosure and transparency, and responsibilities of the board of directors.

CMA has also taken some actions in support of corporate governance by improving the level of quality in the auditing profession. In 2006, it created an auditors registry. The auditors that join this registry are the only ones that are allowed to audit companies that are listed on the stock exchange. Auditors listed on this registry are expected to be of the highest calibre, and this is reflected in the eligibility requirements of this registry.

In 2007, CMA issued a new code of ethics for auditors in Egypt.[7] The code discusses and explains the rules and regulations for important issues such as independence of auditors, objectivity, competence, confidentiality and professional conduct. In addition, it presents conditions and rules for important topics, including hiring auditors, conflict of interest, fees, marketing of services, and gifts.

Several non-profit organizations have also begun to recognize the importance of corporate governance in developing the Egyptian business environment. The Egyptian Junior Businessmen association has focused on creating an awareness campaign comprised of several events, including workshops and roundtables. In addition, the association issued the Corporate Governance Manual for Family Businesses in October 2006, which is considered the first guide in Egypt and the MENA region for family companies seeking growth and sustainability for their business.

.. This has included a number of legal reforms, as well as new institutions and codes of conduct which specifically seek to create awareness of good corporate governance practices. According to the World Bank's ROSC studies of Egypt, the country has made significant progress in implementing its overall regulatory framework for promoting corporate governance, although a number of areas are recognized as requiring additional attention. Chapter II below contributes to the broader work of promoting corporate governance in Egypt by providing a picture of current reporting practices among leading enterprises.

---

[6] OECD (2005). OECD Guidelines on Corporate Governance of State-owned Enterprises.
[7] CMA (2007). Code of Ethics of Accountants and Auditors Listed at CMA Register.

III. Status of implementation of good practices in corporate governance disclosure in Egypt

A.   Background and methodology

The purpose of this study is to evaluate the level of implementation of good practices in corporate governance disclosure in Egypt. It was undertaken by the Accounting Unit of the American University in Cairo, in cooperation with the UNCTAD secretariat. The study compares the corporate reporting practices of a leading set of Egyptian enterprises with the ISAR benchmark of 53 disclosure items. This is based on the UNCTAD publication *Guidance on Good Practices in Corporate Governance Disclosure* and consists of 53 disclosure items covering five broad subject categories:

(a) Financial transparency and information disclosure;

(b) Ownership structure and exercise of control rights;

(c) Board and management structure and process;

(d) Corporate responsibility and compliance; and

(e) Auditing.

The sample of enterprises selected for the study is composed of the 30 enterprises that made up the CASE 30 in 2005. The CASE 30 is the most commonly used index to measure the performance of the Egyptian capital market. It is a price index that includes the CASE's top 30 enterprises measured by market capitalization and adjusted by the free float.[8] Companies constituting the CASE 30 in 2005 represented a range of industries, as indicated in table 1 below.

Table 1. CASE 30 industrial classification

Sector	Number of companies
Building materials and construction	3
Communication	3
Entertainment	2
Financial services	6
Holding companies	2
Housing and real estate	4
Information technology	1
Media	1
Mining and gas	2
Textiles and clothing	6

CASE 30 companies typically represent the largest enterprises in Egypt, making the most significant contribution to the country's economy. Table 2 provides an overview of the aggregate financial data for the CASE 30 index.

---

[8] Note that free float must be at least 15 per cent for a company to be listed on the CASE.

Table 2. CASE 30 financial overview

(All figures Egyptian pounds, 2005 data)

Description	Average	Maximum	Minimum
Sales	1,299,127,195	18,730,653,475	163,506
Assets	6,018,092,334	38,274,231,487	1,145,770
Liabilities	7,210,896,977	87,619,977,251	122,409
Equity	1,143,858,505	9,628,309,993	1,023,361
Net income	316,783,917	3,900,011,434	-31,419,324

This study is mainly dependent on a manual and electronic survey of the public information that is available for the CASE 30 companies. The information covered in the study is primarily taken from 2005 annual reports and other data published in 2006 or early 2007. At the time of data collection, annual reports for 2006 were not yet available for most of the enterprises in the study.

B.   Main outcomes of the survey: overview of all disclosure items

Table 3 provides an overview of the corporate governance disclosure items in the UNCTAD publication *Guidance on Good Practices in Corporate Governance Disclosure*. The disclosure items are organized into five thematic groups. Next to each disclosure item is the number of CASE 30 companies found to be disclosing this item.

Table 3. Main findings of survey on CASE 30 corporate governance disclosure

Disclosure items by category	Number of enterprises disclosing this item (max. = 30)
Ownership structure and exercise of control rights	
Ownership structure	13
Process for holding annual general meetings	4
Changes in shareholdings	3
Control structure	13
Control and corresponding equity stake	13
Availability and accessibility of meeting agenda	5
Control rights	13
Rules and procedures governing the acquisition of corporate control in capital markets	2
Anti-takeover measures	0

Disclosure items by category	Number of enterprises disclosing this item (max. = 30)
Financial transparency	
Financial and operating results	30
Critical accounting estimates	29
Nature, type and elements of related-party transactions	26
Company objectives	30
Impact of alternative accounting decisions	0
Disclosure practices on related party transactions where control exists	20
The decision-making process for approving transactions with related parties	0
Rules and procedures governing extraordinary transactions	1
Board's responsibilities regarding financial communications	4
Auditing	
Process for interaction with internal auditors	1
Process for interaction with external auditors	2
Process for appointment of external auditors	1
Process for appointment of internal auditors/scope of work and responsibilities	2
Board confidence in independence and integrity of external auditors	2
Internal control systems	1
Duration of current auditors	1
Rotation of audit partners	1
Auditors' involvement in non-audit work and the fees paid to the auditors	0
Corporate responsibility and compliance	
Policy and performance in connection with environmental and social responsibility	8
Impact of environmental and social responsibility policies on the firm's sustainability	8
A code of ethics for the board and waivers to the ethics code	1
A code of ethics for all company employees	1
Policy on "whistle blower" protection for all employees	0
Mechanisms protecting the rights of other stakeholders in business	2
The role of employees in corporate governance	1

Disclosure items by category	Number of enterprises disclosing this item (max. = 30)
Board and management structure and process	
Governance structures, such as committees and other mechanisms to prevent conflict of interest	5
"Checks and balances" mechanisms	6
Composition of board of directors (executives and non-executives)	10
Composition and function of governance committee structures	4
Role and functions of the board of directors	4
Risk management objectives, system and activities	24
Qualifications and biographical information on board members	7
Types and duties of outside board and management positions	7
Material interests of members of the board and management	0
Existence of plan of succession	6
Duration of director's contracts	4
Compensation policy for senior executives departing the firm as a result of a merger or acquisition	1
Determination and composition of directors' remuneration	4
Independence of the board of directors	4
Number of outside board and management position directorships held by the directors	7
Existence of procedure(s) for addressing conflicts of interest among board members	1
Professional development and training activities	4
Availability and use of advisorship facility during reporting period	1
Performance evaluation process	1

As shown in table 3 above, the strongest group of disclosure items is financial transparency and the weakest group is auditing. The ownership structure category and the board and management structure category show mixed results, with a number of disclosure items being reported by a majority of CASE 30 firms, while other items are reported by only a few, or even none. Six disclosure items are reported by 20 or more enterprises in the CASE 30. Of these six, five are in the financial transparency category, and one is in the board and management structure category.

Forty-seven of the 53 items in the ISAR benchmark are disclosed by less than half of the CASE 30 enterprises. Five disclosure items in the ISAR benchmark were not found at all among the corporate reporting of the CASE 30. These five included relatively new disclosure practices such as the item "auditor involvement in non-audit work and the fees paid to the auditors" (an item that became more common only after the 2001 Enron/Arthur Anderson scandal), as well as more traditional corporate governance disclosures such as the item *"material interests of the members of the Board of Directors or the item anti-takeover measures"*.

To put these findings in context, it is worth noting that the idea of corporate disclosure in general is a relatively new requirement for Egyptian enterprises that was not introduced until the 1990s with the revitalization of the CASE. It is also important to note that some disclosure items refer to practices that are not very common in Egypt, such as takeovers, whistle blowing, etc. As a result, measures and procedures related to these items are not commonly disclosed. In addition, it is important to note that Egyptian laws explain in detail many of the procedures and rules that companies are expected to follow, especially those related to the general assembly and the board of directors' functions and meetings. Therefore, many companies believe that there is no need to disclose any information about these things because they are described in the law. This logic, although prevalent, is flawed: while the laws indicate in a general way what should happen, the purpose of corporate disclosure is to report specifically what actually happened. The disclosure of actual practices is more relevant for an enterprise's stakeholders, as it assures, among other things, that the enterprise (at a minimum) meets the relevant rules and regulations.

As noted above, disclosure items from the financial transparency category were the most prevalent within the reports of CASE 30 enterprises. Figure 2 below provides a graphical view of the disclosure items in this group. Two of the items are disclosed by all 30 of the enterprises studied, with five of the nine items in this group disclosed by two thirds or more.

Figure 2. Financial transparency
(Disclosure items ranked in order of prevalence among the CASE 30)

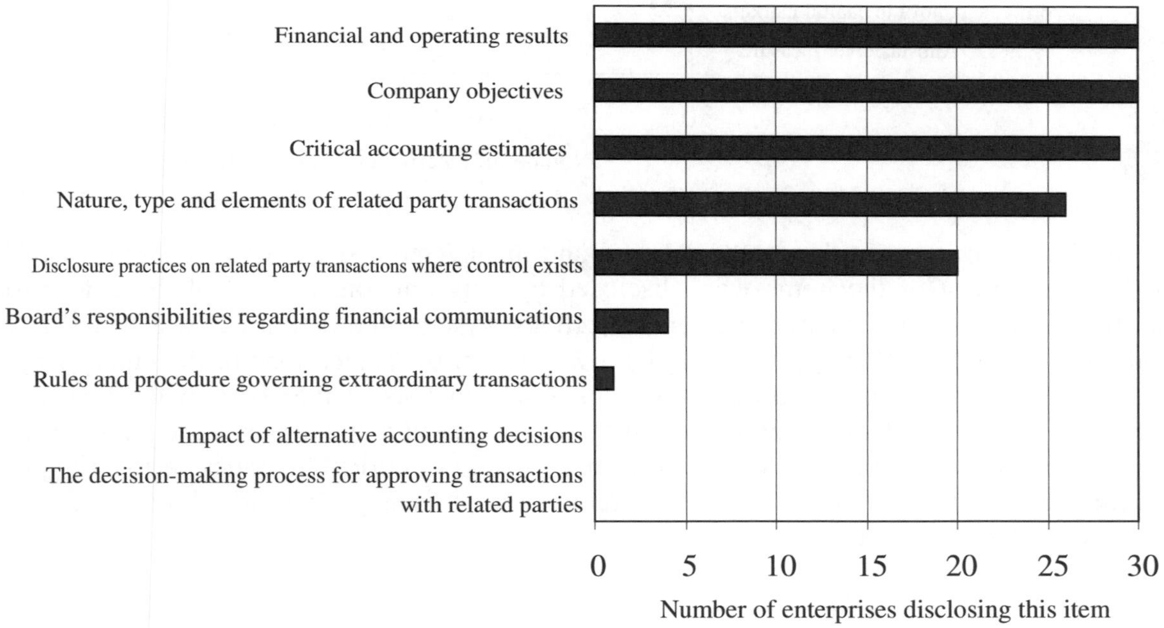

Number of enterprises disclosing this item

The next most prevalent group of disclosure items was ownership structure. As displayed in figure 3 below, four of these items were disclosed by more than one third of CASE 30 enterprises. On the lower end of the scale were disclosure items such as "process for holding annual general meetings and changes in shareholdings" that were disclosed by less than five of the 30 enterprises under review. As noted above, no enterprise in the study disclosed information on anti-takeover measures.

Concerning the disclosure of the item "availability and accessibility of meeting agenda", Egyptian listing rules require that companies publish their meeting invitation and agenda in two widely-read newspapers, but not anywhere else, such as on the websites of the reporting company, CASE or CMA, or through other means of corporate reporting. In this study's examination of a large sample of leading Egyptian newspapers, very few instances of enterprises actually reporting this item were found. Regarding the item on the "process for holding annual general meetings", it is suspected that since Egyptian law provides a generic description of the process of holding an annual general meeting, enterprises do not think they need to report on their actual practices in this area.

Figure 3. Ownership structure and exercise of control rights
(Disclosure items ranked in order of prevalence among the CASE 30)

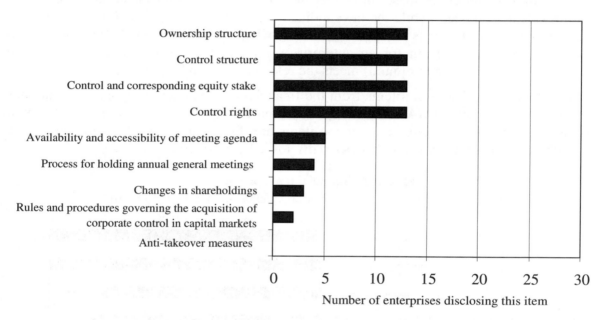

Number of enterprises disclosing this item

Disclosure of items in the category board and management structure varied considerably (figure 4). While most of the items were disclosed by between four and 10 of the enterprises studied, the disclosure on "risk management objectives, system and activities" was found to be reported on by 24 of the 30 enterprises. On the lower end of the scale, none of the enterprises in the study appeared to disclose information on "material interests of members of the board and management". The research team conducting this study observed that compensation packages and an individual's ownership of shares in a firm are typically confidential issues in the Egyptian market. It is very difficult to find details on the remuneration package or insider holdings of most directors, managers and board members.

Figure 4. Board and management structure and process
(Disclosure items ranked in order of prevalence among the CASE 30)

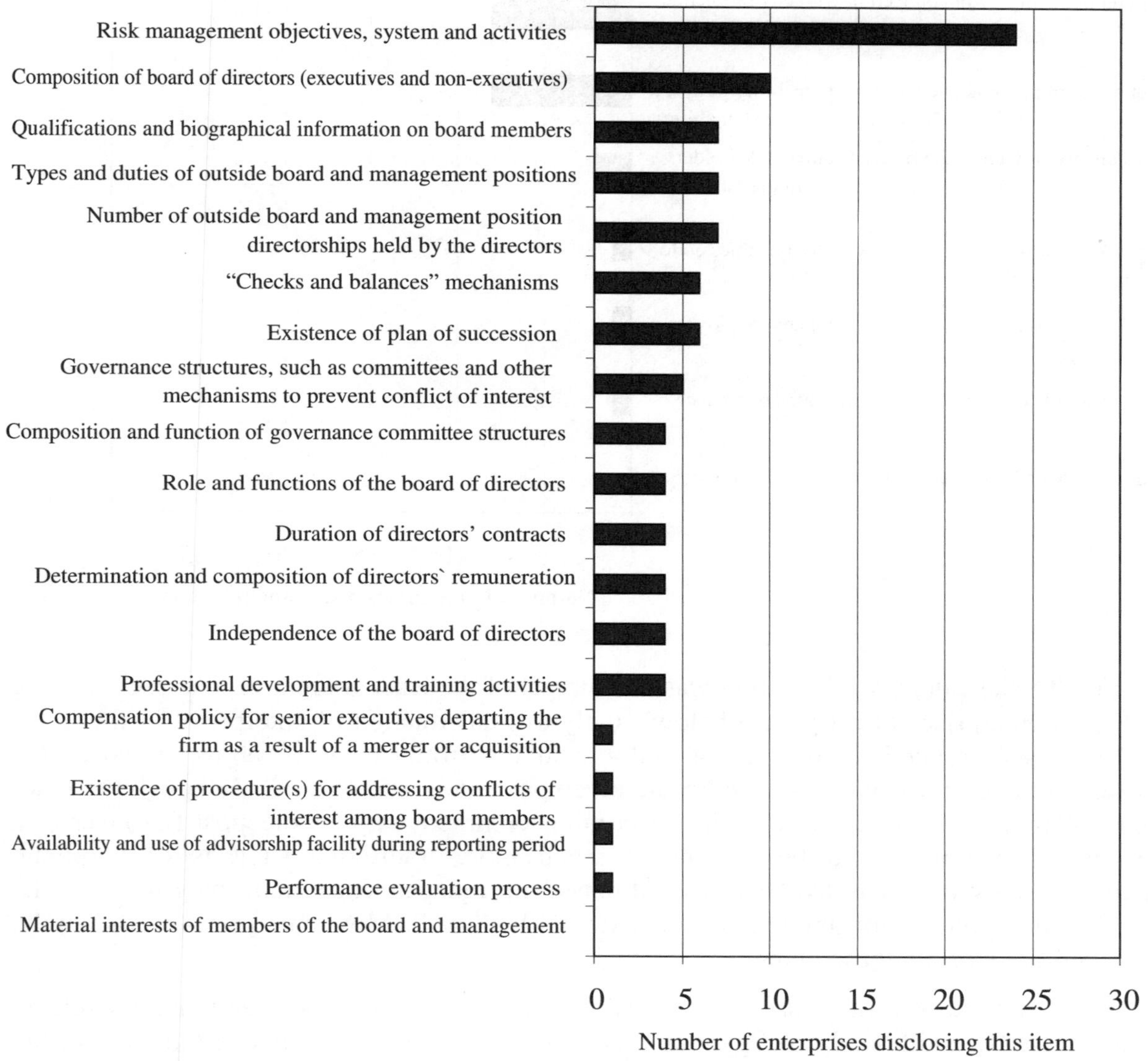

Disclosure item	Number of enterprises disclosing this item
Risk management objectives, system and activities	24
Composition of board of directors (executives and non-executives)	10
Qualifications and biographical information on board members	7
Types and duties of outside board and management positions	7
Number of outside board and management position directorships held by the directors	7
"Checks and balances" mechanisms	6
Existence of plan of succession	6
Governance structures, such as committees and other mechanisms to prevent conflict of interest	5
Composition and function of governance committee structures	4
Role and functions of the board of directors	4
Duration of directors' contracts	4
Determination and composition of directors' remuneration	4
Independence of the board of directors	4
Professional development and training activities	4
Compensation policy for senior executives departing the firm as a result of a merger or acquisition	1
Existence of procedure(s) for addressing conflicts of interest among board members	1
Availability and use of advisorship facility during reporting period	1
Performance evaluation process	1
Material interests of members of the board and management	0

Number of enterprises disclosing this item

Despite the relative novelty of many of the disclosure items in the corporate responsibility category, there was some reporting of these items among a few of the CASE 30 enterprises. In particular, reporting in connection to a firm's environmental and social responsibility was found among several enterprises. In general, however, the reporting in this category was low, with less than one third of CASE 30 enterprises reporting on any of these topics (see figure 5 below).

Figure 5. Corporate responsibility and compliance
(Disclosure items ranked in order of prevalence among the CASE 30)

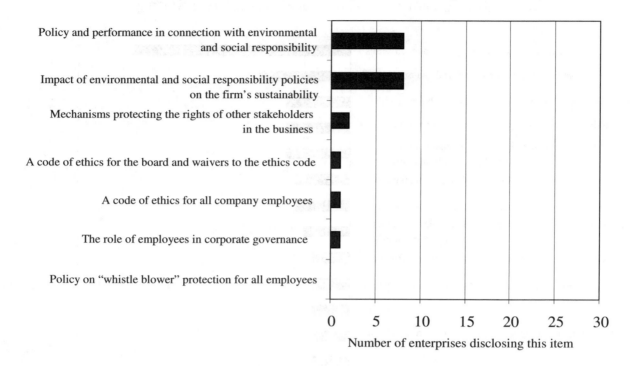

Number of enterprises disclosing this item

Finally, the category of auditing was the subject of the least amount of disclosure among the CASE 30 enterprises (see figure 6 below). Only a small fraction of enterprises in the index reported on issues related to the role of auditors in the firm. As noted above, none of the enterprises reported on the issue of "auditor involvement in non-audit work". Although the latter disclosure item is a relatively new issue (becoming common only in the post-Enron era), a number of other items could be considered much more traditional subjects of corporate governance disclosure, such as "board confidence in independence and integrity external auditors" or the "process for appointment of external auditors". Most enterprises in the study, however, do not report on these items.

There can be several reasons for this low occurrence of audit and auditor-related disclosures. Firstly, traditionally in Egyptian business, the relationship between the auditor, the company and shareholders has been considered confidential information and very few individuals were aware of its details. In addition, the financial arrangements that result from the consulting and auditing activities have been considered even more sensitive. It is worth noting that Egypt does not have rules similar to those in the United States Sarbanes Oxley Act, which prohibits accounting/auditing firms from simultaneously providing both auditing and consulting services to the same client. In Egypt, accounting/auditing firms can perform both auditing and other consulting services for the same company, after approval by the audit committee. Moreover, Egyptian law describes the required processes and procedures for the hiring, firing and resignations of auditors. As a result, many companies may believe that they are not required to disclose their actual processes and procedures in this area. However, it is important to emphasize, as indicated previously, that the law indicates what should happen in a general way, while company disclosure should indicate what actually happens in a specific way.

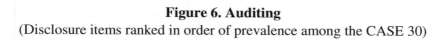

Figure 6. Auditing
(Disclosure items ranked in order of prevalence among the CASE 30)

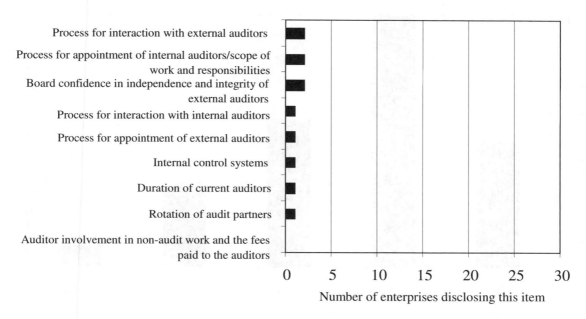

Number of enterprises disclosing this item

The findings presented in this document have so far focused on the disclosure rates of individual items in the ISAR benchmark among the enterprises of the CASE 30. Figure 7 below focuses not on individual disclosure items, but on the total number of disclosure items reported by the enterprises in the study. This is intended to provide a general overview of the disclosure rates for individual enterprises. What the figure indicates is that 25 of the 30 enterprises in the study reported less than 20 of the disclosure items in the ISAR benchmark. Nearly half of the CASE 30 firms disclosed between six and 10 items and six firms disclosed five or less. Only five firms disclosed more than 20 items in the benchmark. The firm with the greatest number of disclosure items reported 36 items, while the enterprise with the least reported just three.

This data is useful in illustrating that some companies are covering many more topics in their corporate reporting than others. This data should also be considered in the context of a separate UNCTAD study of corporate governance disclosure in emerging markets, which found that 41 of the items in the ISAR benchmark are required to be disclosed by enterprises listed on the CASE.[9] In this context, the data may reflect a situation in flux, wherein many of the companies are still in the process of implementing recent reforms, with some enterprises further along in that process than others.

---

[9] UNCTAD (2007). 2007 Review of the Implementation Status of Corporate Governance Disclosures: an inventory of disclosure requirements in 25 emerging markets" (TD/B/COM.2/ISAR/CRP.6).

Figure 7. Reporting by enterprise
(Total number of disclosure items reported by enterprises of the CASE 30)

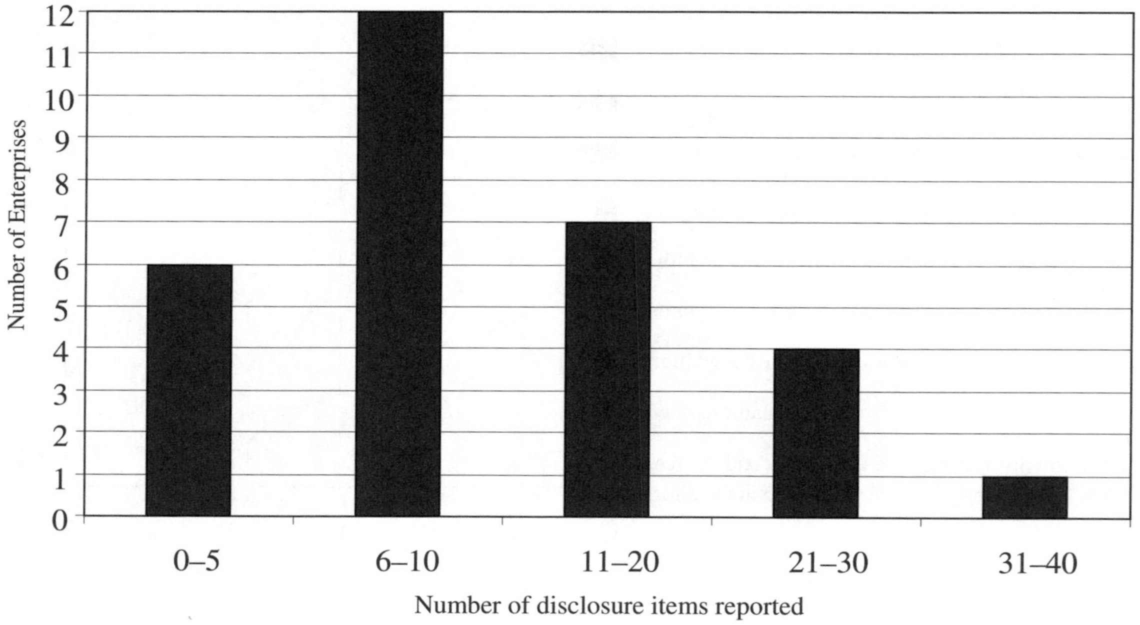

IV. Conclusions

This report is the first study of corporate governance disclosure among the CASE 30 using the ISAR benchmark on good practices in corporate governance disclosure. The ISAR benchmark contains 53 disclosure items spanning five broad categories of disclosure. The CASE 30 is the leading index of publicly listed enterprises in Egypt. The study seeks to provide a picture of what corporate governance information the enterprises in the study are currently reporting.

Chapter I provided an overview of recent developments in Egypt in the area of corporate governance disclosure. One of the significant trends highlighted is the increased pace of reform aimed at improving the quality of corporate governance and enhancing the country's capital markets.

The presentation and analysis of the data in chapter II provides an indication of the implementation status of good practices in corporate governance disclosure in Egypt. The main findings presented in chapter II suggest low rates of corporate governance disclosure among the CASE 30 enterprises when compared to the ISAR benchmark. Some items, however, are widely reported. Six core disclosure items can be found among two thirds or more of CASE 30 enterprises: (a) financial and operating results; (b) company objectives; (c) critical accounting estimates; (d) nature, type and elements of related-party transactions; (e) disclosure practices on related party transactions where control exists; and (f) risk management objectives, system and activities.

A number of observations are offered to help explain the currently low levels of corporate governance disclosure in Egypt. As noted throughout this study, the practice of corporate reporting in general is relatively new in Egypt, and the practice of corporate governance disclosure in particular is even more novel. Thus, the actual rates of disclosure identified here are indicative of new and emerging practices. In this sense, it is important to focus on the rate of increase of disclosure instead of the absolute level of disclosure. Therefore, it would be useful to repeat this study periodically to see the degree of change in the level of disclosure. As noted in chapter I, a number of reforms in the area of corporate governance continue to be implemented in Egypt. Thus, this study of corporate reporting for 2005 may serve as a baseline for future studies of corporate governance disclosure in Egypt.

It is also important to note that lack of adherence to some disclosure requirements should not necessarily be interpreted as intentional defiance of the relevant rules by enterprises. As many of the rules and regulations related to disclosure are relatively new, a possible explanation for the lack of compliance is that many of the officials in the companies studied are simply unaware of the disclosure requirements. Indeed, some of the recent reforms in Egypt have occurred only just before or even after the 2005 annual reports used in this study were prepared. The ECCG, for example, was released in 2005, and companies may not have had time to adopt all of its provisions at the time of preparing their 2005 annual reports. This suggests that future studies, using the same sample and benchmark, might usefully serve to measure the implementation of new disclosure rules by identifying changes in the number and type of subjects reported on by enterprises. It also reinforces the need for education and training among executives and directors to create awareness of the rapidly evolving regulatory environment, as well as the underlying importance of corporate governance disclosure.

Another contributing factor to low levels of disclosure in Egypt is that many company officials appear to believe that the generic description of corporate procedures and processes in the laws of Egypt is sufficient to explain their company's specific procedures and processes. Thus, companies are under the impression that they do not need to disclose information on these subjects as it would be a repetition. This perception fails to recognize that the specific processes of an enterprise, while well within the generic requirements of the law, can be and often are far more complex. This is especially true for leading large enterprises, which often display best practices that exceed legal requirements. And in all cases, investors and other users of corporate reports will be interested to know the specific procedures and processes of a company, not merely the generic requirements of the law.

In addition to these other factors, historic business factors may explain a significant part of the low disclosure rates in Egypt. Before the reforms of the 1990s, enterprises in Egypt placed a high value on confidentiality and did not engage in extensive corporate reporting. This situation was fostered in a business environment marked by closely held public enterprises with low trading volumes, and large numbers of privately held and family owned enterprises. Within this environment, many companies never established the practice of extensive corporate reporting, including corporate governance disclosure. Indeed, in such an environment, the directors of many companies saw little value in corporate governance disclosure or any corporate reporting, feeling that it might only serve to benefit commercial competitors, if anyone. It was not until the late 1990s, when the CASE began introducing a number of reforms in a bid to increase investment in Egypt, that the idea of disclosure became important. In Egypt's new business environment, the role of the stock exchange is growing in importance as a tool for attracting foreign investment and mobilizing domestic savings. In this new environment, enterprises are beginning to learn the value of communicating with the investment community, and the traditional business culture is slowly giving way to a new business culture of corporate transparency.

This study concludes with some policy options. To the extent that lack of awareness is the cause of low rates of corporate governance disclosure in Egypt, then significant improvements may be gained from training and education programmes, such as those provided by the Egyptian Institute of Directors. One policy option to be considered, therefore, is an increased focus on training and education to explain to preparers of company reports the means and benefits of disclosures in general, and disclosures related to corporate governance in particular. To the extent, however, that lack of compliance indicates a lack of penalty for non-compliance, Egyptian regulators may want to consider additional policy options. Such options might include, for example, small fines for failure to report required items, or publishing on the CASE website a list of non-compliant companies, or alternatively, a list ranking the best company reports. The Egyptian Institute of Director, for its part, has already begun annual competitions for the best company reports and best company websites in regards to corporate governance disclosure. This is intended to encourage companies to aspire to best practices. Such aspirational approaches may be best in the long term to encourage companies not to merely do the required minimum, but to instead develop meaningful communication with investors and other stakeholders. However, a "carrot and stick" approach, wherein such aspirational competitions or rankings are complemented with some at least nominal penalties for non-compliance, might be useful for bringing about higher rates of disclosure.

Chapter VIII

2007 Review of the implementation status of corporate governance disclosures: Case study of china [*]

I. Introduction

The Intergovernmental Working Group of Experts on International Standards of Accounting and Reporting (ISAR) has been working in the area of corporate governance since 1989 (E/C.10/AC.3/1989/6). During the twenty-first session of ISAR in 2004, the group of experts requested the development of an annual study to assess the state of reporting on corporate governance. This resulted in a series of annual reviews presented at each of the subsequent ISAR sessions, including the twenty-second and twenty-third sessions. At the twenty-third session, ISAR considered the document 2006 Review of the implementation status of corporate governance disclosures (TD/B/COM.2/ISAR/CRP.3) (hereafter the "2006 Review"). These annual reviews examined corporate governance disclosure practices across the world, including a number of enterprises from different world regions. These studies were facilitated by the development of ISAR's benchmark of good practices in corporate governance disclosure. This benchmark consists of 53 disclosure items and is explained in more detail in the UNCTAD publication *Guidance on Good Practices in Corporate Governance Disclosure*. This publication was the outcome of ISAR deliberations, particularly those of the twenty-second session.

This report is a case study of corporate governance disclosure in China. It was conducted in cooperation with Nankai University and with support from the China Life Insurance Company. The study utilizes the ISAR benchmark and the general methodology employed by the UNCTAD secretariat in the 2006 Review.

The objectives of this study are to: (a) provide a brief overview of key recent developments in China related to corporate governance disclosure; and (b) present and analyse the results of the review of corporate disclosure practices among leading enterprises in China. The overview of recent developments is provided in chapter I, which also examines the statutory framework in China related to corporate governance and recent reforms to China's capital markets and rules and regulations related to corporate practices. Chapter II presents and analyses the results of the review, looking in detail at disclosure rates for each individual item in the ISAR benchmark.

II. Overview of recent developments in the area of corporate governance disclosure

Since China's economic reforms began in the late 1970s, the idea and practice of corporate governance has been steadily developing. Corporate governance reform in China has strengthened investor confidence, and reinforced the economic sustainability of Chinese enterprises. This chapter provides an overview of recent developments in this reform process that effect corporate governance, disclosure practices and capital markets in China.

167

A.   Share structure reform

On 23 August 2005, the China Securities Regulatory Commission (CSRC), the State-owned Assets Supervision and Administration Commission (SASAC), the Ministry of Finance, the People's Bank of China and the Ministry of Commerce jointly issued Guidance Notes on the Split Share Structure Reform of Listed Companies. This joint guidance was a milestone in the reform of China's capital markets. The "split share structure" refers to the existence of both tradable shares on the stock exchange and a large volume of non-tradable shares owned by the state and legally defined entities in China's A-share market. This share reform measure is intended to address historical problems related to these non-tradable shares, and to enhance the overall functioning of the stock market in China. The share reform process in China is proceeding step by step, taking into account the views of all stakeholders while seeking to enhance the value of listed companies. The reform process includes a focus on the regulation of securities companies' operations, the building of stock market institutions and the development of new securities products. The share reform is designed to float the formerly non-tradable shares, rather than for the purpose of selling State-owned shares through the open market. The authorities have indicated that they currently have no intention of selling the State-owned shares in listed companies through the domestic capital market.

With a view to standardizing the work relating to the split share structure reform of listed companies, the Administrative Measures on the Split Share Structure Reform of Listed Companies was enacted, in accordance with the Company Law of the PRC, Securities Law of the PRC, Provisional Regulations on the Administration of Share Issuance and Trading, Guidelines of the State Council for Promoting the Reform and Opening-up and Sustained Development of the Capital Market, and the Guidance Opinions on the Split Share Structure Reform of Listed Companies.

B.   Amendments to the Company Law of the People's Republic of China

The Company Law of the People's Republic of China was revised for the third time at the 18th session of the 10th National People's Congress on 27 October 2005. The revisions affect corporate governance in three main ways. Firstly, the new company law protects the interests of minority shareholders by allowing small shareholders to withdraw from the company under certain conditions, and by allowing listed companies to set up a cumulative voting system. Secondly, the new company law seeks to improve the board system by removing the requirement that the chair of the board of directors is the legal representative of the company and by prescribing more detailed regulations regarding the process for meetings of the board of directors. Thirdly, the new company law strengthens the role of the board of supervisors by expanding its power and scope, and it also requires that workers have a minimum number of seats on the supervisory board.

C.   Improved internal control

Guidelines on internal control for companies listed on the Shanghai Stock Exchange were released on 5 June 2006 and came into effect on 1 July 2007. These guidelines were designed to provide direction to companies listed on the Shanghai Stock Exchange in their establishment of complete, reasonable and effective internal control systems and to protect the legitimate interests of investors. The guidelines require a number of factors that must be considered when establishing and implementing internal control systems, including goals of internal control, corporate culture, risk assessment and evaluation, risk management strategy, information management, inspection and supervision.

The guidelines require listed companies to include their subsidiaries and the trading of financial derivatives in their internal control systems. A listed company should also create a special office directly under its board of directors to conduct regular and ad hoc inspections on the company's implementation of its internal control systems. Any material risks discovered in such inspections must be disclosed to the public through the exchange. Listed companies must also include a self-evaluation report with respect to their internal control systems in their annual reports.

D.   Independent directors and employee representatives

In February 2004, SASAC put forward a proposal to improve the governance of solely State-owned enterprises. In June 2004, it issued documents that specified the main framework and procedures for a pilot project and at the same time determined the first batch of companies to participate in the project. Establishing and strengthening the system of outside directors is one of the more significant features of the pilot project, and one that marks the biggest difference between State-owned enterprise boards under the new rules and State-owned enterprise boards of the past.

Under the SASAC proposal, outside directors are entitled to evaluate the performance of top managers in the companies and also determine their compensation. When the number of outside directors is more than half of the whole board, SASAC will transfer key responsibilities to the company's board, including the authority to selecting the chief executive officer and determine the corporate investment plan.

SASAC rules also stipulate that the board of directors at State-owned enterprises shall comprise representatives of the employees. While other members of the board of directors shall be designated by SASAC, representatives of the employees shall be elected through the meeting of the employees of the company.

In a joint stock limited company, the supervisory board should include both representatives of shareholders and an appropriate percentage of representatives of the company's employees. The percentage of the employee representatives shall account for not less than one third of all the supervisors, but the exact percentage shall be specified in the articles of association. The representatives of employees who serve as members of the board of supervisors shall be democratically elected through a meeting of employee representatives, employees themselves or by other means. No director or senior manager may also act as a member of the supervisory board.

E. Stock incentive plans and insider trading rules

The Administrative Measures on Stock Incentives by Listed Companies, enacted in December 2005 and effective since January 2006 require that directors, supervisors and senior executives fulfil their fiduciary duty in the process of granting stock options and protecting the interests of their corporations and all the shareholders. To prevent the assets of the listed companies from being misappropriated, these measures also identify some basic information that must be included in a stock incentive scheme, outline procedures for using a stock incentive scheme, and define some additional disclosure and filing requirements. The new procedures include requirements for discussion and resolutions regarding stock incentives at board meetings attended by independent directors and by special board committees, as well as shareholder input via voting mechanisms at the company's annual general meetings.

On 5 April 2007, the CSRC issued its Rules on the Management of Shares Held by the Directors, Supervisors and Senior Management Officers of Listed Companies and the Changes Thereof. The purpose of these rules is to strengthen the regulation of insider trading for listed companies. The rules cover the trading of shares held by senior officials of the company, including the directors, supervisors and senior management. Disclosure of the changes of shareholdings has already been put in practice through the website of both the Shenzhen Stock Exchange and the Shanghai Stock Exchange.

F. Procedures for annual general meetings and voting

On 16 March 2006, the CSRC issued the Rules for the General Meetings of Shareholders of Listed Companies. These rules provide listed firms with clear regulatory guidance on holding annual general meetings (AGMs). The rules require, for example, that listed companies clearly state the time of AGMs and procedures for voting, as well as procedures attached to "network voting". One month later, on 20 April 2006, the Shenzhen Stock Exchange issued a complementary set of rules (Detailed Implementation Rules of Network Voting on Shareholders' Meeting of Listed Companies of Shenzhen Stock Exchange, 2006 Amendment), which set regulations on the timing and notice of AGMs and the voting methods to be used. The reforms focused on strengthening the procedures of AGMs were further addressed in March 2007, when the CSRC issued the Notice on Carrying out Related Measures about Strengthening Special Activities of Corporate Governance. This notice requires that listed companies make the responsibilities of AGMs clear, and use a network voting system on major issues.

G. Regulations on information disclosure of listed companies

On 30 January 2007, the CSRC issued its Regulations on Information Disclosure of Listed Companies. According to China's laws, including the Corporate Law and Securities Law and administrative bylaws, these regulations are formulated in order to standardize the information disclosure of stock issuers and listed companies, strengthen the management of information disclosure and protect the legitimate interests of investors. According to the new regulations, the directors, supervisors and senior managers of the issuers and listed companies shall faithfully and assiduously fulfil their obligation of information disclosure, which shall be authentic, accurate, complete, prompt and fair. Documentations to be disclosed include a share offering prospectus, a pro rata offering prospectus, listing announcements, and annual reports.

H.   Investor relationship management

In order to enhance guidance on the investor relationship management practices of listed companies, regulate the work of investor relationship management of listed companies, and protect the legitimate rights and interests of investors, especially public investors, the CSRC formulated and promulgated the Working Guidelines for the Relationship between Listed Companies and Investors. This includes the purpose, basic principles, contents of communication and main duties of investor relationship management.

In order to establish a long-term regulatory framework for securities trading companies and investment fund companies, the Implementation Measures for the Payment of Securities Investor Protection Funds by Securities Companies was put into practice on 1 July 2005. The act is expected to enhance the stability of the capital markets, serve the public interest and protect the legitimate rights and interests of investors. It gives detailed regulations on the duties of investment fund companies and organizations, on how funds are raised and used, and on the management and supervision of investment fund companies.

I.   Corporate social responsibilities

The Guidelines on Corporate Social Responsibilities for Companies Listed on the Shenzhen Stock Exchange, released by Shenzhen Stock Exchange on 25 September 2006, are intended to urge listed companies to produce a social responsibility report along with their annual reports. These guidelines require listed companies to fulfil corporate social responsibilities in the following six areas: (a) protection of shareholders and creditor interests; (b) protection of employees' rights; (c) protection of suppliers, customers and consumers' rights; (d) environmental protection and sustainable development; (e) public relations and community activities; and (f) information disclosure.

J.   Self-inspection report

On 9 March 2007, the CSRC issued its Notice on the Matters concerning Carrying out a Special Campaign to Strengthen the Corporate Governance of Listed Companies. These requirements were set to strengthen the basic institutions of China's capital markets, to promote adaptation to the requirements of the newly revised Company Law and Security Law, and also to the new requirements of the share-trading reform of listed companies. The first stage of this special campaign is that each listed company undergoes a process of self-inspection. The CSRC requires that the stock exchanges improve their supervision of the self-inspection reports and the reorganization plans of listed companies. One aim of this special campaign is clarifying the functioning of AGMs and the role of shareholders. The campaign aims toward the strengthening of specific rules to guide the procedures of AGMs, as well as institutional arrangements which could facilitate public investors to participate in the decision-making process, and the use of electronic voting systems on important matters.

K.   Chapter conclusion

China's rapidly developing capital markets have been the subject of a number of reforms in recent years. Many of these are focused on corporate governance and the disclosure practices of enterprises listed on China's stock exchanges. In addition to new disclosure requirements being placed on listed companies in China, additional reforms are taking place to ensure that investors have an opportunity to effectively participate in AGMs and make use of the information disclosed by enterprises.

III. Status of implementation of good practices in corporate governance disclosure at the company level

A.   Background and methodology

The purpose of this survey is to evaluate the level of implementation of corporate governance disclosure among companies listed on Chinese stock exchanges. The reader should note that, as in UNCTAD's previous annual reviews, this study is not intended as a measure of the *quality* of the disclosure of individual items; rather, it is a measure of the *existence* of the selected disclosure items.

This study was undertaken by the Research Centre for Corporate Governance of Nankai University, in cooperation with the UNCTAD secretariat. The study uses the UNCTAD methodology employed in UNCTAD's earlier 2006 Review, presented at the twenty-third session of ISAR. This methodology compares actual company reports with the ISAR benchmark of 53 disclosure items explained in more detail in UNCTAD's 2006 publication *Guidance on Good Practices in Corporate Governance Disclosure*. A number of comparisons were made between the data gathered in this 2007 study of Chinese company practices and the data found in UNCTAD's 2006 Review, which covered 105 enterprises from 70 economies around the world.

As in the 2006 Review, the 53 disclosure items in the ISAR benchmark are grouped into five broad categories, or subject areas, and are presented and analysed by category in section B below. These categories are:

  (b)   Financial transparency;

(c)   Ownership structure and exercise of control rights;

(d)   Board and management structure and process;

(e)   Corporate responsibility and compliance; and

(f)   Auditing.

The sample of Chinese enterprises reviewed in this study consists of 80 companies that were randomly selected from among the CSI 300 (*Hu Shen 300*). The CSI 300, jointly produced by the Shanghai Stock Exchange and the Shenzhen Stock Exchange, is the leading equity index in China and is widely used to benchmark the performance of the Chinese capital markets (specifically, the China A share market). The CSI 300 is designed for use as a performance benchmark, as well as a basis for derivatives products and index tracking funds. Of the 80 enterprises selected, 56 are from the Shanghai Stock Exchange and 24 are from the Shenzhen Stock Exchange. The enterprises included in the survey represent a wide range of industries including: energy, financial services, telecommunications, pharmaceuticals, manufacturing and retail, among others.

An array of corporate reports was surveyed for the 2007 Review in China, including annual reports, corporate governance reports, and other information available from financial databases and enterprise websites. These included: (a) company websites; (b) annual reports; (c) financial reports; (d) proxy circulars/proxy statements; (e) company by-laws; (f) corporate social responsibility reports/sustainability reports/corporate citizen reports/environmental reports; (g) corporate governance reports/corporate governance charters (codes); (h) board of directors charters; (i) risk management policies; (j) audit and risk management committee charters; (k) shareholders charters; and (l) board of supervisors rules of procedure.

B.   Main outcomes of the survey: overview of all disclosure items

Table 1 below presents the results of the survey of Chinese enterprises. The table displays the average percentage rates of firms reporting on each of the five broad disclosure categories discussed above, alongside the findings of UNCTAD's 2006 Review. The category averages in this table are compiled by averaging the percentage of firms reporting on each individual item, within each category. This allows readers to see in very general terms the rate of reporting for each of the disclosure subject categories.

Table 1. Main findings of survey on corporate governance disclosure: category overview
(number of enterprises in parentheses)

Number of firms reporting on disclosure items, by category (in percentage)	China (80)	Findings of UNCTAD's 2006 Review					
		All (105)	Type of listing		Country income		SOE
			Inter-national listing (72)	Only local listing (29)	OECD* & other high income (42)	Low & middle income (63)	SOEs (24)
Financial transparency and information disclosure	94	77	82	69	82	73	78
Ownership structure and exercise of control rights	88	70	77	59	78	65	70
Board and management structure and process	71	70	80	52	82	63	66
Auditing	62	61	71	43	79	50	54
Corporate responsibility and compliance	40	64	73	45	77	55	55

* Organization for Economic Cooperation and Development.

As shown in table 1, the Chinese enterprises in the study demonstrate relatively high rates of reporting on corporate governance issues for the categories of financial transparency and ownership structure. Indeed, for these two disclosure categories, the percentage of Chinese enterprises surveyed that report on these subjects is significantly higher than the average for all enterprises in the 2006 Review, and also higher than the average for internationally-listed enterprises and enterprises from high-income countries. For the two categories of board and management structure and auditing, the level of reporting for Chinese enterprises is a little higher than the average for all enterprises in the 2006 Review, but is lower than the average level for internationally-listed enterprises and enterprises from high-income countries. Concerning corporate responsibility, the average level of reporting on disclosure items for Chinese enterprises remains significantly lower than the average for all enterprises in the 2006 Review, and also lower than the average for enterprises from low- and middle-income countries.

Figure 1 below presents the spreading range of the rates of the five categories: that is, the range between the highest average reporting rate among the five categories and the lowest average reporting rate among the five categories. This range is provided for the findings of the survey of 80 Chinese enterprises and, for comparison, the findings of the 2006 Review, including its subgroups. The reporting rates of the average for all enterprises in the 2006 Review ranged from 61 per cent of firms to 71 per cent of firms. The reporting rates of enterprises from the OECD and other high-income countries gathered in the region from 77 per cent of firms to 82 per cent. The disclosure rates of enterprises from low- and middle-income countries ranged from 50 per cent to 73 per cent of firms. Finally, the rates of Chinese enterprises spread between 40 per cent and 94 per cent are shown. The very narrow range for enterprises from high-income countries indicates a much more consistent pattern of disclosure across all five categories. The disclosure rates for Chinese enterprises have the broadest range, showing a pattern with polarization: in some subject areas, Chinese enterprises have high rates of disclosure, and in other areas very low rates of disclosure.

Figure 1. Spreading range of disclosure rates compared

(number in parentheses indicates sample size)

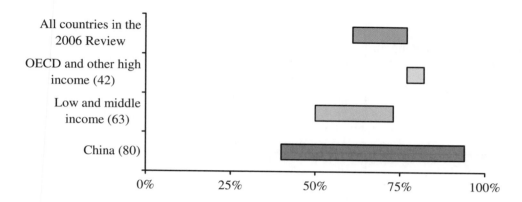

These general observations are the subject of more detailed analysis in the following sections. Table 2 below provides the detailed findings of the study of Chinese enterprises alongside the findings of UNCTAD's 2006 Review.

Table 2. Main findings of the survey on corporate governance disclosure: detailed results

(number of enterprises in parentheses)

Number of firms reporting on disclosure items, by category (in percentage)	China (80)	Findings of UNCTAD's 2006 Review					
		All (105)	Type of listing		Country income		Special focus
			Inter-national listing (72)	Only local listing (29)	OECD & other high income (42)	Low & middle income (63)	SOEs (24)
Financial transparency and information disclosure (in percentage)							
Financial and operating results	**100**	100	100	100	100	100	100
Company objectives	**100**	92	96	86	95	90	88
Nature, type and elements of related-party transactions	**98**	94	99	90	100	90	88
Impact of alternative accounting decisions	**96**	75	82	66	86	68	67
Critical accounting estimates	**94**	90	96	79	98	84	83
Disclosure practices on related party transactions where control exists	**91**	47	51	41	52	43	50
Board responsibilities regarding financial communications	**89**	80	89	66	90	73	88
The decision-making process for approving transactions with related parties	**89**	53	57	48	52	54	63

Number of firms reporting on disclosure items, by category (in percentage)	China (80)	Findings of UNCTAD's 2006 Review					
		All (105)	Type of listing		Country income		Special focus
			Inter-national listing (72)	Only local listing (29)	OECD & other high income (42)	Low & middle income (63)	SOEs (24)
Rules and procedures governing extraordinary transactions	**88**	59	65	48	62	57	75
Ownership structure and exercise of control rights (in percentage)							
Ownership structure	**100**	90	93	90	93	89	96
Control rights	**100**	82	88	76	90	76	79
Availability and accessibility of meeting agenda	**100**	78	89	62	98	65	83
Changes in shareholdings	**100**	69	78	52	74	65	63
Control structure	**99**	86	86	86	86	86	92
Process for holding annual general meetings	**96**	91	96	86	98	87	92
Control and corresponding equity stake	**91**	75	88	52	88	67	58
Rules and procedures governing the acquisition of corporate control in capital markets	**85**	30	35	21	36	25	38
Anti-takeover measures	**18**	30	39	10	40	22	25
Board and management structure and process (in percentage)							
Composition of board of directors (executives and non-executives)	**100**	99	100	97	100	98	96
Qualifications and biographical information on board members	**100**	83	93	66	86	81	79
Independence of the board of directors	**98**	68	82	38	88	54	67
Role and functions of the board of directors	**96**	84	92	69	93	78	83
Duration of directors' contracts	**96**	76	88	55	98	62	63
Governance structures, such as committees and other mechanisms to prevent conflict of interest	**90**	88	96	72	98	81	83
Determination and composition of directors' remuneration	**90**	68	81	41	88	54	75

Number of firms reporting on disclosure items, by category (in percentage)	China (80)	Findings of UNCTAD's 2006 Review					
		All (105)	Type of listing		Country income		Special focus
			Inter-national listing (72)	Only local listing (29)	OECD & other high income (42)	Low & middle income (63)	SOEs (24)
Number of outside board and management position directorships held by the directors	**85**	79	90	59	90	71	71
Types and duties of outside board and management positions	**85**	74	88	48	93	62	58
"Checks and balances" mechanisms	**81**	88	93	79	93	84	83
Existence of procedure(s) for addressing conflicts of interest among board members	**78**	67	75	55	81	57	63
Availability and use of advisorship facility during reporting period	**74**	41	47	28	52	33	33
Composition and function of governance committee structures	**74**	86	94	66	90	83	75
Performance evaluation process	**74**	67	75	52	81	57	71
Risk management objectives, system and activities	**59**	89	96	76	95	84	83
Material interests of members of the board and management	**31**	57	68	34	64	52	58
Professional development and training activities	**20**	36	43	24	50	27	33
Existence of plan of succession	**14**	52	63	28	62	46	50
Compensation policy for senior executives departing the firm as a result of a merger or acquisition	**10**	38	54	3	55	27	21
Auditing (in percentage)							
Board confidence in independence and integrity of external auditors	**95**	58	69	34	83	41	50
Process for appointment of external auditors	**89**	81	92	62	90	75	75
Internal control systems	**88**	75	89	48	88	67	75
The scope of work and	**86**	84	92	69	95	76	75

Number of firms reporting on disclosure items, by category (in percentage)	China (80)	Findings of UNCTAD's 2006 Review					
		All (105)	Type of listing		Country income		Special focus
			International listing (72)	Only local listing (29)	OECD & other high income (42)	Low & middle income (63)	SOEs (24)
responsibilities for the internal audit function and the highest level of leadership to which it reports							
Duration of current auditors	**86**	32	38	21	55	17	33
Process for interaction with external auditors	**78**	70	82	48	90	57	54
Rotation of audit partners	**18**	21	24	14	33	13	17
Process for interaction with internal auditors	**9**	74	82	59	95	60	63
Auditors' involvement in non-audit work and the fees paid to the auditors	**6**	56	71	28	79	41	46
Corporate responsibility and compliance (in percentage)							
The role of employees in corporate governance	**86**	25	25	24	36	17	29
A code of ethics for the board and waivers to the ethics code	**81**	73	88	45	88	63	63
Mechanisms protecting the rights of other stakeholders in business	**45**	57	67	38	71	48	46
Policy and performance in connection with environmental and social responsibility	**36**	91	96	79	98	87	83
Impact of environmental and social responsibility policies on the firm's sustainability	**16**	78	82	66	88	71	63
A code of ethics for all company employees	**11**	72	86	45	83	65	67
Policy on "whistleblower" protection for all employees	**1**	50	64	21	71	35	33

As shown in table 2, in the category of financial transparency, the average level of reporting of the Chinese enterprises surveyed for each of nine items is higher than the average level of reporting on these items for all enterprises in the 2006 Review. In the category ownership structure, except for anti-takeover measures, the reporting levels of other items for Chinese enterprises are higher than for all enterprises in the 2006 Review.

The level of reporting varies significantly among the 19 items in the category board and management structure and process. Among these 19 items, the reporting rates for seven items are above 90 per cent of firms and are higher than the corresponding rates for all enterprises in the

2006 Review. The reporting rates for five items, however, are below 60 per cent of firms and lower than the corresponding rates for all enterprises in the 2006 Review.

In the category corporate responsibility, the level of reporting for Chinese enterprises is relatively low. The disclosure rates for five of the seven items in this category are below 50 per cent of firms and lower than the corresponding figure for all enterprises in the 2006 Review.

Table 2 also shows that the average level of reporting for Chinese enterprises fell below 50 per cent of firms for 13 of the disclosure items: one was in the category ownership structure; four were in the category board and management structure; three in auditing; and five in corporate responsibility. For these 13 items, the level of reporting for Chinese enterprises remains significantly lower than the average for all enterprises in the 2006 Review, and especially so for the internationally-listed enterprises and enterprises from high-income countries.

Table 3. Most prevalent and least prevalent disclosure items in China
(in percentage)

Top 10 most prevalent disclosure items among all 80 enterprises surveyed	Disclosure rate	Bottom 10 least prevalent disclosure items among all 80 enterprises surveyed	Disclosure rate
Financial and operating results	100	Professional development and training activities	20
Company objectives	100	Anti-takeover measures	18
Ownership structure	100	Rotation of audit partners	18
Control rights	100	Impact of environmental and social responsibility policies on the firm's sustainability	16
Availability and accessibility of meeting agenda	100	Existence of plan of succession	14
Changes in shareholdings	100	A code of ethics for all company employees	11
Composition of board of directors (executives and non-executives)	100	Compensation policy for senior executives departing the firm as a result of a merger or acquisition	10
Qualifications and biographical information on board members	100	Process for interaction with internal auditors	9
Control structure	99	Auditors involvement in non-audit work and the fees paid to the auditors	6
Nature, type and elements of related-party transactions	98	Policy on "whistleblower" protection for all employees	1

Concerning the most prevalent disclosure items (table 3), the top eight are reported on by all the Chinese enterprises in the study (100 per cent disclosure rates). Of these eight, four are in the category ownership structure, two are in board and management structure and two are in financial transparency. The high disclosure rates for these items may result from the requirements of the New Company Law.

As to the least prevalent disclosure items, all of the bottom 10 have reporting rates below 30 per cent. The items "policy on 'whistleblower' protection for all employees" and "auditors' involvement in non-audit work and the fees paid to the auditors" have reporting rates of only 1 per cent and 6 per cent, respectively, indicating these are not commonly reported items in China.

C. Comparison between China and international average

Figure 2 below presents the average level of reporting within each category and compares the disclosure practices of Chinese enterprises with the average for enterprises around the world. The figure displays an average for each category of disclosure items: to produce an overview of the level of reporting for a subject area, this category average is calculated by taking the average percentage of enterprises reporting each disclosure item within a category. The upper line in figure 2 represents the sample of 80 Chinese enterprises surveyed, and provides a clear overview of the average level of reporting for the different categories. The lower line represents the average of a sample of 105 enterprises from around the world found in UNCTAD's 2006 Review.

Figure 2. Comparison between China and international average
(number in parentheses indicates sample size)

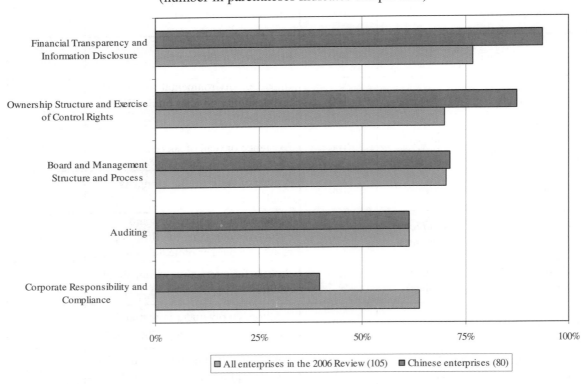

The results presented in figure 2 indicate that for four of the five categories, the level of reporting in China is higher than or equal to the international average found in the 2006 Review. The category of financial transparency, on average, is the subject of the highest rates of reporting for both Chinese enterprises and others around the world. In the two categories financial transparency and ownership structure, the level of reporting for Chinese enterprises is significantly higher than the international average from the 2006 Review. However, the level of report'ng for the category corporate responsibility shows that Chinese enterprises have relatively low levels of reporting on this subject compared to enterprises elsewhere in the world.

The results of this study show that the level of reporting of Chinese enterprises generally follows the same pattern as those of enterprises from around the world studied in the 2006 Review. Both studies show the same top three categories of reporting: financial transparency followed by ownership structure, followed in turn by board and management structure. One difference with the current study lies in the overall reporting rates for the categories auditing and corporate responsibility. The category with the lowest reporting rate for enterprises in China is corporate responsibility. In contrast, that of auditing is the lowest for the average of all enterprises in the 2006 Review.

D. Comparison between China and high-income countries

Figure 3 below examines the level of reporting among the Chinese enterprises surveyed compared with enterprises based in the OECD and other high-income countries. Among the five categories, figure 3 indicates that Chinese companies tended to show higher levels of reporting in two categories: financial transparency and ownership structure. However, the findings also show that Chinese enterprises have lower rates in the other three categories. The largest disparity in reporting practices between enterprises from China and high-income countries is found in the category corporate responsibility.

Figure 3 Comparison of disclosure rates between China and high-income countries
(number in parentheses indicates sample size)

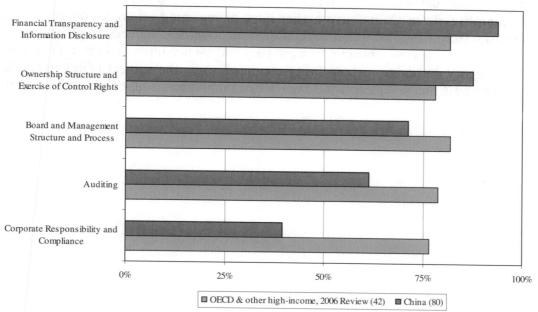

According to the findings of the 2006 Review, enterprises based in the OECD and other high-income countries demonstrated a higher rate of corporate governance disclosure than enterprises from low- and middle-income countries. Although the average level of reporting of Chinese enterprises in this study exceeds those of the OECD and other high-income countries in two categories, enterprises from China have significantly lower levels of reporting for a number

181

of individual items. Table 4 below presents the top five disparities between the reporting rates of enterprises from China and the OECD and other high-income countries.

Table 4. Top five highest disparities in disclosure rates, China and high-income countries
(number in parentheses indicates sample size)

Disclosure item	Disclosure rates (in percentage)		
	China (80)	OECD and other high-income (42)	Disparity
Process for interaction with internal auditors	9	95	86
Auditors' involvement in non-audit work and the fees paid to the auditors	6	79	73
Impact of environmental and social responsibility policies on the firm's sustainability	16	88	72
A code of ethics for all company employees	11	83	72
Policy on "whistleblower" protection for all employees	1	71	70

E.   Comparison of disclosure rates between China and low- and middle-income countries

Figure 4 below compares the reporting rates of enterprises from China with those from low- and middle-income countries in the 2006 Review. The analysis indicates that in four of the five categories, enterprises from China have higher rates of reporting on corporate governance items than enterprises from other low- and middle-income countries. Indeed, large differences exist in the rates for two categories: financial transparency and ownership structure. Figure 4 also indicates that the category corporate responsibility continues to be the subject of relatively low rates of reporting among Chinese enterprises, even when compared to other low- and middle-income countries.

Figure 4 . Comparison of disclosure rates between China and low- and middle-income countries
(number in parentheses indicates sample size)

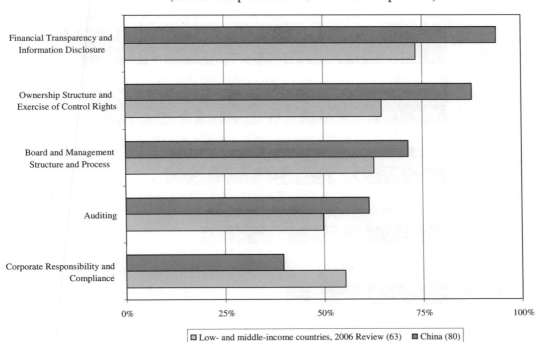

F.   State-owned enterprises

One observation of the 2006 Review was that the State-owned enterprise model continues to be a common feature of the industrial strategy of many developing countries, where State-owned enterprises are often among the largest enterprises. This is true for China. In this survey, 69 of the 80 the enterprises studied in China were State-owned enterprises. However, the number of non-State-owned enterprises, while small, may nevertheless provide some useful comparisons. Figure 5 compares the level of reporting of State-owned enterprises and non-State-owned enterprises in China. The reporting practices of the two groups are relatively similar, with the only significant difference found in the category corporate responsibility, where State-owned enterprises have somewhat higher rates.

Figure 5. Comparison of disclosure practices between State-owned enterprises and non-State-owned enterprises in China

(number in parentheses indicates sample size)

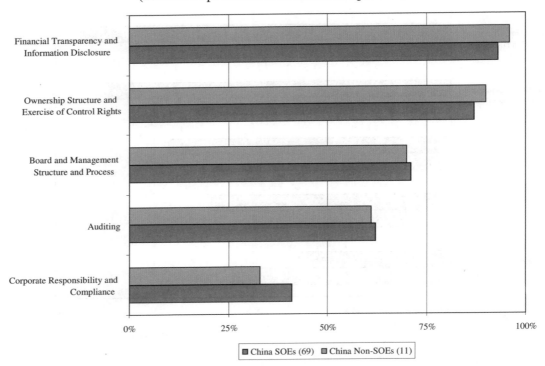

Table 6 below highlights the top five greatest disparities between reporting of individual items by State-owned enterprises and Non-State-owned enterprises. Two of the top three items with the greatest disparities belong to the category corporate responsibility. Table 6 also shows that among the items with the greatest disparity between State-owned enterprise and non-State-owned enterprise reporting, State-owned enterprises have the higher rate for four of the five items. It is only for the item "Existence of procedures for addressing conflicts of interest among board members" that the sample of non-State-owned enterprises has a higher rate of reporting than the State-owned enterprises in the study.

Table 6. Top five highest disparities in disclosure rates, by company type

(number in parentheses indicates sample size)

Disclosure item	Disclosure rates (in percentage)		
	Non-SOEs (11)	SOEs (69)	Disparity
Policy and performance in connection with environmental and social responsibility	9	41	32
Risk management objectives, system and activities	36	62	26
Impact of environmental and social responsibility policies on the firm's sustainability	0	19	19
Rules and procedure governing extraordinary transactions	73	90	17
Existence of procedure(s) for addressing conflicts of interest among board members	91	75	16

Figure 6. Comparison of State-owned enterprise disclosure rates between China and other countries
(number in parentheses indicates sample size)

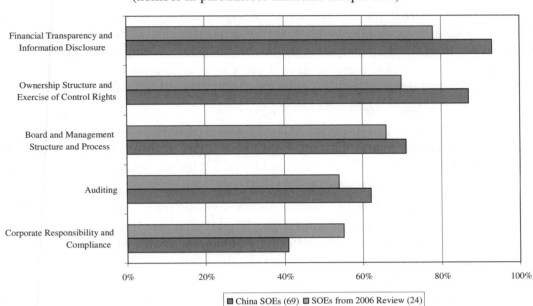

Figure 6 above presents a comparison between the sample of State-owned enterprises surveyed in ISAR's 2006 Review and the State-owned enterprises from China surveyed in this study. As Figure 6 indicates, the State-owned enterprises from China demonstrate a higher level of reporting on corporate governance items across four of the five categories. The one category where the rates are relatively lower is that of corporate responsibility. This result is consistent with the findings elsewhere in this study that show a relatively low level of reporting among Chinese enterprises in this category.

IV. Conclusions

This report is part of a series of annual studies on corporate governance disclosure prepared for ISAR. This is the first report to specifically assess the corporate governance reporting practices of Chinese enterprises. The report was developed in cooperation between the UNCTAD secretariat and the Research Centre for Corporate Governance of Nankai University. It uses the ISAR benchmark of good practices in corporate governance disclosure and the general methodology of previous UNCTAD studies on corporate governance disclosure. The purpose of this report is to provide an indication of the current corporate governance disclosure practices of publicly listed enterprises in China. A sample of 80 enterprises was randomly selected from the CSI 300, a leading Chinese index that is broadly representative of the Chinese equity market.

The main findings of this case study show that Chinese enterprises have relatively high levels of reporting for four of the five categories studied. The exception is for the category corporate responsibility. Chinese enterprises have relatively low rates of reporting on this subject when compared to enterprises in other countries. Of all five categories, that of financial transparency has the highest level of reporting, while the category corporate responsibility is lowest. For the two categories financial transparency and ownership structure, the level of reporting among Chinese enterprises is significantly higher than the average for all enterprises in the 2006 Review. The reporting of Chinese enterprises on items in these two categories is also higher than the average among enterprises from high-income countries in the 2006 Review. For the two categories of auditing and board and management structure, the level of reporting for Chinese enterprises is nearly the same as the average for all enterprises in the 2006 Review, but is significantly lower than that for enterprises from high-income countries in the 2006 Review. Concerning corporate responsibility, the level of reporting for Chinese enterprises remains significantly lower than for the enterprises in the 2006 Review. Compared with the State-owned enterprises surveyed in the 2006 Review, those from China demonstrate a higher rate of reporting on corporate governance items across all categories except the category corporate responsibility.

A number of factors contribute to the reporting practices of enterprises in any country. One factor that seems to be driving reporting practices in China is the number of reforms that have taken place in recent years. Chapter I discusses these reforms in more detail, but they include the Company Law of the People's Republic of China, the Securities Law, and a number of new rules and regulations introduced by the CSRC.

These rules have all sought to promote greater reporting and standardization of corporate information among listed companies in China. These changes have also strengthened the protection of small and medium-sized investors, by enhancing their effective participation in the decision-making process of companies. As a result, these investors are playing an increasingly important role in China, increasing demand for more corporate information. The results of this study, namely the relatively high rates of reporting among Chinese enterprises, may be a result of these recent reforms.

Despite these reforms and the relatively high levels of reporting in other categories, there are several possible reasons for the lower level of reporting among Chinese enterprises in the category of corporate responsibility. Many Chinese enterprises have not adopted formal corporate responsibility management programmes, and specific mechanisms such as "whistleblower" protections are not widely implemented in Chinese companies. Thus, the low rate of reporting is likely indicative of the low rate of adoption of many of these practices, and not an indication of a lack of transparency. Going forward, this situation may change. In China, regulators and other institutional bodies are placing greater emphasis on corporate responsibility issues. The Shenzhen Stock Exchange, for example, published its Social Responsibility Listing Guidelines of the Shenzhen Stock Exchange which took effect on 25 September 2006. These guidelines are expected to have an influence on the reporting rates in this category, but this will probably first be seen in 2007 annual reports, published in 2008, which were not available at the time this study was conducted.

This study has established a useful picture of current practices of corporate governance disclosure in China. As noted earlier, this study is not intended as a measure of the quality of the disclosure of individual items; rather, it is a measure of the existence of the selected disclosure items. Future researchers may wish to revisit these results using the ISAR benchmark on good practices in corporate governance disclosure to gauge changes in company reporting.